BECAUSE WE ARE CANADIANS

A BATTLEFIELD MEMOIR

BECAUSE WE ARE

FOREWORD BY
Pierre Berton

CANADIANS

Sgt. Charles D. Kipp

EDITED BY *Lynda Sykes*

DOUGLAS & MCINTYRE
VANCOUVER/TORONTO

Douglas & McIntyre
2323 Quebec Street, Suite 201
Vancouver, British Columbia V5T 4S7
www.douglas-mcintyre.com

National Library of Canada Cataloguing in Publication Data

Kipp, Charles D. (Charles Disbrowe), 1918–2000
Because we are Canadians : a battlefield memoir / Charles D. Kipp ;
edited by Lynda Sykes.

Includes index.

ISBN 1-55054-955-3

1. Kipp, Charles D. (Charles Disbrowe), 1918–2000. 2. World War,
1939–1945—Personal narratives, Canadian. 3. Canada. Canadian Army.
Lincoln and Welland Regiment—Biography. 4. Soldiers—Canada—Biography.
I. Sykes, Lynda. II. Title.

D811.K56 2003   940.54'8171   C2002-911044-0

Editing by Brian Scrivener
Copy-editing by Kathryn Spracklin
Jacket and text design by Peter Cocking
Jacket photographs of Charles Kipp courtesy of Margaret Kipp
Typesetting by Rhonda Ganz & Val Speidel
Maps on pages vii–x are from *The Lincs: A History of the Lincoln and Welland
Regiment at War* (Alma, Ontario: Maple Leaf Route, 1986). They are used with
the permission of the author, Geoffrey Hayes, and the Laurier Centre for
Military, Strategic and Disarmament Studies, Wilfrid Laurier University.
Letter in Appendix from Charles to his parents reprinted courtesy of Rosemary
Hopper. Other letters courtesy of Charles Kipp.
Printed and bound in Canada by Friesens
Printed on acid-free paper

The publisher gratefully acknowledges the financial support of the Canada
Council for the Arts, the British Columbia Ministry of Tourism, Small Business
and Culture, and the Government of Canada through the Book Publishing
Industry Development Program (BPIDP) for our publishing activities.

CONTENTS

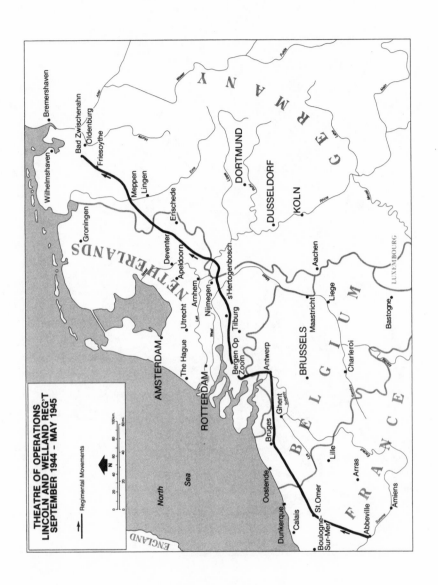

THEATRE OF OPERATIONS
LINCOLN AND WELLAND REG'T
SEPTEMBER 1944 – MAY 1945

→ Regimental Movements

N

0 20 40 60 80 100km.
0 20 40 60mi.

ENGLAND

North Sea

NETHERLANDS

GERMANY

BELGIUM

FRANCE

LUXEMBOURG

Bremershaven
Wilhelmshaven
Bad Zwischenahn
Oldenburg
Friesoythe
Meppen
Lingen
Groningen
Enschede
Deventer
Apeldoorn
Arnhem
Nijmegen
Utrecht
The Hague
AMSTERDAM
ROTTERDAM
s'Hertogenbosch
Tilburg
Bergen Op Zoom
Antwerp
Ghent
Bruges
Oostende
Dunkerque
Calais
Boulogne-Sur-Mer
St.Omer
Abbeville
Amiens
Arras
Lille
Charleroi
BRUSSELS
Maastricht
Liege
Aachen
Bastogne
DORTMUND
DUSSELDORF
KOLN

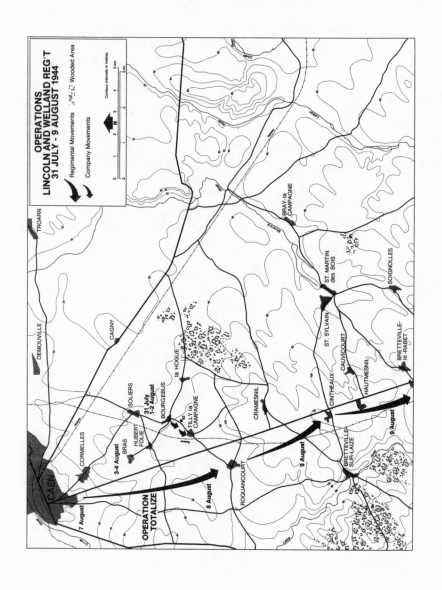

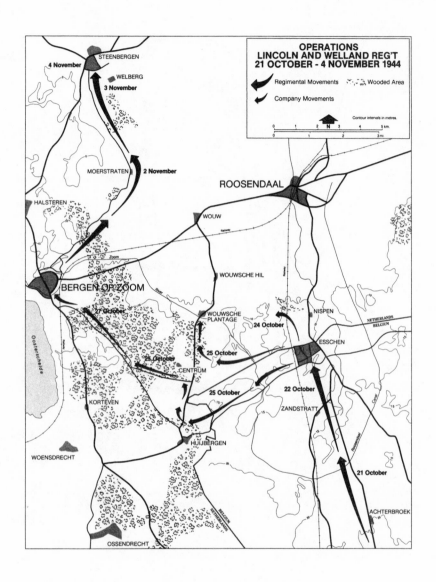

OPERATIONS
LINCOLN AND WELLAND REG'T
21 OCTOBER - 4 NOVEMBER 1944

Regimental Movements   Wooded Area
Company Movements

Contour intervals in metres.

0   1   2   N   3   4   5 km.
0   1   2   3 mi.

STEENBERGEN
4 November
WELBERG
3 November
MOERSTRATEN   2 November
HALSTEREN

ROOSENDAAL
WOUW
Railway
WOUWSCHE HIL

Zoom

BERGEN OP ZOOM

27 October
WOUWSCHE
PLANTAGE
24 October
NISPEN
NETHERLANDS
BELGIUM
ESSCHEN
River
25 October
26 October
CENTRUM
25 October
22 October
Oosterschelde
KORTEVEN
ZANDSTRATT
15
19
15
21 October
WOENSDRECHT
HUIJBERGEN
BELGIUM
NETHERLANDS
20
ACHTERBROEK
OSSENDRECHT

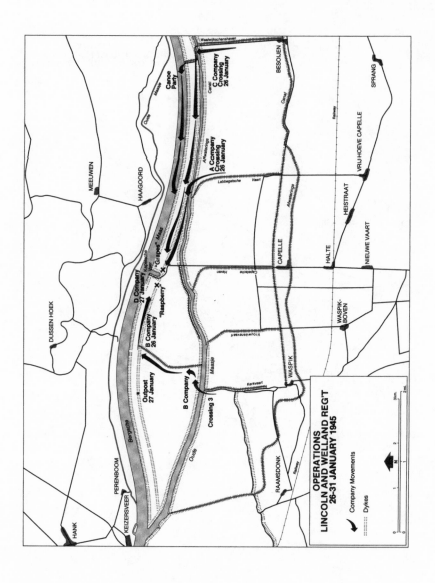

OPERATIONS
LINCOLN AND WELLAND REG'T
26-31 JANUARY 1945

Company Movements
Dykes

N

0   1   2   3   3km.
0   1   2   2mi.

FOREWORD

THIS IS A REMARKABLE BOOK—and an important one. Since the end of World War II, we have been inundated with a tidal wave of memoirs and reports about the various campaigns and the politics and strategies involved. In most cases, however, the authors have been generals, politicians, officers and war correspondents, who have viewed the conflict from a distance. But this is war seen from the point of view of a bayonet, closer than a sniper's bullet—war as it appeared to a man in the mud, hemmed in by the contorted corpses of his comrades, or the cadavers of the flaxen-haired soldiers whom he was forced to kill to save his own life.

Charles Kipp's unadorned and unsentimental prose, remarkable in its remembered detail, tells it like it is: the commanding officer who "did not have the guts of a rabbit," the young German who died in his arms, the soldier who slowly burned to death before his eyes.

Some of his tales are truly horrifying. Others will bring a catch to the reader's throat. The book's greatest asset is that it is not ghost written: these are Kipp's own words, and the story rings true!

Kipp joined the Lincoln and Welland Regiment as a corporal and ended up as a platoon sergeant. He was wounded nine times in action, but the worst scars came from the battle fatigue, which was once known as shell shock. In eight months of hard fighting, he scarcely had a free moment, for his platoon was rarely up to strength.

His unemotional narrative stands as an indictment of Canada's haphazard recruiting system, which produced an army top-heavy with cooks and bottle-washers, who, in an act of military desperation, had to be mustered into the infantry, while Canadian politicians argued about the need for conscription, and two divisions of "zombies" sat on their rumps on the West Coast.

Kipp watches the new men arrive—green troops, half-trained— and knows they will be dead by midnight, as indeed they often were. Much of the time, his platoon was without an officer, and Kipp took on the responsibility himself. Under those circumstances, leave was almost non-existent.

Kipp soldiers on, half-drugged from lack of sleep, unable to take his boots off for days until his feet give out, saved often from a sniper's bullet by an instinct born of battle.

Of all the reading I have done on the war in northern Europe, this is the most memorable. Anyone who really wants to know what the war was like will benefit from reading it.

PIERRE BERTON

A TRIBUTE TO CHARLES KIPP

AT A QUARTER PAST THREE in the afternoon on Friday, October 27, 1944, I saw a Canadian armoured vehicle entering the street in Bergen-op-Zoom, where I lived in those days. I then realized that we were liberated after over four years of occupation.

The day after, I met Charles Kipp for the first time. He and a young corporal came into the basement of our house, where we had taken refuge from the fighting since the beginning of October. Our basement soon became an information and communication centre, where my father, a teacher of English, one of the few people who spoke English in those days, served as an interpreter between the Canadian and underground forces. It was in that cellar, on October 28, that Charles and his commander, Major Lambert, planned what later became known as the Battle of Bergen-op-Zoom, which took place that very night. After Lambert had left, Charles and the corporal prepared for battle.

My father poured three glasses of wine as a toast to their success in the battle. Only his hand trembled as they raised their glasses, and he asked why they, who faced possible death, were so steady. "Because we are Canadians," they answered together.

That became the title of Charles's book about his war.

After that battle, Charles returned to our house, completely exhausted by many hours of fighting. On October 30, after having slept

3

for a very long time, he described the battle to my father, and told him that the battle was even worse than the one he had fought at Falaise. At the end of that day, he left us to return to his unit; that was the last we saw of him. He did not return to our town. Not until forty years later, when he returned to Bergen-op-Zoom as a war veteran, did we learn that he had survived the war. It was an emotional reunion, especially for my father, who was by then almost ninety years old.

As he describes the fighting in his book, the Battle of Bergen-op-Zoom was one of the ferocious battles of the Second World War. In October 1999, I visited Charles in Canada, and on October 28, we both raised our glasses in commemoration of the toast to the battle fifty-five years earlier in the cellar of our house in Bergen-op-Zoom.

Dear Charles, we owe you and your comrades-in-arms so much. We will always remember what your people did for us so that we could live our lives in liberty.

Canada can be proud of her son Charles and of his fellow soldiers!

DR. J.A.F.M. LUIJTEN
Soest, Netherlands, January 2000

PREFACE

THIS BOOK IS NOT WRITTEN with the intention of telling how the generals and top brass won the war. Two people could be in the same company, in the same battle, and still give two different versions of that battle. This is the way I saw it, and this is my version of it, and no one else's. This is not a "story"; this is an account of my war, in my words. There is no way I can tell every detail—this account merely covers the high spots.

After the breakout in France following D-Day, the fighting was very hard and fast. Every day, we fought different battles—attack! . . . attack! . . . attack! Many days, it was several times a day—battles long forgotten, and towns and positions, I never did know where. And many times the enemy gave us a terrible beating. All we could do was lick our wounds and then go back at it, with nothing but death at the end of the road. Was it any wonder that many good men broke and could not go on? And although I have told of many gruesome events, there is no way I can describe the terror or the horror of things I did, or saw done.

I have very great sympathy for parents who watched as their children went off to war and then received telegrams telling them they would never come back. After going through the war, I could not sit back and watch my family going off to war. The thought of it is too much even to contemplate. Just the thought of my grandson or my granddaughter having to do or see what I did is beyond contemplation.

And last, but nowhere near least, this book could not have been done without the help of my very dear friend and neighbour, Lynda Sykes. For years, we talked of writing a book of memoirs of my war. I cannot describe the work and the details of her help and know-how. Typing, correcting spelling and punctuation, sentence and paragraph structure, rewriting, and looking after many of the small details of writing. There is no way to count the hours she has spent on my book, or, I should say, our book. Thank you, Lynda.

I would like to dedicate this book, firstly, to *all* the good men who trusted my leadership and followed me as I led them into battle. Sadly, too many of them did not survive the war. And secondly, I would especially like to dedicate it to the brave young corporal, whose name I never knew and whom I never saw again, who sat side by side with me on the basement steps of the Luijten home in Bergen-op-Zoom, and, when asked how we could be so steady before going into battle, replied so fervently and without hesitation, in perfect unison with me, "Because we are Canadians."

SGT. CHARLES D. KIPP
Lincoln and Welland Regiment
Brownsville, June 1999

I

PREPARING FOR WAR

I WAS BORN at Keswick Ridge Farm, just one mile north of the village of Delmer, Ontario, on what was known then as the 9th Concession of Dereham Township (now Keswick Road), on November 22, 1918, just eleven days after the First World War ended. As I always wanted to be a soldier, I think I must have been a reincarnation of a soldier who was killed in the war.

The first memory I have is of standing with my sister, Audrey, at the window of my father's house, at the top of the stairway, watching my grandfather's house, across the laneway from our house, burn to the ground. That was in 1919, and I was not very old, but I do remember Audrey and me being taken out of bed, and standing looking out the window at the fire. At that time I had one brother, Arthur, and one sister, Audrey. I, Charles Disbrowe Kipp, was the third child, followed by Donald and William in that order. My parents were Clarence and Stella Kipp, my mother being born Stella Mellisa Disbrowe.

The first things I learned to do were to ride a horse and swim. We all learned these things almost as soon as we could walk. Life passed very quickly, and it was very good. We were not rich, but we did have good food to eat. And every year I got a hand-me-down coat to wear. When Arthur outgrew his, he got a new one and I got the old one.

When I was six years old, I started school in the old Delmer schoolhouse. My first teacher's name was Jessie Harrington. I hated school. It was much more fun to be out riding horseback or fishing in the creek that went through our farm or just going to the woods to play. I could see no sense in going to school. To me, that was a waste of time. As a result, I had no trouble being at the wrong end of the class most of the time. As for arithmetic, anything past 2 + 2 and the wheels in my head just stopped turning. I simply could not do arithmetic. Consequently, I was always in trouble with it and had to stay in at recess or after school. This was very bad for me, and I think the reason I hated school so much. As for spelling, I could get up in a spelling match and spell down the whole room, but I couldn't write it on paper. Every other subject, I got top marks. I was very good at reading and read everything I could get my hands on. To me, a book was a book, and I read it. When I was fourteen years old, my father was very sick. One morning in the spring of the year, he called me into his room and told me to bring my books home that night. I was done school. But not many years later, I realized what a mistake that was. Without an education, a person was very limited as to what he could do. It was very fortunate for me that I liked to read. It was from this that I got my education.

However, now I was getting a different education. I was given a team of horses and set to work. But it was not all work and no play. I got myself a .22 rifle and learned to shoot. In the summertime, I hunted woodchucks and learned a lot about fieldcraft, which stood me in good stead in later life. I learned to crawl up to within a shooting distance on a woodchuck and how to hide on a flat piece of ground. In the wintertime, I hunted jackrabbits and cottontails. It was nothing for me to shoot a running jackrabbit at more than a hundred yards. From this experience, I was later to be the best rifle shot in my regiment.

Time passed in this way, and I grew up just like all farm boys. But in the mid-1930s, something new came along—a man named Adolf Hitler, chancellor of Germany. He was going to rule the world, and he made no secret of it. He worked on the younger folks in Germany, preaching that the Germans were a "super-race" and that it was their right to rule the world.

He brought propaganda into its own. I can remember hearing his speeches on the radio. He would hold massive assemblies with thousands of people. They would start with very stirring band music. All around would be loudspeakers, and as the bands played, out of the speakers would come loud cheering, and they chanted "Sieg heil, sieg heil, sieg heil!" and "Deutschland über alles." When everyone was properly worked up, Hitler would give his speech. He would rant and rave, and you could just imagine him foaming at the mouth, the spit flying. All the while, his speech was interspersed with music and cries of "Sieg heil, sieg heil, sieg heil!" Even though he was crazy, his people listened to him. And even though he told everyone he was going to war, the rest of the world paid no attention. By the time people started to take him seriously, it was too late. They woke up to the fact that he had the largest army and air force in the world. By 1939, the world was at war.

On September 1, 1939, German forces attacked Poland. Hitler signed the order to attack at noon and German forces moved up to the frontier. At eight o'clock in the evening the German radio station at Gliewitz was attacked. The attackers were members of the German ss in Polish uniforms, and they left behind some bodies of concentration camp inmates in Polish uniforms to convince the world that Poland was the aggressor.

On September 2, 1939, both the British and the French presented ultimatums to Germany. Fifteen minutes after those ultimatums expired, at eight o'clock in the morning on September 3, 1939, British Prime Minister Neville Chamberlain announced that war had begun. Australia and New Zealand declared war on Germany the same day. On September 10, Canada declared war on Germany.

That same day, the first major units of the British Expeditionary Force landed in France, with Field Marshall Lord Gort in command. September 10 was a Sunday and a special session of Parliament had been called. All the Kipp family had gone to church except for me. I stayed home to follow the events. I made myself a big dish of popcorn and sat down in front of the radio to listen. I knew that if there was a war, I was going to be there. I heard the announcement that Canada had declared war on Germany. On Monday morning, many of the military-aged men were in London to enlist, but I was in no hurry. This was going to be a long war. Besides that, I had a bad hernia, and they were not accepting men with hernias. To be able to get in the service, I had a lot of planning I had to do. I would have to play this by ear. A war without me was unthinkable.

Canada went ahead making war plans and discussing what to do. I sat and waited. The government announced that farmers were exempt, but they also started to make plans to give everyone over twenty-one years of age thirty days of military training, and I could see a way to get in the service.

Our neighbour, Jack Woodbine, and I talked about going to London to enlist. We decided that we would go as soon as our fall work was done on the farm. He did the fall plowing on their farm and I did it on ours. We finished about the same day, in the middle of November, and it was now time to go and try our luck. My father drove every day to his office in Ingersoll, so we rode there with him in the morning and thumbed our way to London from there.

I will never forget what my father said to me that morning when we started out: "You are young and tough, just the kind of man they want in the army. And when you come home with your health in ruins, they will do nothing for you." I thought he did not know what he was talking about. After all, the papers were full of government promises—medical care, big pensions. They would always look after us with the best of care. And if we were killed, we would get a wonderful burial in an army bed blanket. We all paid one dollar for our blanket. I did not use mine, so when I was discharged from the service, my one dollar was given back to me.

Jack and I decided we would try for the air force. I was quickly turned down because I did not have enough education. Jack signed up, and he was promptly sent to a hospital in Westminster for a medical. There, it was discovered he had problems with his feet, but they took him anyway. They sent him to Toronto to drive a tractor clearing snow from the airport runway, and that was where he spent the winter. In the spring they did not need him, so they offered him a discharge. He wanted to stay in, so he joined the air force police, and that was how he fought the war. After the war ended, he was sent as a police officer to England to bring back a prisoner. In England, he jumped off the back of a truck and hurt his feet. He went to the medical officer, who made a record of it. On his return to Canada, he was given a discharge and a big pension. He spent four days in England and drew a good pension for the rest of his life. My experience was quite different.

While Jack was having his medical, I was exploring other options. The boys in the recruiting office were really giving me a good going-over. They had a green farm boy here, and they were telling me what a good life the army was: "Just sign here, and we'll have you in England in two weeks." They showed me their new uniforms, even let me feel them while they were showing me that they were bullet-proof. They assured me that bullets just could not go through and that there was nothing to worry about. (One day overseas when I got five different bullet holes through my uniform, I thought back to what they had said.) I decided I would join the infantry and just go wherever I was sent, so the recruiters started to fill out the forms. But when they came to the question "Do you have a hernia?" what could I say? I had to say yes. I was then told that they would not accept me but just sign here, anyway. They would send me for a medical, I would be turned down, and then I could go home and forget about it. I asked them, "If I am turned down now, will I be called up for training?" I was told that I would never be called. But this was not what I had in mind. I was going to war, one way or another. I just picked up the forms and tore them up, and then I left the office. There had to be a way, and I was going to find it.

I returned home and waited. I waited for almost a year. In 1940, they called up the first batch of men who came to be called the "thirty-day wonders." I was in the first group called up. One day, Mrs. Yates, the mailman's wife, called and informed my mother that my "call-up" was in the mail. I was to go to my family doctor for a medical. We made an appointment, and I went in. The doctor looked me all over, and when he was done, he said, "Well, you're lucky. With that hernia, I will have to give you a c.1 category. You will not have to go." I said, "Doctor, I want to go. I want in the army." He just said, "Well, in that case, we'll try it, and see what they do." He changed the category from c.1 to a.1. A few weeks later, I got my notice to report to Woodstock for training. Allan Rice was called at the same time. We talked it over, and it was decided he would pick me up that morning and we would go together.

We arrived in Woodstock about nine o'clock in the morning, showed our letters, and were told to get our clothes off and to get in line. There was already a line of bare-naked men. I let Al go first, as I wanted to see what happened and be prepared. Al went right through, no problem. The first doctor who looked at me said, "How did you get here? You get your clothes on and go home." But I had different ideas. I said to the doctor, "Nothing doing. I have a letter telling me to be here, and I am going to stay." He could not believe what he was hearing. He looked at me, then at the letter, and just stood there trying to make up his mind. He looked at my name and said, "Are you any relation to Clarence Kipp?" I said, "He's my father." He replied, "Oh, then you want in, do you?" And I said, "Yes, this is my only chance." "Well, I'll see," he said. He then talked it over with a couple of other doctors. When he came back, he said, "All right, just go on in. No one else wants to look at you." I ran in and caught up to Al just as he was getting his uniform. I got mine right behind him, and we were marched away in the same platoon and put in the same hut. Al was in the bottom bunk and I was in the top. As it turned out, the doctor was a friend of my father's in Ingersoll, and for that reason he let me in. Later, when Al tried to join active service, he failed his medical and never did have to go to war.

I took to the training like a duck to water. The only thing I had trouble with was "left" and "right," but that didn't last long. I soon learned that for farm boys it wasn't "left" and "right." It was "hay" foot and "straw" foot. Everything else was easy. Rifle drill was *very* easy. I had handled a rifle since I was fourteen, and I was soon the best marksman in the company. My years spent hunting woodchucks stood me in good stead. Every day, someone came to our platoon asking for men to join active service. If anyone volunteered, he was sent to the medical officer for a checkup, but I did not dare to volunteer. I knew as soon as a medical officer looked at me, he would send me home, so I just played the waiting game. The thirty days' training went fast, and when we were tested on our exams, even though I didn't have much education, I passed with one of the highest marks in my platoon.

Finally, our basic training was over. On that day, we turned in all of our equipment. At a certain hour, we would be allowed out the gate to go home, with orders to report to the Oxford Rifles in Tillsonburg. We were known as reserves, or non-permanent active militia. I sat wondering, "What can I do? What can I do?" I wanted to go active, but as I said before, if I did, I would be discharged. Just fifteen minutes before it was time to go home, the door opened, and in came one of the company instructors, Cpl. Ted Shaddock. He hollered at everyone to be quiet, and after everyone fell silent, he said, "They want instructors to go to Chatham No. 12 Basic Training Centre. Are there any volunteers?" This was it! I volunteered on the spot. After a short interview with the company commander, I was accepted and told to go home. They would call me when they were ready for me. I was a bit closer to being in active service, and knew I was going to make it. Luck was with me now.

I reported to the Oxford Rifles in Tillsonburg. We trained one night a week all winter long, building rifle pits with sandbags and doing every kind of training—rifle drill, foot drill—the same as in Woodstock. It was suggested that I be promoted to lance corporal, but when they learned I was to go to Chatham, they didn't think they should send me to NCO school, only to lose me when I came home. Then came summer camp. We were to go to Carling Heights for two weeks under canvas. We left Tillsonburg by train for Iona Station. There, we were picked up by trucks to go into London, where we were all put into tents by platoons. We had no sooner got settled when the company runner came for me and told me I was to report to the medical officer, who told me I was to be sent home and discharged. I went straight to Sergeant Major Moir and my platoon commander, Lt. "Baldy" Armstrong, to protest. They told me to go back to my tent and they would see what they could do. Moir came back later and said, "It's okay. You can stay." Another hurdle had been passed.

The training at Carling Heights was designed for fun. The more fun it was being in the service, the more men they could get to go active. We did have a good time with competition between platoons and companies. I never did get put on fatigue duty, which was dish-washing and picking up around camp. But I did get put on guard duty, which was on the gate, checking for men coming in late or without a pass to be out. We made agreements with all the other regiments there: you do not charge our men, we do not charge yours. This worked very well. Instead of asking for their passes when they came in late at night, we just asked what regiments they were with. There was one regiment that wouldn't cooperate. Anyone late or without a pass, they charged. So all the other regiments charged them. They really hollered about that. Every day, they had the biggest defaulters parade in the whole camp and wondered why we picked on them.

The camp was on one side of the river, and the Wonderland Dance Hall was on the other side, just at the top of the hill. There was a footbridge across the river and a guard post at the bridge. The NCOs who were in charge of the guard could pick their own men. Harley Meyers and Norm Moir, both First World War veterans, always picked me. They looked after me and taught me all the tricks. One Saturday night, we drew guard duty on the footbridge. About nine o'clock they said to me, "A young fellow like you should be out having fun, not down here playing guard duty. You beat it. Go up and dance at the dance hall. We'll look after your job here. Just don't get caught."

I went across the bridge and up the hill to have a look. I knew the military police would not be far away, and I was going to find them before they found me. After all, it was past curfew, and I did not have a pass. The place was full of servicemen, both reserve and active. There was bound to be a fight. The active servicemen thought it was their right to beat up on any reserve man they could catch alone. In their opinion, the reserve men were too yellow to fight, or else they would have joined active service. Most of the reserve men did, in fact, eventually join active service, but now they were just not ready. Fights at the dance hall were very common, but they had never had a riot yet. It all changed that night. I could see reserve men on one side of the floor and active men on the other, eyeing each other. It was not long before the pushing began, and soon pushing came to shoving, and then it started. The whole dance floor was full of fighting men. This was no place for me to get caught. It was an open-air dance hall, so I went over the side and headed for the pathway to the bridge. I was the first one out. Sirens went off, whistles blew, women screamed, and I was down the hill and across the bridge as fast as I could run. Harley and Norm heard the commotion and ran to see what it was all about. I said, "There's a big fight up there. Get ready." In just a few minutes, we could hear men coming down the hill, their feet pounding on the bridge as they ran across. We just stood back and let them through. The police had been ready for trouble and were there in a hurry. The dance hall was a wreck. I had survived my first big fight in the service by running—a very good lesson. The next day, the Wonderland Dance Hall was put out of bounds for all servicemen, and, to my knowledge, that was never lifted all through the war. Shortly after we came home from Carling Heights, my notice came to report to Chatham. I was on my way.

2

MY LIFE IN CHATHAM

I RODE TO INGERSOLL with my father in the morning when he went to his office. He put me out on Highway No. 2 and told me to follow it to Chatham. In those days, we hitchhiked all over. If a car had an empty seat, the driver gave someone a ride. I rode in several different cars and arrived in Chatham at just about twelve o'clock. I had no idea where the training centre was, so I went into a restaurant to get a bite to eat and ask directions. When I asked the waitress where it was, she said, "Just a minute. I'll get you a ride." There was a man in uniform in the restaurant, and she went over and spoke to him. He looked up and nodded his head. When he was ready, he said, "Let's go," and I rode into No. 12 Basic Training Centre in an army truck. He was a driver from there. He let me off at the guard-house and told me to go in and report.

I was taken from the guardhouse to the adjutant's office. He asked me a few questions, and then said, "I see you have a hernia." I told him it was not a hernia, but something like it, and that it didn't bother me. The adjutant sent me to a clerk to fill out enlistment papers. The clerk told me that I didn't have to go active service and that if I wanted to, I could stay reserve. I said I wanted to go active, and was duly sworn in. It had taken about a year and a half, but I was now in the service. What I did not know was that once I was taken on the staff of No. 12, I was frozen and would be there for the duration. The army had to have instructors. I was made a lance corporal and assigned to "D" Coy. Although I knew the work very well, I had never given an order or taught a class. The first few days were a disaster, but I got down to work and soon learned to give orders with the best. But it was some time before I could give lectures. I had never been trained to do that. Later on, I learned to after much hard work and help from some of the other instructors. They were mostly good guys, and I got along well with most of them. There were Wilford "Wimpy" Hays, Bill Nicholson, Jim Bell, Andy McCormack, Walter Johnson, Howard Hicks, Harry Jones, Lyle Ryan, Reg Sutton—who was the company sergeant major—and many more whose names I have forgotten. Of these instructors, Bill Nicholson, Jim Bell, Howard Hicks and I were all in the Lincoln and Welland Regiment together later on. When the war ended, Howard Hicks and I were together, he being the company commander, and I, the acting sergeant major.

As basic training instructors, we taught new recruits everything they had to learn to be soldiers. Some of them were active servicemen and some were reserve. They came from all walks of life—farmers, doctors, lawyers and everything in between, all mixed in together. There were preachers, German sympathizers, hillbillies from the United States, even bank robbers. One man had been a member of the "Purple Gang" from Detroit, the mob who did the Valentine's Day murders years earlier. I remembered them from when I was a kid. There was another chap from Toronto who had worked parking cars. Many of these cars belonged to people who worked nearby and were there every day. He had devised a foolproof plan to hold up a bank in St. Catharines. Every day when he got off work at noon, he would take a car from the parking lot, drive to St. Catharines and plan the job. Finally, the day came to do the job. He took a car, disconnected the speedometer, drove it to St. Catharines and held up the bank. A very neat job, so he thought. But someone had gotten the licence number of the car, and when he drove back onto the lot in Toronto, the police were there waiting for him. Two other men who had been good friends of mine became holdup men after the war was over. One time, we had a platoon of men who were all deserters. By the time their training was over, most of them had deserted again.

Every day, the recruits had to be on parade at 8:00 A.M. They were taught platoon drill: how to march; how to make left, right or about turns, either standing still or on the march; and how, when and who to salute. Then they were issued rifles and taught rifle drill, musketry and all small arms. They learned how to clean and take care of their weapons, how to use them and how to fix a bayonet. Then we taught them how to kill a man with a bayonet. We had to be fencing instructors, teaching them how to fight with a bayonet—how to parry, point and withdraw a bayonet from a body. Real gruesome work. I was also sent to Long Branch, a school of chemical warfare, and learned to instruct in how to use a respirator, how to identify the different gases (chlorine, phosgene, diaphosgene and mustard gas) and what action to take if you were gassed. Fortunately, gas was never used. Basic training lasted two months. Then, men had to pass tests in everything we had taught them. If they were reserve soldiers, they then went home. If they were active servicemen, they went to advanced training for whatever branch of the service they were going to. This meant that every two months, we got new men to train, and the process started all over again. It also meant that we got very raw throats out on the parade square.

Just like the recruits, the instructors were from all walks of life, but most of them were young men just out of school. It was the first job many of them had ever had. Most of them were good instructors, were well liked and got along fine with the men. I can say that I was always very popular and made many good friends. But some of the instructors were bullies, and as soon as they were given some authority, they used it. Consequently, they were hated, and in a place like that, anything could happen.

We had just completed this one group's two months' training, and they were ready to move on the next day. We had just finished our supper, and I was on my way back to my hut. A man walked up behind me, and, as he went past, he didn't even look at me. He just said, "Get lost." I did not let on I had heard him, but I got the message. "Lights out" was at ten o'clock, and I had my bed all made up and ready to get in. The minute the lights went out, I rolled up my blankets and put them under my arm, and out the door I went. The other side of our hut was empty, so I ran in there to a corner bed, threw my blankets on it and crawled in. I was just in time. The centre door of the hut opened, and in came about a half-dozen men, all carrying fire pails full of water, on their way to get one of the instructors who had been giving them a hard time for the last two months. I was the only one who had been warned about what they were going to do, and I just settled down and went to sleep. No one bothered me. The rumpus soon spread from one platoon to another until it boiled over into the other companies. They rioted nearly all night. I never did ask how they got things settled down, and no one ever asked me where I had gotten to or what I had been doing, but I was not very popular with several of the NCOs from then on.

One Friday morning when I woke up, I did not feel well. My throat was swollen and my neck was very stiff, so I thought I had better see the doctor. He took one look at me and said, "Mumps. Go get your things. You're going to the hospital." They put me in a truck, took me into town and dumped me off in front of a building with a red cross on it. It was a small military hospital. I went inside and looked around, but there was no one there. It was all fixed up and had six beds in it. I waited around for a while, but no one came in, so I picked out a bed and got into it and went to sleep. About one o'clock a girl came in and asked me what I was doing there. Her job was to keep the place clean. I asked her where the doctor was, and she said there was no doctor there. Doctors were supposed to come from London every morning, but they had not been there for weeks. She stayed around for a while and then left. I stayed there until four o'clock, and then finally got up, put my clothes back on, went back to the training centre and went to bed. On Monday morning, I went to the doctor again. He said, "What are you doing here? You're supposed to be in the hospital." By this time, they had about thirty cases of mumps, so they put us all in one side of a hut and closed the centre off so we couldn't get out. There was a black man by the name of Lucas who had already had the mumps, so he was given the job of looking after us. Some of us could not get out of bed and could not even get to the food when it was brought in. We nearly starved. My friend Buzz Hannam crawled over the partition one night just to see how I was. I told him I was hungry, so every night thereafter he brought food in for me until I could get up and get my own. We were in there for about three weeks and it was a pretty rough time.

The next thing that happened to me was my hernia started to give me trouble. One day, I fell down on the parade square, and they put me on a stretcher, took me to the medical officer's office and left me on the floor while they went to get the doctor. I got off the stretcher and left. Later that day, Sergeant Major Sutton came and told me that I was excused of all duties until further notice. I thought, "This is it. They will discharge me from the service." Several days later he came to me and said, "You can have a discharge, or they will give you an operation." I did not hesitate; I said I'd have the operation. I was sent to Trafalgar Street military hospital in London, where they performed the operation. Six weeks later, I was back in Chatham.

About this time, we began hearing rumours that all the active force men were to be sent overseas, and some of them started to leave—some to regiments overseas, and some to officer training school. I went to the company sergeant major and said, "Will you see that I am put on draft for overseas?" He said okay, and a few days later he told me I was on the list. I thought if I was going overseas, I should get married before I went. On June 26, 1943, I married Margaret Leach and rented an apartment in Chatham for her, but she was not there very long. We were put on notice and given embarkation leave for two weeks. All of our furniture was moved to my parents' home in Ingersoll, and Margaret went back to work at her aunt and uncle's store in London.

The day came that our company was to go. We were all packed, and had been given instructions to turn in our blankets the following morning and be on parade down by the gate at eight o'clock, ready to leave. Then the blow fell. About four o'clock that afternoon, Sutton came in and said, "I got news for you. You've been taken off the draft. You're still a c.1 medical." There was nothing I could say. My friends Jim Bell and Bill Nicholson, or "Nick," as we called him, with whom I was supposed to be going, came to say, "Too bad. We'll miss you." But I said nothing. I was all ready to go. After all I had done to get in the service and come this far, I was not done yet. In the morning, I turned in my blankets, picked up my pack, and fell in the parade with Jim and Nick. It was not long before Company Sergeant Major Sutton saw me there. He came over and looked at me, but I didn't look at him. He said, "You're going, are you?" I replied, "Yes." He said, "I'll take care of it for you." My name was not on the list, and I left Chatham with no documentation or anything. As far as Chatham was concerned, I was a deserter, as I had gone without authorization. When my documents caught up to me, I was an A.1 medical category and on my way to England.

We were sent to Stratford, Ontario, as a staging area. When everyone was assembled there, it was discovered that although many of the men had been in the service since 1939, many of them did not have very much training. As every man going overseas had to pass tests on elementary training, they were given thirty days to take the training and pass the tests. They were divided into platoons, and instructors were appointed; I was one of them. Then we went to work on them, teaching them how to be soldiers. They all passed their tests, and we were ready to go.

One weekend, I made arrangements for Margaret to come to Stratford for a visit. That morning, we were all confined to barracks. I had planned to find a place for her to stay that morning, but I wasn't allowed out of the barracks. She arrived about the middle of the afternoon, and I went down to meet her. There we were—me on one side of the fence and her on the other. By this time, the news that we were leaving that night had gotten out, and there must have been five hundred to a thousand people there to say goodbye. It must have been about eight o'clock when we were all assembled on the parade square. That was the last I saw of Margaret. I had no idea where she was to spend the night, and I could do nothing about it. She went to the train station and waited most of the night for a train back to London.

Meanwhile, we were all formed up and ready to go. Every so often, a name would be called and the man would leave. In a few minutes, he would be back to announce that he had been taken off the draft and could go home. Then my name was called. This was it. I went to the orderly room expecting the worst, but it wasn't that at all. I was asked if I would consider staying in Canada to take officer training. If I did that, it would be at least another year before I would get overseas. I said I was not interested. Shortly afterwards, we marched out to the station and were on our way to Windsor, Nova Scotia.

Our stay in Windsor was mercifully brief. We nearly starved to death as they had no regular cooks. On a Saturday afternoon, Jim Bell and I decided to go into town and find something to eat. There were no restaurants there, but we did find some food. It was a kind of kelp and smelled like sardines, only worse. We bought a big bag of it. Then, we found half a gallon of homemade root beer. We went down on the dock and sat down to enjoy our lunch. We took one bite of the kelp and pitched it off the end of the dock. We took one taste of the root beer and pitched it in there, too. We decided to go back to camp and get whatever we could. We were nearly there when a taxi pulled up beside us and stopped. A girl was driving. She opened the door and said, "Hop in." We said, "No, we're nearly there, we don't need a ride," but she insisted, saying she wanted to talk to us, so we got in. She said, "I want three men to come to dinner Sunday night. You guys get someone else, and I'll pick you up at the gate at five o'clock on Sunday." We wondered what we were getting into but collared Bill Nicholson to go with us. At five o'clock we were out there, and along she came. She drove us to a big house, where her mother and father were waiting and a big roast beef dinner was ready for us to eat. We all sat down at the table, and it was delicious. They told us that this was their war effort and that every week they had someone there for dinner. The mother said that they had recently invited some sailors whose ship had been torpedoed and sunk. She said one of them looked just like me, only he was better looking than I was. After a wonderful supper and a delightful evening, the girl drove us back to camp. The next day, we were taken by truck to Halifax and put aboard the *Queen Elizabeth,* a luxury liner converted into a troopship, to begin an uneventful trip to Glasgow, Scotland.

3

TRAINING IN ENGLAND

As THE QUEEN ELIZABETH could stay in port for only a brief period, we were all unloaded in a very short time. If the German air force ever found her there, they would have been right after her. That would have been a great prize. Tied up to a dock in Glasgow, the ship wouldn't stand a chance, so she had to be unloaded and back out to sea in about two hours. You can imagine the mad rush there was. We were taken off at a dead run and put on trains for Aldershot. It was nearly dark when we boarded a train and headed out. We had not gone very far before it was completely dark. The train was all blacked out, and every once in a while it would slow right down or even stop, and we could hear planes overhead. We knew then we were in the war. Several times when we stopped, bombs landed close enough to rock the train. But we did eventually arrive at our destination, where we unloaded and marched to the Balaclava barracks. All this time, Bill Nicholson, Jim Bell, Jim Marr and I had stayed together. We had resolved to keep together if we could. We had no idea what was in store for us, so we enjoyed our first glimpse of England. We spent the next week looking over the town and getting used to the money and the beer. We had trouble with both until we learned how to handle them.

Then, one morning, we heard, "Everyone out!" We dashed out and formed up in three ranks, which was the thing to do. The four of us were still together. They started to call out, "Ten volunteers here!" When they had ten men, they marched them away, and then it was eight volunteers, or maybe six. We soon learned they were being assigned to different regiments. We decided that when they called for four, we would volunteer. It was not long in coming, and we put our hands up and stepped out. We were marched away and told we were to go to the Lincoln and Welland Regiment.

This was a regiment from Niagara and St. Catharines with a long and illustrious history in both Britain and Canada. The Lincolnshire Regiment of the British army was formed in England in 1685 as the 10th Regiment of Foot, and fought in the Low Countries in the reign of William and Mary; in the Low Countries again in the War of the Spanish Succession, 1701–1714; in America during the Indian Wars and Revolutionary War, 1775–1783, and the Fenian Raids, 1866–1870; in Egypt, Italy and Spain during the Napoleonic Wars, 1800–1815, and in India in 1846. The county of Lincoln, Ontario, was so named after Lincolnshire in England, making the Lincolnshire Regiment of England the home regiment of the 19th Lincoln Regiment of Canada when it was formed. It was known for a while as the 19th St. Catharines Regiment, but in 1912, just before returning to its former territorial designation as the 19th Lincoln Regiment, it established an alliance with its namesake in England. It was at this time that the Lincoln and Welland Regiment was authorized to use "The Lincolnshire Poacher" as its regimental march, and it continues to do so to this day. After the Second World War was over and we were waiting in Holland to come home, both regiments entertained members of the other, thus keeping up the friendship.

During the Indian Wars and the Revolutionary War, the British mode of fighting was not very successful. When moving from one place to another, they were very vulnerable to attack from camouflaged and fast-moving Indian warriors. The Lincolnshire Regiment got together with Col. John Butler of Butler's Rangers fame, who fought as the Indians did. Under the training of Colonel Butler's Rangers, the Lincolnshire Regiment became the first English regiment to don buckskins and war paint, and fight as the Indians fought, with very effective results.

In the Battle of Queenston Heights, there were men of the Lincolns with Maj. Gen. Isaac Brock when he was killed leading an assault on an enemy position. It was also at this time that Laura Secord, wife of Sgt. James Secord of the 1st Lincolns, escaped from the Americans under the pretext of going to visit a sick relative. She walked for eighteen hours until she reached an Indian camp and gave the alarm that the Americans were planning to attack. The Indians laid an ambush near Beaver Dams, where they were joined by a small detachment of the Lincolns and by a special force under Fitzgibbon, and together they bluffed the Americans into surrendering their whole force.

In the Great War of 1914–1918, the Lincoln and Welland Regiment was given battle honours for each of the battles they fought at Ypres, Festubert, the Somme, Arras, Hill 70, Amiens, the Hindenburg Line and Mons. It was a very old and highly respected regiment. My own great-great-grandfather, William Kipp, had been a seventeen-year-old private in the Lincoln and Welland Regiment. This was the regiment I had now joined and would fight with through the Second World War. I couldn't believe my luck. We were issued regimental shoulder flashes and green divisional patches. We would be in the 4th Canadian Armoured Division.

The next morning we were driven by truck to Victoria Station in London. As Nick was the senior of the group, he was put in charge. We had no idea where we were going. All we had was a train number, but we soon learned that the Lincoln and Welland Regiment was in Nissen huts near Thetford in the southeast part of England. As well, we soon found out Victoria Station was a pretty big place. We also learned to check all telephones for money the last caller had not picked up when it was returned. We picked up a lot of money that way. When our train number was called, we piled in, found a seat for four, and were on our way. As we were coming to a stop at one station, I saw a familiar face on a man sitting on a kit bag and waiting for a train. I hollered at Nick and both Jims to come, and they followed me off the train. There was our old friend Howard Hicks, from our Chatham days. We all piled on him and rolled him around on the ground just for good measure. He was an officer in the Lincoln and

Welland Regiment and was on his way to take a course in something. The train whistle blew and we jumped back on the train, leaving him to pick himself up.

We arrived in Thetford about 4:30 in the afternoon and looked for our transportation to the regiment, but there was none. What to do? We did the only thing any good soldier would do. We took all of our equipment and found a pub in which to talk it over. Nick, as he was in charge, approached the barmaid and had a talk with her. She told him we should just stay put, as there would be someone in later who would give us a ride out to the camp. She would see to it.

About 10:30 P.M., an English girl from the Army Service Corps came over to us and asked if we were the blokes who wanted a ride out to the Lincoln and Welland camp. We said we were, and she said she would pick us up in about half an hour, and then she left. Half an hour later she was back, and she stuck her head in the door and said to come on, she was ready to go. We grabbed our gear and put it in a fifteen hundred weight truck. She was standing by the truck calling, "Anyone want a ride? I'm leaving." A few more people appeared and climbed in. She slammed the back up, climbed in and started the motor. The night was so black you could not see 10 feet in front. She left town for the open road, put her foot on the floor, and we were off just as if someone was chasing us, wide open down the road in the dark, no headlights on because of the blackout. Every once in a while she would stop at the gates of a camp and call out its name. Anyone for that camp climbed out, and we took off again. After several stops, she called out Lincoln and Welland, then came around and opened the back tailgate so we could get our stuff out. We said thanks, but she was not listening. She just jumped in and rode away off into the dark.

We went to the guardhouse and reported in. The orderly officer was called, and he said that we were not expected and that he didn't know what to do with us. We were finally given blankets, taken to an empty hut and told to go to bed. Someone would see us in the morning. We went to bed in the dark, but at least we now belonged to a regiment. The regiment is a soldier's home, and all the members are his family. It was October 20, 1943, that I was taken on strength of the Lincoln and Welland Regiment, four years after the outbreak of war.

But I had finally found my home and family. I had been fighting for this since 1939. I always knew I was going to get there, but the way had been rough and hard. Many times I had been ready to call it quits and go home. But now there was no backing out. I went to my bed in the dark very satisfied with my effort to go to war and serve my country.

The next morning a runner came to the hut where we had been quartered the night before and told us we were to report to the battalion orderly room at nine o'clock for an interview. We had no idea what to expect, but here we were, all very good NCOs and better trained than many of the officers, and we knew we could be an asset to any regiment. So at nine o'clock sharp, we reported to the orderly room—pants pressed, shoes shined, and brass in which you could see yourself. We knew every move and every answer. Nick, the senior amongst us, was called in first. It was a very short interview. He came out very pale and absolutely livid. Jim Bell was next. He also had a very short interview. We knew we were not being interviewed; we were being given an ultimatum. My turn came.

I stepped into the room, stopped, saluted smartly, took two steps forward, stood at attention and said, "I am A57319, Corporal Kipp, Sir." Behind the table sitting in a chair was a man with the rank of major. He looked down his nose at me as if I was just so much scum, and with a very deliberate sneer, gave me his ultimatum: "We did not ask for you, and we don't want you. You will revert to a private, or you will *be* reverted to one. We have our ways of doing that. If you are any good, you will be promoted when your turn comes." I answered, "I am a good NCO. I know my job, and I will not revert to a private." I was confirmed in my rank, and the only way they could take that away was by court martial. He said, "You will report to Able Company, and you will get *nothing* from this regiment." And he was as good as his word. Although I had more citations by the end of the war than any man in the regiment, I did not get a decoration. Every citation was thrown out.

I went back to the hut where the others were waiting. They were all pretty mad and were getting ready to report to the company to which they had been assigned. That was one of the stupidest things, amongst many stupid things, the army did. This regiment had very few NCOs trained as well as we were. We were capable of teaching any subject, and we were being asked to revert to private soldiers and to be led by other men who did not have the training. The Lincoln and Welland Regiment had many NCOs who, although they were good men, were not trained for the job.

I picked up my things and went to find Able Coy., which was at the far end of the camp. When I found their orderly room, I put my things down and stepped inside. The proper way to enter an orderly room was to step inside, come to attention, salute and state who you were and why you were there. This I did. Everyone just looked at me. What gives with this guy? Most of their NCOs just slouched in and stood there. A first lieutenant was there and he said, "I have been expecting you, Corporal. Just come with me." We started to the platoon area. He introduced himself as my platoon leader, and told me that I would be in No. 9 Plt., and that I would be leading No. 9 section. When we got there, he introduced me to the platoon. What a reception I got! No one spoke or even acknowledged me. I thought, "If that's the way it is, so be it." I looked around, picked an empty bed in the corner and took possession of it. I turned my back on them and ignored them all. After all, I was now the senior corporal in the platoon and was quite capable of looking after myself. There I was—all pressed and shined, and looking like a real parade ground soldier. I soon found out I was referred to as "that shit-hot NCO who knows it all." The men hated me and let me know it. The platoon was soon called out for the afternoon, and I was told to just follow along until I learned the routine.

The Nissen huts we were housed in were made of steel, and that night I had just gotten into bed when something dropped with a bang on the roof, rolled down the incline and thudded onto the ground. This went on all night long. First thing in the morning, I went out to see what it was, and found the ground was covered with sweet chestnuts. I picked up a handful, took them back inside and put them on the top of the stove to roast. When they popped and fell on the floor, I let them cool, then picked them up and ate them. Everyone watched me and thought I was crazy. Then I was spoken to for the first time. One of the corporals, Cpl. Reg Sheppard, said, "Don't eat those. They're poison and will kill you." I handed him one and told him to try it. In a couple of days, everyone in the hut was roasting chestnuts, and I had to get up early if I wanted any.

The first period of the morning was platoon drill. It was the job of the platoon sergeant to get everyone out by eight o'clock, form them into platoon and take roll call. By that time, the platoon officer was there, and the platoon was turned over to him for inspection. After all this was done, the officer turned them back to the sergeant. We had a very good sergeant, one of the few sergeants in the regiment with NCO training. His name was "Curly" Mackrow, a very capable man and soldier. After the lieutenant was gone, he would give a bit of platoon drill, then turn the platoon over to either Corporal Sheppard or Corporal Thorne. It was deemed to be work I didn't know how to do yet. Neither one of these corporals knew how to give platoon drill. In five minutes, the men would be so tangled up they did not know in which direction they were going. Ten minutes of this, and the men were mad at everyone and swearing at each other. There is a way to give platoon drill. Every order has to be given at just the precise time, and on the right foot. If an order for a turn is given on the wrong foot, it's trouble. Everything is out of order. These guys did not know how to do it.

I watched for two mornings and felt sorry for the men. On the third morning, Corporal Sheppard was in charge. When the men were so mad they were just about ready to rebel, he turned around to me and said, "How be you take over for a while." I took a position at the edge of the drill square. If it had been big enough, I would have gone to the centre and worked the platoon around me. But this would do. I gave them ten minutes of drill without stop, then drew them up in front of me in an advanced position and halted them. I had given every order at the correct time and had not made one mistake. The men all came up smiling. Maybe this "shit-hot NCO" did know a little bit of something. I turned around to "Shep" and he was gone. Every morning after that, platoon drill was my job. And every morning, I called a lance corporal out to stand beside me and gave him instructions on how it was to be done. "Shep" was all right, but he had never been trained for the job. And he was the only one who had spoken to me so far. But after that, the boys in the platoon started to acknowledge me. This was my introduction to the Lincoln and Welland Regiment.

The 4th Division was just being formed. It was the biggest and most heavily armed division in the Canadian army. This division was formed for one thing: to spearhead the Canadian army across France and break through into Germany. The Lincoln and Welland Regiment was newly arrived in England, so there was a lot of hard training to do.

The end of the week came. Saturday afternoon we had nothing to do. Jim Bell and Nick came to get me to go for a walk. We went to the edge of the woods where there was an open field. Out in the field was a great big chestnut tree. We walked out to it, picked up the nuts, and sat down to eat them and talk. We decided this would be our meeting place.

Every night after that, after we had had our supper and prepared everything for the next day, we met under the chestnut tree. The first one there gathered the nuts that had fallen and put them in three piles. When we were all there, we would sit and eat the nuts, and talk over the events of the day and how each of us was getting along. Everything that had happened through the day, we discussed, and gave each other advice on how to handle it. After "shop talk" was taken care of, we would talk over our letters from home and share how things were going there. Nick and I were both married, and now Nick had a son whom he had yet to see. One of the things we talked about was what our chances were of living through the war and getting home. Naturally, we all supposed we would get through the war and go home and live happily ever after. We supposed we might be wounded at some time or another, but not killed. Jim was always poking fun at Nick and me for being old married men and tied down, whereas he was free to do as he wished—no apron strings. After our serious talks were over, and we were preparing to return to the camp and go to the NAFFI (a British canteen) for tea and cakes before going to bed, Jim would always say, "Well, if you guys get killed, don't worry. I'll go home and look after the widows." Nick and I would always reply, "You won't get the chance to look after my widow; I'll be there to do it myself," or words to that effect. We would then jump on him and pummel him good, and roll him around on the ground until one of us would jump up and holler, "Last one to the NAFFI has to pay!" Then we'd race back to the camp. We spent a lot of evenings out there under the tree, Jim and Nick and me. They are amongst the best memories I have of the war.

And then one night, it all ended, which is one of the most regrettable things in my life. But at the time, it was all in fun. There came an evening when, after Jim's inevitable ribbing about taking care of our widows, Nick said, "We'll settle this right now." He took three coins from his pocket. They were three Canadian pennies from home, and he gave Jim and me each one, and kept one for himself. "There," he said. "We'll just flip these coins, and that will decide once and for all who is going home and who isn't. And after the war is over, we'll put our coins back together, so be sure and save them." It was to be "odd man out," and so we tossed our coins and then uncovered them. Jim and I had heads and Nick had a tail. Immediately, Jim and I started to holler and laugh at Nick, but one look at him stopped us dead in our tracks. Only then did we think of the enormity of what we had just done. The look that came over Nick's face—the blood just went right out of it and he turned as white as a sheet. Jim and I very quickly said, "This doesn't mean anything! It's just a stupid superstition! Doesn't mean a thing!" But it was too late; the fun was gone, and we very quietly walked back to camp. When we got there, Nick said, "Good night, I think I'll pass on the tea and cakes. I have some work to do," and abruptly left. Jim and I decided we didn't want anything to eat, either, and very sober faced, went to our beds. The next night, Jim and I went to the tree. There we talked about what we had done and were so very sorry about it, but it was too late. Nick did not come to the tree that night to meet us, and although Jim and I occasionally met there, Nick never again came to our tree. Although Jim and I remained very good friends, Nick avoided the both of us. If we went to him, he talked to us, but I saw him again just a few times. All over the flip of three little coins.

None of us had seen Jim Marr, and we were all wondering how he was getting along. We soon found out. His company commander had started right in to give him a hard time, and after several days, Jim gave in. He had reverted to a private and had been sent to Headquarters Coy. There, they promoted him to a lance corporal, gave him a motorcycle and made a dispatch rider out of him. We did not see very much of him after that, but he and I always stayed in touch, and when it was time to go on leave, we went together. Jim Bell and I started getting along where they put us, and before long, we were both amongst the most popular NCOs in the regiment.

The Lincoln and Welland Regiment was, at this time, organized into its final war establishment, with a full strength of 38 officers and 812 other ranks. Approximately one hundred of these men, in all ranks, were in Headquarters Coy. The balance of the regiment consisted of Support Coy. and four rifle companies. The rifle companies were the core of the fighting strength of the regiment. Each had a full strength of five officers: a company commander (a major), a second-in-command (a captain), and three platoon commanders (first lieutenants), with a sergeant as second-in-command. A platoon was composed of three sections, each led by a corporal, with a lance corporal as second-in-command. I was a section leader. Only about half of a regiment's establishment was constantly exposed to battle. Some were LOOB (left out of battle), ready to re-form a compnay in case it suffered severe losses. With this arrangement, some men did not see too much fighting. They were used instead as chore boys, carrying up supplies. I was always of the opinion that some of them had a very easy war. I was never at any time designated as LOOB. Others were part of the regiment's rear echelons, responsible for supply and maintenance of approximately 150 vehicles to service the fighting companies.

In early September, the regiment had moved to Norfolk, the site of the Stamford battle area. There, they were introduced to the other units of the 10th Canadian Infantry Brigade and learned to operate with them, taking part in a long series of tactical exercises known by such names as "Takex 1," "Obsex 1," "Grizzly 11" and "Harrow 6." These were all done living in the open. Throughout the fall of 1943, we worked with other supporting arms of the brigade and division.

The most important thing we had to learn was to coordinate with artillery, machine guns and tanks. The 10th Canadian Infantry Brigade was considered armoured infantry because we worked very closely with tanks, either attacking with them or riding into battle on top of them. The regiment was also supplied with TCVs (troop carrying vehicles). We also rode into battle on these. We had to learn to ride into position and jump out at 30 miles per hour, carrying full equipment. The first jump, we broke arms and legs and suffered many sore backs. I broke a vertebra in my back, but I did not go to the doctor. That was a big mistake. Years later, it caused me a lot of trouble and I could do nothing about it because it was not on my medical records.

Living in the open as we did during these tactical exercises was very rough. October weather was cold and miserable, and, at times, we did not eat for a couple of days. I believe it was during "Grizzly II" that we were up near the border of Scotland in the rain and the mud. The whole 4th Division was ordered back to the Stamford area. What a time that was. In my regiment, only one TCV arrived at our destination. We spent hours on the road and arrived there about four o'clock in the morning. That night, some dispatch riders were killed or hurt from being run over by tanks or trucks in the dark. We used no lights and many vehicles ran out of gas. The men just holed up where they could and waited, sometimes for days, for someone to come and find them. They were lost.

The regiment took part in many mock attacks on a feature known as "Frog Hill." How many times we captured that place, I don't remember. One exercise we did, named "Brigadoon," was a tactical advance of divisional strength against enemy attacks made by the 9th British Armoured Division. Our role was to hold bridgeheads along the line of their advance. Our regimental pioneer platoon put up a tent on the position I was to hold with my section. Then everyone forgot us. When noon came, the rations that were to be brought out to us never appeared. Nighttime—still no rations. Then down the road came an enemy truck with two English girls in it, taking rations to their men. We took them both as prisoners, and as it had started to rain, we took them in the tent and lived on their rations for three days. I told them they could take their truck and go anytime, but they didn't want to go—they were having too much fun. They stayed until the exercise was over.

Another time when we were out and no rations came, they told us the cook truck had got lost. About four o'clock in the afternoon, we went into a wood. We always stayed in a wood so the German planes could not see us at night. I went for a walk just to look the place over and came to the edge of the woods where there were people working in the field. I quickly saw that they were digging potatoes, so I kept out of sight. At five o'clock, they stopped work and left. As soon as they were gone, I went over the fence, dug up all the potatoes I could carry and took them back to my men. We dug a hole, put the potatoes in and covered them up, and started a fire over them. Before we went to sleep, we stuffed ourselves on potatoes, and we did not share them, either.

One of the last exercises we did in November of 1943 was to make a mock attack on a small town somewhere in the Stamford area. I was detailed to take my section into a part of the town and secure the area. It was evening and very cold when we entered the town. It began to rain and sleet with a harsh wind. We secured the position and settled down to wait for supper, which didn't come; we were just left there to take care of ourselves. When it got dark, we knew we were in for a long wait, so we found a shed to get in out of the cold and wet. But someone had to be out on watch in case we were called in. I told the men to get inside and I would stay out and watch. The houses in that town were very old, with walls a foot and a half thick. This set the doorway way back in. I found one of those doorways, and got back in it as close to the door as I could. I sat down and went to sleep for a while, but it was too cold and wet for that.

About four o'clock in the morning, a baker came down the street with a big basket of fresh, warm bread. I stopped him and bought a big loaf of bread. I broke off a big piece for myself and took the rest of it to the men. Then I returned to the doorway.

About 6:30 A.M. I heard movement in the house. All of a sudden the door opened, and then closed just as quickly. I could hear talking, and soon the door opened again, and an old man looked out. He opened the door and said, "Come in." I was soaked right through and nearly frozen, so I didn't need a second invitation. The old man and his wife got me out of my wet clothes and put a robe around me, then set me up to the fireplace to get warm. I think they gave me most of their breakfast and hot tea. Then they hung up my clothes to dry. Boy, that was nice.

About nine o'clock, the word came down to assemble in the town square to return to our camp. My men all went in, and when they were asked where I was, they said they didn't know. They hunted all over town for me, but the boys would not tell where I was. About noon, they decided I had had enough time to get warm, and one of the men came to the house and said, "Come on, we can't keep quiet any longer." I put on my dry clothes, thanked the old couple and went to the TCVS. The major looked at me and could see that I was the only man in dry clothing. He just smiled a little bit and gave the order to move off. My men knew by now that if they looked after me, I would look after them. And I now knew that amongst the men, I had been accepted.

About this time, we were told that we were to go on two weeks' leave, and we were to report to the orderly room and let them know where we wanted to go. I had no idea where I wanted to go, so I said I would go up north to Inverness in Scotland. That way, I could just work my way back south from there and I would see a lot of country along the way.

A few days later, I found myself walking down a street in Inverness and wondering, now that I was there, what I was going to do. A man I became acquainted with gave me a bus ticket and put me on a bus to an estate called Killmarten in Glen Urquhart. With no idea where I was going or what I was going to do once I got there, I sat down at the back of the bus, and we headed out into the hills down along Loch Ness.

We travelled for a couple of hours, and, by now, I was the only one left on the bus and it was getting dark. We had just passed a big estate with a stone wall about eight feet high, when the bus driver suddenly stopped the bus, turned around and said, "This is where you get off." So off I got and away he went, leaving me standing in the road in a very rugged glen. This was in one of the wildest parts of the highlands of Scotland, way deep in the hills. A big iron gate in the wall opened, and out came two Scottish ladies. They apologized for being late, but explained that they had just gotten a telephone call informing them that I was on that bus. I was made very welcome and given a large, beautiful room on the second floor. That night, I slept in white sheets for the first time since I had left Canada.

After I had gone to bed, several times I heard people talking outside of the house. There seemed to be people going through the property. When it happened again the second night, I asked my hostess, Mrs. Tinker, who it was. These people from way back in the hills were very superstitious people. There are ghosts and haunts all over the place; everywhere you go, really. A short distance up the road from the estate was a small stream running through a culvert under the road. This place was haunted, and at nighttime, people would not cross it. A gate had been put in at the end of the wall around the estate so people could go through there, past the house and back out onto the road at the other end of the wall.

During our conversation about this, she also told me that the bedroom I was sleeping in had its own private ghost, but that it would not bother me. Then she told me about a small loch back in the hills, but warned me not to go there. She said it was very bad, but refused to discuss it further. This, of course, just aroused my curiosity, and I resolved that I would go and look for it myself.

The next morning, armed with a shotgun and a lunch in a bag, I headed into the hills. Just at noon, I came out on top of a very high precipice and looked over and down. I had found the loch. It was in a large bowl-shaped hole about three or four hundred feet down. I sat down and ate my lunch, all the while looking the place over. I saw that about a mile away there was a small stream that came out from the loch and made its way down through the low land, providing an opening where I could get in. It was about a two-mile walk in and around the loch and out the other side of the stream.

Taking my gun with me and leaving my lunch bag there, I started off. I quickly made the short distance to the opening. The sun was shining bright and birds were twittering in the trees as I made my way down to the stream. Once there, I decided I would cross the stream and go in on the other side, walk all the way around the loch and come back out on this side, so I crossed the stream and headed up towards the loch. As I went into the bowl and towards the loch, it suddenly turned dark. There was not a ray of sunshine down there, and the water in the loch was just as black as ink. I came across the remains of a small wharf and the frame of a small boat. They looked as if they had been there for a lot of years. I started around it and soon came to the far side of the loch. It was then I noticed that there were no birds there—no life except for me. I made my way up to go around the end of the loch and out the other side. The side of the cliff was straight up, and I could see there were holes and small caves up there. I was about halfway there by now, and suddenly, cold chills started up and down my spine. My hair felt as if it were standing straight up. There was something in one of those caves watching me. I could not see a thing, but I could *feel* it watching me. I did not feel terror from it; I could feel the hate—just outright, malevolent, venomous hate! Whatever it was, it was there, and it was not an animal! As I went farther in, the feeling of hate grew stronger. It was getting the message through to me: "If you come here, something terrible will happen to you." I started and stopped several times. I never felt such hate as that in all my life! It just boiled around me! I did not continue around the loch. I turned back, and as I went out of there, I could feel the hate receding. As I walked back out into the sunshine, it left me completely. I made my way back up to the top and looked back down in there. All I could see were my tracks in the snow.

I never told Mrs. Tinker that I had gone there, but I knew then that it was as she had said. It was a bad, *very bad,* place. I know that if I had tried to go around the end of the loch, I would not have made it.

Shortly after our leave we went into winter quarters in the town of Crowborough in the south of England. This was the town of Sir Arthur Conan Doyle, famous as the creator of Sherlock Holmes. We were quartered in a large house. The NCOs—Reg Sheppard, Red Irwin, Bill Thorne and I—were bunked in a small upstairs room. The rest of the platoon was in a big room on the first floor, along with the company kitchen. Behind the house was a small hall with a stage in it. This was where we trained in cold weather. The other two platoons would come there, and it was generally my job to train them in whatever subject was on for that day, be it map-reading, first aid or chemical warfare. I was informed at that time that I had been designated NCO in charge of chemical warfare for the regiment.

On January 2, 1944, we were given a new lieutenant colonel, J.G. McQueen, formerly of the Calgary Highlanders. He had also been the senior commanding officer of the 1st Canadian Special Service Battalion. Together with the Americans, this was the regiment that took Monte Cassino in Italy. He was a fine-looking soldier, a strict disciplinarian and training officer, but otherwise, just no damn good, as we learned later, much to our sorrow. After he came, the training was very stiff, especially weapons training.

In February 1944, we went to Scotland and practised assault landings on the beaches of Loch Fyne. The water was very cold. While there, we were billeted at Inverary Castle, which was also the place where commandos were trained. There was an assault course up the side of the mountain—a long, hard climb. Many of the men could not do it. They started at the bottom with a 40-pound pack on their back and carrying a weapon. An English commando held the record for the fastest time to the top. I put on a 50-pound pack, and, three times a day, I went up the mountain. I asked for a try at the record. In training, I carried 50 pounds, but when trying for the record I would carry only 40 pounds. This made a very big difference. After 50 pounds, 40 pounds seemed very light. But I never got the opportunity to try for the record. In the middle of one night, we were ordered from our beds and returned to the south of England. I was very disappointed, as I was sure I could have broken the record.

By February 23, we were back in Crowborough and back to the old grind. We started to train with live ammunition. This was done on an obstacle course, which the men crawled through as live ammo was fired over them. I was the best shot in the regiment with a rifle, so another man who was a sniper and I did the shooting with .303 rifles. We would start in the morning with a safety man to watch us and make sure we did not fire too close to the men. We each fired hundreds of rounds. By noon, we were very tired and shaky. They would not start the afternoon shoot until we were ready to go again.

This went on day after day. Some days, we would start to shake so badly that we just dropped our rifles and walked away. The first day it was fun, but before it was over, our nerves were shattered.

One corporal, Bill Thorne, was not very popular with us. We just couldn't wait for him to come through. We were not to put a bullet any closer to a person than about 12 inches, but when he came through, we both went after him. We put bullets two inches in front of his nose, and, when he was almost through, we shot the heels off his shoes. We heard about that, too. But it was very good shooting. They put the whole regiment through several times, officers and all, and we never had a casualty. But when it was all over, we were very glad to stop.

Almost before we knew it, winter was over and we went into spring training. This consisted of tactical training without troops and street fighting in Brighton. About this time, it came to light that many of the NCOs in the regiment had never passed a test of elementary training. Since Jim Bell, Jim Marr, Bill Nicholson and I were about the only qualified instructors in the regiment, we were detailed to test them. We gave any that failed a crash course, and then passed them. We spent a couple of weeks at this job.

Jim Bell and I got together whenever we could. Jim Marr we very seldom saw, and we suspected Nick was having a rough time. His company had one sergeant too many, and his company commander never forgot that he had refused to revert to a private when we came to the regiment. One night, Jim Bell and Nick came to my billet and hollered at me to come for a walk. When we came back to my billet from our walk, Nick said he had something to tell us. The day before, they had been to Brighton for street fighting. In street fighting, we used thunderflashes to simulate grenades. When the exercise was over, any that were not used were collected and turned in to be used another day. The platoon officer had collected them and gone to turn them in, but one man had kept one in his pocket. When they were getting in their TCV to go home, he exploded it, and although the other sergeant was right there also, they had charged Nick with not having control over his platoon. He was given the option of either reverting to a private or being court-martialled. Now he had come to tell Jim and me about it. I never saw Nick again. He reverted to a private and asked to be sent back to the holding unit. This was nothing but a frame-up to get him. He was both a top-notch instructor and a disciplinarian, and one of the best NCOs in the regiment. All for jealousy. He eventually went to the Canadian Scottish Regiment.

On May 29, 1944, the Lincoln and Welland Regiment moved into a bivouac on Crowborough Common, right on the edge of a golf course about a mile south of downtown Crowborough. The men were ready—fully trained—and our equipment was prepared for the sea voyage to France. All we could do now was wait for the invasion.

We were now into what could be described as a "lovely war." We spent our days just lying around. The only thing that was compulsory was PT training, which we did at some time every day. I generally put the platoon through it myself. The weather was beautiful, so every afternoon we took a blanket and slept out in the sun to get a good tan.

Many of the boys had English girlfriends. Jim Bell and I used to think it was great sport to take binoculars out in the evenings and watch what was going on. Every evening at about 6:30 the girls would come streaming out to visit their boyfriends. Just before dark, most of them headed back to town, but some stayed all night.

As soon as we finished our supper at five o'clock, one man was detailed to get newspapers and go into town to line up for fish and chips. Sometimes they stood in line for a couple of hours, and many a time the fish and chips ran out before they got close enough to get any. Some nights there would be a lineup of at least 150 people for them, so you had to get there early. When the man with the fish and chips came back, we would sit in a group to eat, talk and visit. Sometimes, we would build a fire and sit around it. But come dark, the fire was put out. In fact, all lights were extinguished. Even smoking was forbidden. A cigarette could be spotted from miles away by an enemy plane.

In this way, we passed a lot of time. I guess it could be said it was an idyllic life. As for living quarters, some of the men slept out in the open woods when we moved there at first. But gradually, they would pair up and put two groundsheets together to make a small tent. As for myself, I slept alone. At first, I put my groundsheet up on stakes.

But just one groundsheet left one side open, and you had to change it every day, depending on which way the wind was blowing. Although it was very good for one night, it was not very good for a permanent place to stay. I had developed a way to put mine up with a pocket at one end. As there was generally a lot of dew at night, the pocket would be full of water when I woke up in the morning. When I crawled out in the morning, I had water to wash and shave. All the boys would gather around and beg shaving water from me.

After a couple of nights, I decided I would have to make a change. We could be there for quite a while. I had a friend by the name of Leo LaRue who drove for the colonel. He kept asking me if there was anything I wanted. He would say, "Anything you want, I'll steal it for you." When he asked me if there was anything I needed, I said, "Yes, I could use another groundsheet," and away he went.

I began to gather some sticks for corner posts. In about twenty minutes, he was back with a groundsheet. I put two groundsheets together up on top of my framework to make a roof. Then I went to the quartermaster and asked for some canvas. He gave me a roll and said to bring back what I didn't need. With the canvas, I had a wall around me and enough to block up the ends to make a door. I got a box to stand on end, and this made a dresser for me. I could put my things in the box—paper, shaving gear, all that kind of stuff. All I needed now was a bed. Down at the far end of the golf course was a small barn. In the barn was a car, and in the car was a good back seat. After dark, I went down to the barn and stole the seat. It made a very good bed, but my feet went over the end. That was not very comfortable, so I got some wood and raised the bed up about 14 inches from the ground. Then I dug sod, and built up the foot of the bed even with the car seat. I now had the best shelter in the camp. I could go in there at night, light a candle and read or write to my heart's content.

I was very comfortable now. I could live here until the war ended. I had three good meals a day, a good home and $1.30 a day; *and* my burial blanket was paid for. What more did I need?

One thing I needed now was a place to take a bath and clean up. Every day, I would go for a run, usually about five miles across country. One day, I headed out across the golf course over on the other side where I had never been before. And there was the answer—a small stream of water, only half a mile from camp.

Every morning, I would jump out of bed, grab a towel and a razor and run over to the stream to wash and shave. Again in the evening, I would go to the stream and have a bath, usually after my run. One nice, warm evening I decided to see what was on the other side of the stream, so I walked up to have a look. There was a large house sitting in a big flower garden. Evidently, some big shot lived there. It was a regular English gentleman's home, garden and all. No one could see me from the house, so I pushed on the garden gate, which opened just far enough for me to get in. It was certainly a very well kept flower garden. Rows and rows of flowers, planted in steps—a typical English flower garden.

In a small nook back in a corner, out of sight, was a seat. This was a wonderful place to come and sit in the sun, and read, write or nap. Many an afternoon and evening I spent in there, all by myself. The English family that lived there never, ever knew that a Canadian soldier had made it his home. I think it was one of the loveliest spots I've ever seen.

On June 13, 1944, just one week after D-Day, the first buzz bomb came over England. We had just gotten to bed. We had gotten used to seeing and hearing planes limping home. They would come over, motors going full blast, some of them nearly on the ground. More than once, we had watched as a big bomber came over, and a few minutes later, there would be a big bang and a cloud of black smoke. One of them had just not made it home.

By the sound of the buzz bomb, we thought it was another plane that was not going to make it. I opened my door and looked out. It was down low, with a big streak of fire at the back. It didn't look right, but no one knew anything about it. We had a fellow with us named Ely Snake, a Native Canadian from the Muncey Reserve west of London, Ontario, who always slept naked. When this thing went over us, it really scared him. He jumped out of bed and took off across the field in his birthday suit. All around us were clumps of thorn trees. They had big, long thorns and grew up so thick even a rabbit could not go through them. Ely hit one of those clumps of bushes and went right in. And there he was caught and could not get out. They had to call out the pioneer platoon to cut him out and take him to the hospital.

Ely was a very good friend of mine. I first met him in 1942 when he enlisted for active service and came to Chatham No. 12 for basic training in my platoon. He came to the Lincoln and Welland Regiment in January 1944 while we were stationed in Crowborough. He was a very good man, and nearly made it through the war. Unfortunately, he was one of the last men killed, on January 28, 1945, at the Battle of Kapelsche Veer.

All that night of June 13, the buzz bombs went over. In the morning, we got a good look at them. No one knew just what they were, but we soon learned. If they kept on going, it was all right, but if the motor cut out, look out. The bomb would circle around and come down with a big bang. Neither the air force nor the anti-aircraft guns could shoot them down as this was a heavily populated area, but the air force did not take long to get to know how to handle them. Two fighter planes would come up behind a bomb, one on each side, and they would both put their wing tips under the wing tips of the bomb. They could then turn it around, and as we were not far off from the sea, they would take it out over the water and shoot it down. After a day or so, one plane could do it. The bomb did not travel very fast and a plane could go right around it. It was really something to see them do it. They would just head out to sea, and then, in the distance, we would hear the shooting, followed by a big bang. The air force destroyed a lot of them.

That very same day, June 13, 1944, our regiment was put on six hours' notice. Embarkation tags were issued, and everything was prepared to go to France. The division was to have landed in France twenty-two days after D-Day, June 28, but as Caen had not yet fallen, there was not room in France for us. D-Day had been a brilliant success, but right from the first day, the German 12th ss Division and the 3rd Canadian Division were locked in an almost personal feud that would last until one or the other was destroyed.

The Canadians and the British were to fight inland, in the hopes of drawing all the German strength onto the British-Canadian front, thereby allowing the American armies to break out on the western flank and sweep south and east to the Seine. It was there that the Allies hoped to trap the Germans. The Canadians had a tough and thankless job. The Germans concentrated seven of their eight armoured divisions, and half of their twelve other divisions, against the British and Canadians. The front stayed pretty much where it had been on D-Day + 2, and for weeks, the Canadians took a pounding. By the end of June, Caen had still not fallen.

Then on July 5, back in England, our regiment suffered the most casualties of any Canadian regiment based in England. In anticipation of being sent into the fray, we would go on a route march two or three times a week just to keep in shape. About two o'clock that afternoon, we were told we were going on a route march and would stay out all night. We packed up and away we went. We had gone only about four miles when, at about five o'clock, we came to where we were to spend the night, so we started to make up our beds. I had just put my blanket down when we heard a buzz bomb coming. We could tell by the sound it was going down. Sure enough, the motor stopped, and, about a minute later, there was a big bang and a cloud of smoke. I heard someone say, "I'll bet it hit our camp." Half an hour later our sergeant major came in and told us. The bomb had come over the hill and right straight into the door of our kitchen, killing seven men and wounding eighteen, two of whom died later. One of my men, Braiden Henry from Tillsonburg, had been left in camp. When the buzz bomb came over the hill, he had just finished his supper, washed his mess tins and started back to his bed about 60 yards away. He was very lucky he did not get there. He later found a piece of steel from the bomb right on his bed. If he had been in it, he would have been killed. If we had not gone on that march, there would have been about two hundred men in there eating their evening meal, and many more would have died. They found pieces of some of the dead in a tennis net four miles away. Some of the bodies were never found. It was the worst disaster experienced by a Canadian military unit based in the United Kingdom.

On the night of July 7, the attack on Caen began with a devastating bombing raid made by 467 British and Canadian bombers. Two days later, but thirty-three days later than planned, Caen was finally taken by the 3rd Canadian Division and two British divisions. None of it was easy. For July 8 and 9 alone, total Canadian casualties were 1,194—more than on D-Day.

By July 10, Caen had fallen completely. Eight days later, the code "Vassal tomorrow" was sent to all our company positions. On July 18, the Lincoln and Welland Regiment left Crowborough for a marshalling area near Tilbury docks. We were on our way to France.

It was nearly three years since I had fought my way into the service. I was now far better trained than many of our officers. It just remained to be seen if I was capable of doing the job for which I had been trained.

4

OFF TO FRANCE

D-DAY HAD BEEN JUNE 6. The 4th Canadian Division was to have gone to France on June 28, but war on paper is just not the same as the real thing. So, after much delay, on July 18, we finally broke camp and headed out. I am not sure, but I think I went over on the ss *Will Rogers*.

On our way from Crowborough to where the ships were docked, we had to go through London. London was no place for a convoy of TCVs to get caught. Our trip was planned right to the second. At the edge of London, we were met by our military police, who were to take us through the city and to the docks. All went well until we were about halfway across the city. I was in the last TCV in the convoy, and somehow we got lost and left behind. The driver did not know where to go. It only took the MPs a few minutes to miss us, and back they came, motorbikes wide open. They got in front and in back of us, and hollered, "Go!" And we went! The TCVs were a top-heavy outfit. Why we did not upset, I do not know. Wide open down the street, around corners on two wheels, slewing all over the place, over curbs and everything. People had to run to get out of our way. It was the wildest ride I've ever had in my life—just like a police chase on television. We eventually got to the docks. There was no waiting. We just jumped off the TCVs and on board the ship. We put our equipment away, and in a few minutes we were back on deck to see what was going on.

We had only been on board a short time when over the horizon came a buzz bomb straight at us. All we could do was watch. The ships were packed right in side by side. We could almost step from one to the other. Ships as far as we could see—all being loaded to go to France. The motor on the bomb cut out. It made a circle and started down. There was nothing we could do but watch as it came closer—right at us. Finally, the nose came down and the bomb dived right into the third ship away from us. Just a big bang.

Down came the gangplanks and away we went out into the Thames. At last, we were on our way to France. Nothing to do now but eat and sleep. We ate from compo packs—one box of compo rations held three meals a day for fourteen men. By the time we got to France, most of the men were ready for something else to eat, but I was brought up to eat everything, so the food did not bother me.

We sailed on July 19, and for three days, we just sailed in a circle at the mouth of the Thames and watched the buzz bombs being shot down. On July 22 towards the end of the day, our convoy slipped downriver into the Channel, where it followed close to the southern shore of England and next morning marshalled in the Solent. On July 24, we finally put out to sea and sailed, very slowly because of a new type of mine, towards Normandy. Finally, on the afternoon of July 25, we anchored off Courseulles in a sprawling fleet of ships. We could not see too much—just a few burned-out tanks. So we knew there had been fighting there.

We all lined up on the ship's deck. Each of us wanted to see all he could. It was not long before we could see infantry landing craft coming out to meet us. They came right in close to our ships and tied up. Scramble nets were put over the side of the ship. We put on full packs—all of our belongings were on our backs—and over the side we went. Scramble nets were made of rope and looked like big nets. It would take too long going down one man at a time on a rope ladder. This way, we just swarmed down the side of the ship all together. I was one of the first to go down. The landing craft were manned by British navy men. They were a happy lot. Each craft carried about sixty men, and when we were loaded, we headed for shore. We had about two miles to go and the tide was out. Our landing craft went right into the shore, the front of it coming down like a drawbridge. They moved right up onto the beach and we stepped out onto the sand. I didn't even get my shoes wet.

A platoon was made up of three sections, each led by a corporal, with a lance corporal as second-in-command, and seven privates. Each platoon was led by a lieutenant, with a sergeant as second-in-command. My platoon officer at that time was Lieutenant Armstrong. I was in No. 9 Plt., and the sergeant was Sgt. Art Winterford. My platoon had thirty men, all ranks. I was responsible for my section—No. 9 Section. I gathered my men and joined the rest of the platoon. We had to wait for our TCVs to come in. Just as it was getting dark, they came in and formed a convoy on the road. They had come across from England at the same time we did.

It was getting dark by now, and we were hungry, but we would not eat until we were in the camp where we would spend the night. We climbed into our TCVs and started to move, but we only went a short way before the German air force found us. They came in shooting and dropping bombs, and our air force came in after them. All around us the anti-aircraft guns started to fire. Not too often did our air force come in over the aircraft guns, but this was an emergency. The whole 4th Division was on the beach. The planes buzzed around us like flies. At the same time, we were treated to the best fireworks show we had ever seen. Our defences had very powerful searchlights that went several miles in the sky. One light would catch a German plane—it would just be a speck in the sky—then several lights would pick it up. It must have been something for the German pilot. He was just sitting there. It looked as if he was standing still, though he was moving very fast. Then we would see him go into a spin and come down. The lights would stay on him until he was down. Sometimes, we would see a parachute puff out and come down, but they came down in water and there was no one to pick them up.

This went on for an hour or so. All we could do was watch, but it was a good show. Finally, the fight was over and we started to move again. We went to a concentration area north of the village of Tierceville, where we were given our supper and told to dig in for the night. I dug a hole just big enough to crawl down into, digging out one side for my feet and the other side for my head, and went to sleep. During the night, the Germans came back over and bombed us. Some of our men were buried by bombs landing close to them, and several men were wounded. As for me, I slept through it all and never heard a thing. That was our first night in Normandy.

On July 26, the day was spent just looking things over. There was a lot to see. I decided to go for a walk just to see what was over the other side of the hill. Off to our right, I could see some trees and bushes and, behind them, a small village, so I went that way. We had been warned not to go into the towns as there were still some German sympathizers around. Just a few days before, a French girl who was married to a German soldier had shot and killed a Canadian from the Royal 22nd Regiment (the Van Doos). His friend went after her and killed her. When I came to the bushes, I knew I had gone far enough. Downhill from the bushes was a good-sized creek, and several of our boys were sitting on the bank watching a bunch of women doing their washing, while an old man sat there fishing for eels. We all sat down and watched. More of our men came in and sat down. There must have been about fifteen or twenty by then. The weather was hot and we had not had a bath for at least a week, maybe longer. We talked about it, but no one had a bathing suit and there were at least half a dozen women there. Then one of the boys said, "What difference does it make?" and he jumped up, peeled off his clothes and leaped in. In a few minutes we were all in our birthday suits and in the water. The women did not even look at us. The water was lovely, and we all had a good swim.

That night, the Germans came again, but this time there were no casualties. We stayed there until July 28, when we were moved to a concentration area at Fleury-sur-Orne. The route to Fleury was through the city of Caen, which had been very badly bombed. There wasn't much left of it. The Germans had put all the French civilians in the city, and then they had gone outside. If any of the French tried to leave, they were shot. The Allies bombed the city and killed all the people in it, and there were a lot of them. When we went through, we had to hold our noses, the smell was so bad.

We arrived at our new position, and it was here we had our dinner. Someone said there had been a big fight a few days before about a quarter of a mile away. I decided to go over and have a look. It was time I had a run, anyway. I had just reached the area and started to look around when, back at camp, a great commotion broke out. I could hear hollering and people running. Someone was hollering, "Where's Kipp?" People were pointing in all directions. Something was definitely up, so I took off on the run and was there in about two minutes. The company runner was there, looking for me. "Get your equipment and get to Company Headquarters as fast as you can!" I grabbed my things and ran. When I got there, the company commander, Major Gilles, was going wild. He was screaming at me, "Where were you? Don't you know there is a war going on? Get in the jeep and let's go!" What a ride that was! He drove wide open all the way into the town of Fleury-sur-Orne. He stopped in front of the Battalion Headquarters and told me to wait there while he went inside. There were three sergeants waiting there, one of whom was my old pal Jim Bell. It was now about 1:30 P.M. Major Gilles came out, got in his jeep and drove away. No one seemed to know what it was all about. They had been brought in like me and told nothing. We all sat with our backs against a building and slept most of the afternoon.

Five o'clock came and headquarters all went to supper. The adjutant, Major Rogers, came out and went to get his supper. When he was done, he looked at us still sitting there, came over and said, "You fellows better get something to eat." He asked us if we knew why we were here. When we said no, he told us we would soon know. Just eat and wait to find out—that was the army. A great rush to get us there, and then sit and wait. About 7:30 P.M., another friend of Jim's and mine came along, Captain Dickie. We had all been instructors together at Chatham. He told us that we had been picked to go as a reconnaissance party with the Queen's Own Rifles to a town called Bourguébus, and we would leave as soon as it was dark. The other three companies had each sent a sergeant. My company commander had picked me, a corporal, to go. That was a pat on the back for me. Now, at last, we knew what we were to do.

5

BOURGUÉBUS

THE FOUR OF US had sat on the street in Fleury-sur-Orne for eight and a half hours. Finally, about nine o'clock that night, Captain Dickie came out and told us what we were to do. The four of us would go into Bourguébus as scouts and take up positions with the Queen's Own Rifles in preparation for our own regiment to take over the town two nights later. We would scout their position and act as guides for our own men when they arrived. He told us how to get to Bourguébus, then gave us orders to move out, saying he would meet us there later. Why he didn't load us all in the jeep and take us with him, I don't know. He was going all alone, but that was the way things were done in the army.

One of the other sergeants took the lead and we all fell in behind. Being a corporal, I brought up the rear, with my friend Jim Bell right in front of me. We followed the road as it led out of town, five yards apart, just as we had been trained to do. Infantrymen do not bunch up. They keep well apart. That way, only one man gets hit at a time. Out in the night ahead of us, we could hear the occasional machine gun or rifle fire. In the distance, there would be artillery fire, causing the whole sky to light up. At last, the great adventure had begun.

After a while, I moved up with Jim and we started to talk. Jim and I had been together for about three years and were very close friends.

We talked about how we were going to act, now that this was the real thing. Would we be able to stand up to it or not? What was going to happen when we had to kill a man? For three years we had taught other men how to kill—how to shoot and how to use a bayonet. Although we were well trained for it, we had never yet had to do it. While we were moving along the road talking, we could hear a plane in the distance just flying around. Soon, it came in behind us and flew right up the road after us. We all promptly forgot our training, and, instead of hiding, we all stopped in the road and looked up. It was a bright, moonlit night and our faces must have showed up just like a candle in the dark. The plane flew right over us, about 40 feet in the air, and came back around. We still stood in the road looking up, wondering whose it was, whether it was German or Allied. This time we soon found out. There was a big bang, and a ball of fire flashed about 10 feet to the right of us, and then another. But by that time, we were all in the ditch on the other side of the road. We knew now whose it was. It had dropped two land mines on us. Why no one was hurt, I don't know, but it sure taught us a lesson. Our very first time, and we had made a mistake in a place where mistakes could be fatal.

Bourguébus was a small town about two and a half miles south of Caen. It sat just off the top of the high ground known as Bourguébus Ridge. The Germans held the high ground and they intended to keep it. Most of the Canadian regiments had tried to crack the German lines, and all had failed, with the loss of many men. The name Bourguébus still sends a cold chill down many a Canadian soldier's back—mine included! It was a terrible place.

Out to the south of Bourguébus was the town of Tilly-la-Campagne and a small airport named Carpiquet. Farther to the left was a small town named La Hogue, and on the far right of Tilly another small town called Verrières (Verrières was held by the Canadians). Bourguébus was a salient—the very forward point of the Canadian army. We were on our way out to that point. The Bourguébus Ridge was held by the 12th ss Panzer Division under Major General Kurt Meyer, and by the German 89th Infantry Division. Meyer was a tough soldier. After the war was over, he was tried as a war criminal and convicted, but he was too good a man to be locked up. So, after serving a part of his sentence, he was released and given a high place in the West German army as they were preparing to fight the Russians at the beginning of the Cold War.

Somewhere around ten o'clock, we came into Bourguébus, where we were split up and sent out to different companies. I was sent to "A" Coy., and handed over to one of their corporals. He took me out to the front, way down to the last slit trench in the line. He suggested that as he had been there long enough, he was tired and needed to sleep. Therefore, he would go to sleep, and I would stay awake and watch. He climbed down into the trench, and, in a few minutes, he was fast asleep. There was now no one between me and the Germans, and I had no idea how close they were.

I was too excited by now to do much sleeping anyway, so I watched most of the night. As daylight came, I could see our position. We were about 300 yards south of Bourguébus, behind a hedgerow running north and south. The company position was formed like a horizontal zigzag. I was positioned at the far left end of the top of the zigzag. Two hundred yards straight south was another hedgerow running east and west, where it connected with the southwest corner of the town. In front of it was an open field, and about a mile and a half across it I could see the Carpiquet airport.

Our slit trench was right behind and under a tree that stood out above the hedge. As soon as it got light enough to see, I made a small peephole in the hedge. I was very careful to camouflage it to look as it did before, and I was very careful not to be seen when I looked out. No sudden moves or showing of any white face. I could see that it was a hay field with several haystacks sitting in it, one of which was about 75 yards out from the hedge. Beside it were a couple of dead horses and a dead German. I don't know how long they had been there, but they were all bloated up to twice their normal size. As they got bigger, they would roll around, and we could hear the gas escaping. Eventually, one of the horses exploded. What a stink! The smell out there was terrible!

After we had our breakfast, I struck up a conversation with the Queen's Own corporal. He told me that just the day before, they had attacked the airport and gotten right up to it, but were driven back.

Eleven of their men had been wounded and several killed. When their stretcher-bearers went back to pick up the wounded men, they found that the Germans had shot each one of them in the head and killed them. It was for these murders that Major General Meyer was later tried and convicted. All day long, our artillery fired on the airport. There was so much dust that everything looked hazy. We watched several dogfights in the air and watched the planes come down. All around us, we could hear fighting going on, so I did not get much sleep that day.

I believe I was there forty-eight hours when I was called back into town and informed that the "Lincs" were on their way in. We four men had been the first of our regiment to be committed to battle.

About ten o'clock, our company came into Bourguébus and I led each platoon to their positions. My No. 9 Plt. was split up and my No. 9 Section was put back on the bottom section of the zigzag facing out the same direction. There was a short piece of hedge to the left with a gap going through it into the field, but most of the position was out in the open. I was in a slit trench to the far right. I had expected my platoon officer, Lieutenant Armstrong, would be in it with me, but the company commander, Major Gilles, had different ideas. He took all the platoon officers back into town to stay with him. That left me in the slit trench all alone.

Then we were given the most stupid order we could ever have been given. We were ordered that under no circumstances were we to fire our guns. When I asked what we should do if we were attacked, I was told that in that case, I was to send a man back into town to get my platoon officer. He would come up and assess the situation, then go back to Company Headquarters and tell the company commander, who would then issue orders as to what we should do. After we were given that order, the officers all went back into the town 200 yards behind us, crawled into their sleeping bags and went to sleep. I could see this was going to be a long night.

In training, we had practised all this, but this was not training any more. In training, it was very easy to overlook some things, one of which was sleeping at night. In training, one man was supposed to be awake all night—one hour on and one hour off. Some men

Charles Kipp as a twelve-year-old schoolboy, c. 1930.
COURTESY MARGARET KIPP

Keswick Ridge Farm, the Kipp ancestral home and Charles's birthplace, c. 1920.
COURTESY MARGARET KIPP

Top: The author's hometown, looking north, c. 1919.
COURTESY JOHN GRUSZKA

Pte. Charles D. Kipp, Oxford Rifles Coy., in front of the town hall,
Tillsonburg, Ontario, c. 1941.
COURTESY MARGARET KIPP

*Lance Corporal Kipp as an instructor at the No. 12
Basic Training Centre, Chatham, Ontario, c. 1941–43.*
COURTESY MARGARET KIPP

The author's wife, Margaret Kipp (née Leach), c. 1945.
COURTESY MARGARET KIPP

*Cpl. Charles D. Kipp during training
in Crowborough, England, April 1944.*
COURTESY MARGARET KIPP

Cpl. Charles Kipp (left) and Cpl. McKenzie,
Crowborough, England, c. April 1944.
COURTESY MARGARET KIPP

The villa at Camp de Brasschaet, Belgium, where Charles walked through the minefield when he was sick and feeling light-headed.
COURTESY MARGARET KIPP

never recognized the difference between training and the real thing, and now, when it got dark, they just lay down and went to sleep. There were two men to every slit trench. All night long, every hour on the hour, I had to go around and check on them to make sure that one man was awake and watching. And that night, I found more than one man asleep. I would give them a good bawling out and then have to stay with them to make sure one of them stayed awake. Then I would go back to my own hole in the ground. After a few hours of this, I started to think that maybe when I got back to my own hole, there could be a German waiting in it for me. After all, my hole was the one way out on the end. After a while, I quit going back to it. I crawled back someplace where I could see and stayed there. I could not go to sleep because I had to make my rounds again in the next hour. It was the platoon officers' job to be there to help, but they had not learned that yet, nor did they see the difference from training.

It was a warm summer night. The moon was shining, with a few clouds drifting across the sky. It made some things out in front of us look as if they were moving. About three o'clock, I went to make sure everything was all right. Two of the boys were sitting up in their trench, huddled up to each other, so scared they could hardly talk. They said there was a man out in front crawling around, and they pointed him out to me. Sure enough, there was something moving out there. It had to be a German—and we had orders not to shoot.

We watched it for a while. Even though it kept moving, it seemed to me that it was staying in the same place. It was under a tree and seemed to stay about the same distance from the tree all the time. I watched the clouds and the moonlight. I tried to tell them it was imagination, but they wouldn't buy that. Finally, I said, "I'll go out and have a look."

I followed the hedge up past the spot. There was a hole in the hedge, so I crawled through it and back to the spot. I carried a knife between my teeth just in case. Before I got to it, I could see that I was right. It was only a branch of the tree that had fallen down. This was the way I spent that night. I never got a wink of sleep. When daylight came, I tried to go to sleep, but it was too late for that. About eight o'clock, the company runner came out and told us that we were to come in, a platoon at a time, and get our breakfast.

After breakfast, we cleaned all our weapons and checked over our ammunition. Major Gilles sent word that he was coming out to check our positions. Shortly, I could see them coming, the major in the lead, all decked out just like an officer—map case hanging around his neck; binoculars hanging down over the map case. No one could miss seeing that he was an officer. The three platoon commanders and their batmen were right behind him, all with map cases and binoculars around their necks. I watched in amazement as he walked up into the gap in the hedge and stood up, looking out across the field. That was the way he had done it in training.

There was a loud crack and a bullet snapped past his ear. He just stood there for a second, then turned around and said, "Who the hell did that?" But he was all alone! Everyone else had ducked for cover. Only then did he realize what had happened. He sure hit the dirt in a hurry. That was a lesson for him and all the officers, too. They took off their map cases and binoculars and sent half of their party back into town while they continued on very carefully.

We had a very quiet day—a bit of mortar shelling on us and we did a lot of shelling on the Carpiquet airport. That night, we were told the Calgary Highlanders were going to attack Tilly from the direction of Verrières. "D" Coy. of the Lincoln and Welland Regiment would make a frontal attack on Tilly from Bourguébus to provide support in the form of a diversion. Again, it was a very beautiful night. The attack by "D" Coy., under Major Swayze, went in at one o'clock in the morning on August 1. After very hard fighting, Major Swayze and ten men established themselves astride a railroad track running south from Caen. I lay beside my slit trench and watched as "D" Coy. made their attack straight in front of me. For the next hour, I watched a terrible battle being fought—machine guns, rifle fire, mortar and tanks. Meanwhile, the Calgary Highlanders had entered Tilly, but they had been driven out again by fourteen German tanks sent from La Hogue, with more than sixty men killed and two hundred wounded. But the army brass still insisted that one company should be able to take the town of Tilly and refused to see why not.

Later in the war, I took a German prisoner who spoke English, and he asked me if I had been in the fighting around Tilly. I answered yes, and he said it was the hardest fighting he was ever in.

That day, I was given orders I was to move my section up to the top of the zigzag and take up my position where I had been the first night I came in, on the far left end of the position. This was the most dangerous spot we had. I moved back into my original slit trench—all alone.

That night, although I did not know it until the next morning, Lieutenant Armstrong, my platoon officer, moved out with his batman, Braiden Henry, and took up a position in the centre of the platoon. Braiden and Armstrong were sitting in a slit trench, and Braiden decided he should look to the front and see that everything was all right. He looked out through a hole and nearly fainted. Two feet out in front lay a German soldier, listening to them talk. Braiden pulled back and told Armstrong, who did not believe him and so took a look himself. Sure enough, two feet in front of them lay a German. Armstrong pulled the pin out of a grenade, reached through the hedge, dropped it beside the German and killed him. That German had crawled right up past me, right up to their position, and I didn't even know it.

Once again, I checked my men every hour all night long. And once again, I got no sleep. When daylight came, I was sitting in my hole trying to stay awake. A German fighter plane came diving in, right straight up the hedge towards me, guns blazing. It was only about 15 feet over my head. I could have brought him down with my Bren gun, but I had been given orders not to shoot at anything. The German and I looked each other right in the eyes as he went over. He went straight up our line shooting and then headed off over the Calgarys, who shot him down with rifle fire, and I watched as he came down out in front of us.

That day we got orders that the Argyll and Sutherland Regiment was to come in and take over the town. We were to attack and take the town of La Hogue about 1,000 yards to the south. Our battalion commander was Colonel McQueen, a very fine-looking man and the youngest colonel in the Canadian army to command a regiment. He looked like a real soldier, but he was one of the yellowest men in the army. He spent most of the day getting his briefing and orders. We were not to attack until about two o'clock in the morning. We were to have artillery and tank support, and this would give our tanks lots of time to come up to Bourguébus and join us. About nine o'clock, the Argylls came in to take over our positions, and we went to our attack positions. "A" Coy.'s position was on the southeast corner of the town, while the colonel was in his position in a town two miles behind us where he said he could observe. By ten o'clock, we were in our position and getting settled down for some sleep while waiting for the tank support when, much to our surprise, we received orders: "We will not wait for the tanks. Move out!" And move out we did.

Down the street at the edge of town was a stone fence. Past this stone fence was German territory. No. 8 Plt. was in the lead, followed by No. 7 Plt. My platoon was in reserve, so we were last. No. 8 Plt. went out around the fence, followed by No. 7 Plt. As soon as they were out in the open, the shooting started. The Germans had a line of 42s up on the top of the ridge, and did they plaster us! At the same time, they started firing mortars and "moanin' minnies." The "moanin' minnies" were rockets with eight barrels, I believe, which were all fired at once. They made a horrible noise, which was how they got their name.

My section was the first of No. 9 Plt. to go around the wall. I didn't get very far before I was stopped by men from the other two platoons coming back. Some were running, and some were helping wounded friends. I tried to find out what was going on, but all I was told was to go back. My own men were mixed up with the men coming back and were lost, pushed back around the wall.

I helped in getting the wounded back, then located my men and took them out again. But again, we did not get far. The whole sky was a sheet of fire over our heads and the bombs were coming in like hailstones. We had been issued what were called "sticky" bombs. These were bombs to burn tanks. The idea was to let a tank go over the top of you and then stick the bomb on the bottom of the tank. I had one of these bombs. If that bomb was hit, I would go up in flames, so I dropped it behind the wall and left it there.

This night was one of the darkest nights we had encountered since coming into France. The men could not see a thing out there. A man would be shot and go down. The man behind him wondered why he was stopping, so he would stop and go down also. Some of the men at the front didn't realize those coming behind had stopped and they kept going. In just a few minutes, they were so disorganized that no one knew what was going on. When they finally realized what had happened, there was nothing they could do but come back. In the dark, no one knew anything.

To make matters worse, the company commander came up to see what was going on, and he was so drunk he could hardly stand up. While some of us were trying to get things sorted out, he was screaming and hollering at everyone. He drew his pistol and threatened to shoot Lieutenant Armstrong if he didn't get out there. Lieutenant Armstrong took the commander's gun away and someone else took the commander away. Then someone said the Germans were coming in on a counterattack.

My men were gone, I didn't know where; they had just been swept away. I went out several more times until someone said he was the last man coming in. I lay down behind the stone wall and the Germans just plastered everything. They showered us with hundreds of bullets and hundreds of bombs. The whole ground shook! Someone ordered the men to get back to their slit trenches, which had been taken over by the Argylls to help fight off the counterattack that never came. I was really disgusted! If we had waited for our tank support, they could have taken out the machine guns. The way it was done, we didn't have a chance! This was the first of many mistakes made by Lieutenant Colonel McQueen. In our first fight, we had taken a terrible beating over that blunder. And I never even got to fire my gun. It was now two or three o'clock in the morning, so I crawled away by myself where no one could find me and went to sleep.

I woke up in the morning just as daylight was coming. The more I thought about what had happened, the madder I got! I would go and get me a German! I picked up a Bren gun. There was equipment all over the place. We had been loaded down with almost everything we owned, and the boys had just dumped it when they got into trouble.

A lot of it was out in the field, and I guess the Germans got it. I went back down to the stone fence. In the daylight, I could see there was a road out over the ridge. Along this there was a shallow ditch just deep enough for me to crawl in. I crawled out almost to the top of the ridge looking for Germans and stopped just short of the top. On the other side of the ridge was the whole German army. *That* I knew I could not fight. I went back to the fence and crawled in behind it. I heard a noise behind me and very nearly shot an artillery spotter. He hollered just in time. Down the wall about 30 yards there was a shell hole. I slithered down there and stuck my head out for a look.

I thought a freight train had just gone through over my head, and I pulled my head back in a hurry. I had found my German! But now that I'd found him, how was I going to get him? I sure couldn't stick my head up for a look. I took off my helmet and made movements with it in the hole. And in came another freight train! I shoved the end of my Bren gun through the hole and fired a shot in his direction. I knew he had to be out in the open on the side of the hill somewhere, so I kept firing a bullet here and a bullet there. And he kept firing back. Soon I noticed his bullets were hitting the side of a brick house about 12 feet behind me. It was a very old house; probably about three hundred years old. It was built very low with a low doorway and small windows. Bourguébus was a very old town. I could see what direction his bullets were coming from just by the way they were hitting the house and glancing off. I was moving my gun around, trying to line him up that way.

I was so busy with what I was doing, I didn't know someone else was getting in on the game. There was a noise behind me. My heart nearly stopped! I looked around and there was Cpl. Fred Storey behind me. Storey was a big, rough fellow. He was in No. 7 Plt. and liked to spend his time sharpening a bayonet or a knife and bragging about what he was going to do when he got in action. He was known as "Windy" Fred Storey. Earlier, back in England when he and I were walking down the street together, he had said to me, "Everyone thinks I'm just a windbag, but I'm not. When we get there, I'll show 'em what I can do." I'd thought to myself, "Boy, am I glad this guy's not in my section!"

But now here he was, coming out to help me. He said he heard the shooting and someone told him I was missing, so he thought it might be me doing the shooting. Fred turned out to be one of the best men in the regiment, and I always felt better when he was with me. One day when I was in a very bad spot, he came in and saved my life. Although he was badly wounded at least twice, he did survive the war. He died sometime in the early 1980s.

I told Fred what was going on. He said, "I have some binoculars. I'll go out in the field and see if I can see him." He went around the fence and crawled down the road a little ways. I got the German shooting again, and Fred said, "I see him!" He was lying on the side of the ridge, right out in the open. I put my gun back out the hole and fired a few shots. Fred saw where my bullets were hitting and directed my fire. "Up a little bit" or "to the left," he would say. "You're getting closer. Just up a bit more." Finally, he said, "You're almost on him," and then he started to holler, "Shoot! Shoot!" I let go a good burst, and he said, "You got him! He's down!" Whether he was dead or not, I don't know. But I had got me a German and had not even seen him. We decided this was the way to fight a war. Let's go and get some more of them.

We went back into town where the rest of the men from "A" Coy. were. There we met a man by the name of MacInnis who said he would like to go with us, so he got his Bren gun. We each had a Bren gun, and three Bren guns were a lot of firepower in the hands of men who knew how to use them.

We went back up to the left of the zigzag position. When we came to my old slit trench, there was a dead Argyll man in it, shot square in the forehead. I asked his buddy what had happened, and he said his friend had been looking through the hole in the hedge I had made, and a German out in the field had shot him.

We went south down to the other hedge, which ran east and west and looked over the top. And there, about 75 yards out in the field, were five or six Germans. They were standing up walking around as if they were looking for something. We lined up along the hedge and laid our guns over the top. I said, "Ready, aim, fire!" The Germans all went down. We gave them a few more for good measure, then, thinking we had done our job for the day, went back to "A" Coy.

In that attack out of Bourguébus, we had lost about forty men—killed, wounded, or taken prisoner. That attack, our first, was one of the most ill-conceived attacks we were ever in. It was doomed to failure right from the start, but McQueen blamed it on the men and officers. He said he was observing, and that we hadn't even tried. He was observing from two miles behind us, and in the dark. Our drunk company commander didn't help, either. There was not a braver man in the regiment, but he was drunk most of the time and could not operate without his bottle. Nothing was said to me for going off on my own. They all knew what I had been doing. It was now nearly dinnertime, so we sat around and talked until noon. We were a pretty sick bunch of men. But I had learned a very good lesson: give no quarter. And the safest place to be was right on top of the enemy with a gun down his throat. I soon had a reputation for shooting too fast and not taking enough prisoners. My reasoning, and I was right, was that if you gave them a chance, they would kill you. We had good men killed by trying to take prisoners, and I had made up my mind I was going to get through this war.

After dinner we were told to pack up for we were leaving. We were to go back to the town of Bras about a mile and a quarter from Bourguébus. This proved to be a farm headquarters of a big estate, less than half a mile from the German lines and in plain sight of the top of the Bourguébus Ridge. We could see the Germans walking around, and they could see us. They had some heavy mortar up there, and, every once in a while, they would plaster us. They would fire a few rounds and then our 25-pounders would open up on them and we could see them running for their holes. Then after the dust settled, out they would come, and soon they would fire at us again. In between, we would all sit around and talk about what had happened. We all knew now what war was.

While we sat there, we could see a line of English soldiers coming in. They were the roughest soldiers we had ever seen. Dirty, unshaven and scruffy-looking. There's always someone who has to say something. Some of our men started to make smart remarks to them, but they ignored it and strode on past. Then someone said, "It's the Desert Rats." They were just getting here from Egypt. There were no more smart remarks. They stopped about 50 yards from us, took off their packs and looked as if they were going to stay. I was doing some sewing when someone said, "Look!" I looked up just in time to see one of them put a revolver to his head and pull the trigger. He jumped a good three feet in the air and came down dead. He had had all the war he could take. They didn't waste much time. In about two minutes, a jeep picked him up and took him away.

The next time the Germans fired our way, the Brits packed up and moved to a safer spot. Someone from our company decided that was a good idea, too, so they packed up and prepared to move. When they were ready, they lined up five yards apart and headed down our way, marching right past our position. I was doing some sewing that needed to be done while the inevitable crap game was going on. I had left my slit trench and gone down where I could watch the game and listen to the talk.

We had a guy with us by the name of Casler who was from Woodstock, Ontario. He was one of those people who always has to be talking. He talked and grumbled away most of the time. As a rule, no one listened to him, but he talked anyway. He was saying, "Boy, would I ever like to get one in my hands. I wouldn't be able to do anything, and then they'd have to send me home and give me a pension." Up on the hill, the mortars started. *Bang! Bang! Bang!* The company that was moving was right even with us. We all jumped and streaked for our holes. Mine was about 20 feet away. I dropped my sewing and ran.

As I ran, I had one ear cocked to listen to the mortar bombs. I could tell that most of them would either go over me or behind me, but one was coming down ahead of me. It was heading straight for my slit trench. Out of the corner of my eye, I could see another man running for that hole, but I would have time to get in the hole ahead of him. I made it to the hole—all I had to do was get in it. I can hardly believe what happened next. As I said, all I had to do was dive in the hole. It was a very good one; about four feet deep with a top on it. Instead of diving in that hole, at that moment, from somewhere, I got a message: "Stay out of there, and go back." This was stupid! I was right at the hole! But I didn't stop to reason why. I just turned and ran back in the direction I'd just come from, which was about 30 feet away and where most of the shells were coming down. As I dived into a hole with three or four other men in it, shells were exploding all around me, and I could hear the shrapnel flying around. Just then, I heard a man start to scream, and I knew someone was hit, but we couldn't do a thing about it until the shelling stopped.

When it was finally over, we all came out of the holes. And there was Casler, on the ground, screaming, both hands riddled with shrapnel. They took him away. He got his wish, and we never saw him again. I went over to my hole, and in it was a sergeant from the other company. It had taken a direct hit and he was dead. But for the warning, I would have been in that hole also. There were several other men wounded as well, but I don't know how many. Thinking that lightning doesn't strike the same place twice, I decided I would sleep in the hole later that night.

The afternoon was getting on now. About four o'clock, my platoon sergeant, Sergeant Winterford, came to me and said that a man had just come in from the field out in front of Bourguébus where we had had the fight. He said that several of our men who had been missing were out there hiding in some bushes, and that one of them, Stan Gibson, was very badly wounded in the stomach. He asked me if I would go out with him that night and bring them in, if we could get permission. I said yes, so he said he would go to Major Gilles and ask him for permission, but permission was not given. Sometime later, those men were picked up by the Germans and taken prisoner. Stan Gibson died from his wounds in a hospital in Paris, the very day Paris was liberated. He was about eighteen years old, and one of the best.

The next morning, we were told there was a mobile bath set up close by, and that anyone who wanted to have a bath and clean underwear was to be ready when they were called. Even though our artillery kept working on those Germans on the hill, they were still there, firing at us and taking a toll. I watched as a bunch of our guys went out for a shower. As every bunch went out, they lost a few men, either killed or wounded. I was not so sure I wanted to go, but when the time came I was ready and we moved out. We lost one man. The Germans shelled us both going out and coming back, but we sure had a good shower. The shower was rigged up with a bunch of shower heads on pipes about eight feet off the ground. Everything was out in the open field. We just pulled off our clothes and everyone waded in. There would be thirty or forty bare-naked men in at a time; they all looked the same, rich or poor.

When we arrived back in Bras, I decided I would go over to "D" Coy. and see if Jim Bell was all right. But while I had been away, something new had been added. The Germans had brought in an 88-millimetre gun loaded with an armour-piercing shell, which they fired straight up in the air. When it came down on our position, it made a terrible screaming sound. It would drill straight in the ground, throwing up chalk 50 feet in the air, just like "Old Faithful." The ground there had only about six inches of topsoil, with white chalk underneath. When that chalk came down, it spread out like an umbrella. I was almost over to "D" Coy. position when they fired one of these shells. Jim had just come back from having a shower, wearing clean clothes, and he thought he would have a sleep. He had just lain down in his hole when one of these shells hit about six feet from him. The chalk rained down all around and half-filled his hole with him in it. He was buried right up to his neck in chalk. I got there just in time to pull him out. Was he an awful mess! His mouth, eyes and ears and every other opening in his body were full of chalk, and he was spitting and swearing—and Jim was not a swearing man. After it was all over, we sat down and had a good laugh.

On August 4, "B" Coy. sent a patrol comprised of a sergeant and three men to the town of Tilly. The big brass way back behind the lines had predicted that the Germans had retreated and left that town, but the Argylls still in Bourguébus knew better. That night they were ordered to attack Tilly. Only one company, "D" Coy. of the Lincoln and Welland Regiment, was sent back into Bourguébus to act as a firm base. The rest of the regiment was to be ready to return to Bourguébus if the attack was successful and to garrison the town. That night the Argylls put in a three-company attack but were driven back, as had been the North Nova Scotia Highlanders, the Calgary Highlanders and the Lincoln and Welland Regiment, all with very high loss of men and equipment.

"D" Coy. of the Lincoln and Welland Regiment provided a patrol of forty men for the engineer mine-detector parties who were clearing out mines. On August 6, we moved back to an area near Caen and turned the area of Bourguébus over to the 51st Highland Division, a British division made up of Scotsmen, which had been attached to the Canadian army. The British were a great bunch of guys—always cheerful and laughing. No matter how warm the weather was, they always carried their greatcoats. They would stop along the road, and the first thing they would do was build a fire and make a pot of tea. They couldn't do anything until they had their tea. I think they would have stopped a battle to make a cup of tea.

One night while we were in Bourguébus, a Churchill tank came into our position and out climbed a bunch of Englishmen. They made a fire and had a cup of tea while they were waiting for it to get dark. We asked them what they were up to and they told us they were doing tank recovery. Out by Carpiquet airport was a Canadian tank that had been hit, and they were going out to fix it and bring it in. We thought they were crazy! And I guess they were. As soon as it was dark, they climbed into their tank and away they went, right out through the German lines. We waited to see what was going to happen. They drove right out to the tank, and then, instead of trying to be quiet, they set out a radio and turned it right up as high as it would go. They talked and laughed, pounded and sang all night long. Just before daylight, they had the tank back in operation and drove it out. If we had even stuck our heads up, the Germans would have blown them off. But they got away with it.

Out in the field in front of us at Bourguébus there were numerous haystacks. Several times through the day, there would be a rifle shot from out there, and the bullet would whiz through the hedge right over our heads. It happened quite regularly, and we didn't know where it was coming from. One day, after it had happened several times, Sergeant Winterford decided it had come from a haystack about 75 yards out in front of us, so he decided he was going to burn it. He got some incendiary bullets, loaded up a rifle, and started to shoot at the haystack. Imagine his surprise when he could not set it on fire. The bullets just bounced off. The haystack was a camouflaged

German tank sitting out in front of us. I suppose they were using it as an observation post.

We were very glad to see the last of Bourguébus. We had taken an awful beating there and lost a lot of good men. But the men who were left had been given a very instructive lesson in war. It sure made us think.

We returned to the area of Caen to reorganize and prepare for an operation named "Totalize." The original plan by General Montgomery was to force the German army back to the Seine River and destroy them south of Paris. This plan was now changed to take advantage of a mistake made by the Germans. The plan was now to trap the German army in a pocket that had its western edge at Mortain in the U.S. sector and its neck at Falaise and Argentan south of Caen. On August 7, the Germans had attacked from Mortain in a drive south to the sea with the idea of cutting off the U.S. forces, but this had failed. And now the Allies had an opportunity of trapping a large part of the German 7th Army in the pocket.

In "Totalize," the Americans would go around to the south through Mortain, the Canadians would go around to the north, and they would all meet at Falaise. This became known as the Falaise Pocket.

The Canadians would attack on a two-division front, the 51st Highland Division on the left and the 2nd Canadian Division on the right. Behind them, ready to exploit their success, were the 1st Polish Armoured Division on the left, and the 4th Canadian Armoured Division on the right. The infantry divisions were to penetrate three miles into the enemy defenses. Then the armoured divisions were to go through them and seize the high ground north of Falaise.

On August 7, 1944, after staying at Caen less than twenty-four hours, we formed up on foot at ten o'clock at night. At twelve o'clock we moved off, "A" Coy. in the lead. Where we went or what we did, I haven't the faintest idea. The next few days were all a maze to me. We got shot at, bombed and kicked around. We just took a terrible beating as far as I'm concerned. I remember riding on tanks into battle somewhere. It was a dusty, dirty ride. On August 8 after dark, we came into a town called Rocquancourt and were told to go to bed.

This town had been cleared by the South Saskatchewan Regiment. I took my section into a house. It was dark and we couldn't see a thing. There were seven of us, and as there was only one bed, we all slept crossways with our feet all hanging over the one side. We were all so tired we just went to sleep. No one rolled over all night. In the morning I looked outside. At the back of the house was a small yard where I found a dead pig swelled up to twice its normal size. Beside it were two shallow graves where someone had buried two German soldiers. The dirt was piled about two feet high on top of them. Their rifles, with their helmets on top, were stuck in the ground by their bayonets.

I decided to have a shave and a wash. The town well, which was in the town square, was about 50 feet deep, with a winch and a pail to get water. I hauled up half a pail of water and went back to the house, where I used it to wash and shave. Then I went to get my breakfast, where I was told, "Don't use the water in the well. There is a dead German in it." Well, at least I hadn't drunk any of it.

The padre came in and suggested he would like to have a church service, so the whole company gathered in the yard behind the house where we had spent the night. I sat on one of the German graves, and we had a church service. Later in the morning we moved out of Rocquancourt, through the town of Gaumesnil to a bare field and stopped. We were just south of the town of Cintheaux. Up ahead of us, we could hear the Argylls as they cleared a small gravel pit.

6

GRAINVILLE-LANGANNERIE

AUGUST 9, 1944, was, for me, a very quiet morning. We were on the main highway from Caen to Falaise, not far from the small town of Cintheaux. It was a beautiful morning. No one seemed to be in a hurry. I had the feeling that there was not much to do, and all day to do it in.

Outside of a bit of shelling, the war seemed a long way away. In front of us, the Argylls were in a fight. We could hear the shooting from where we were. They were fighting to clear a gravel pit where some Germans were holed up. We had our breakfast and then climbed into our TCVs. When the battle was over in front of us, we moved up and passed through the position. Up the road a little way, we stopped and were told to unload, as we would be there for a while.

It was a beautiful meadow, almost like a park. Some of the boys started a crap game. I debated whether to go for a walk or to get caught up on my sleep. Of that, I had had very little for the past week. I decided it was not very safe to go for a walk because there could be Germans anywhere. Even now, they could be watching us. So, I lay down and went to sleep.

That did not last long. Lieutenant Armstrong woke me up to brief me on what we were to do. We had been in action in France for about a week and a half and were just getting the rough edges of our training knocked off. The plan now was that we would have an early dinner and then attack the towns of Langannerie, Vielle Langannerie and Grainville-Langannerie. As support we would have "A" Squadron of South Alberta tanks and a troop of 17-pounders. The plan was that it would be a regimental attack. "C" Coy. would attack Langannerie, "B" Coy. would attack Vielle Langannerie, while "A" and "D" Companies would wait and pass through and exploit where there was the most success. "A" Coy.'s plan was that we would ride into battle in the carriers from our carrier platoon. The cook got dinner ready early, and it was brought up to us. Then all we could do, like the army always did, was sit down and wait.

It must have been two o'clock in the afternoon when our carriers came and we got our orders. "A" Coy. would attack Grainville-Langannerie. There were three carriers and three platoons, not enough room to all go at once. Three carriers would only carry a platoon and a half, so they would have to make two trips. No. 9 Plt. would go in the first wave, and my section was put on the first carrier. We would lead the way.

Only after we were loaded did it strike me that we were drawn up behind what was a raised road about 100 yards in front of us. It was about 10 or 12 feet high. With me sitting on the front of the carrier, we were given orders to move. The company commander, Major Gilles, was in the second carrier.

My driver was a bit hesitant. We went about halfway up the raised road and rolled back down. We tried several times to get over. No way—we could not make it. The second carrier tried and failed. Major Gilles was going wild. He was screaming, "Get over there!" The drivers turned and went back to where we had started. We headed for it again, motors wide open. We were all screaming at the top of our lungs, "Go! Go! Go!" And we did! This time when we hit the road, we went straight up in the air, with me on the front. When we got to the top, I looked straight down about 25 feet. I thought, "This is it!" and I hung on with both hands. I think I even dug in my toenails. The driver eased off on the gas, and we dropped down on the other side. Before I could even catch my breath, we were going flat out for Grainville-Langannerie, which I could now see about a mile in front of us.

Major Gilles's carrier was now in the front. I was screaming to get past them, "Go! Go! Go!" In not much more than a minute, we were there. We crashed through a board fence, my carrier even with the back end of the front carrier. Boards and pieces of board flew every which way, some from the front carrier coming down all over us, and I suppose the third carrier got some of ours. We slewed around on a back street that was not much more than a farm lane. Up the street from us was a shed. I always thought it was a cow shed, but forty years later, I learned it was half full of implements at the time.

Major Gilles hollered, "Into the shed! And regroup!" I called to my men to follow me into the shed. I just went in partway, and I could see my section was right behind me. I could also see that we had taken the town by complete surprise, and I was not about to lose that advantage, so I did not wait for orders. I turned around, calling for my men to follow me, and headed up the street on the run. The laneway we were on came to a "T" intersection about 60 yards up from the shed. There were houses down that street both ways. To say that the Germans were surprised does not even begin to express it. They were dumbfounded! I was spraying bullets left and right as I went up the street. The windows in the house in front of me were already shot out. Just as I got there, the door opened and out came some Germans. I never saw such shocked looks on anyone's faces in all my life. Their mouths just dropped open. I fired a burst of Sten gun bullets over their heads and called for them to put up their hands. They had to do it or die; there was nothing they could do. They threw down their guns and put up their hands and I called to someone behind me to look after them. I had not even stopped running. By this time, I was shooting into the second house and calling on them to surrender. More Germans came out. They took just one look and put up their hands.

I cleared three houses this way and went on to a fourth. The fourth house was on a corner, and the door was on the other side of the house. As I went around the corner, I could see I was all alone. I had gone so fast, I was way ahead of my men, who had all stopped and were looking after the prisoners, going through their pockets searching for money.

It was too late to stop. I had to go on alone. As I came in front of the door of the fourth house, the door opened and out stepped a German NCO with a Schmeisser machine gun. He could not believe his eyes when he saw me, and that gave me the advantage. I fired a burst of bullets past him. I could have killed him just as easy, but I did not. He threw down his gun, called to someone behind him, and two more Germans came out with their hands up. I sent them back down the street to the shed. The rest of the company, led by Major Gilles, had gone down the street in the opposite direction. By now, only about two minutes since we had broken through the fence in our carriers, the fight for Grainville-Langannerie was over. We had taken about a dozen prisoners, and the Germans did not get a chance to even fire a shot. This was "A" Coy.'s part in the fight for Grainville-Langannerie. On the other side of the town, we could hear "B" and "D" Companies coming up the street. They did not take the rest of the town until about an hour later, about six o'clock.

As for me, I could see "A" Coy. gathering in a group behind the houses we had just captured. I looked around and went through some other houses down the road from where I was standing. I thought it was a good place for a German sniper to be, so to be on the safe side, I went through them to make sure there was no one there.

One of the houses was just a concrete shell built by the Germans to fight from, but it looked just like the other houses. It was two storeys high, but, inside, there was no upstairs, just one big room. Thinking it was just an ordinary house, I kicked the door open and fired a burst into the room. What a surprise I got when my bullets ricocheted all over the room! I backed out—and then I made a mistake. I closed the door. Later, I was told that one of our men went to look over the house. He threw a grenade through what he thought was an upstairs window and then ran into the house. As there was no upstairs floor, his grenade came down and killed him.

I sat down on the steps of one of the houses. It was very quiet, and I could see "A" Coy. men sitting down about 200 yards from me. I lit my pipe and sat there to have a rest. Down the road about 80 yards, there was a coniferous woods about maybe an acre and a half in size. I sat and smoked my pipe for maybe fifteen or twenty minutes. The temptation got to be too much. I put my pipe in my pocket, picked up my Sten gun and went for a walk in the woods.

I went down the road to the gate and turned in. It had been a German camp. Down the centre of the woods was a road that went straight through. On each side of the road it had been marked out in platoon areas. Along each side were slit trenches and the floor of the woods had been swept clean, just like a cement floor. I looked it all over and could see the Germans had not been gone long. Down at the far end there was a mobile kitchen. I looked in there to find it spotless, but empty.

I decided to look on the far side of the woods. It was just the same as the side I had just seen. As I was going to the other side, I could *feel* danger. The closer I got, the more I could feel it. The cold chills just snapped up and down my spine. I could almost hear someone saying, "Don't do it! Don't do it!" I knew I had gone far enough. I could see out of the woods now into an open field that went about 100 yards up a hill to a ridge. I knew behind that ridge lay the danger whose ominous presence was making my nerve endings tingle. That was where the Germans were, but I did not know until later how many of them there were.

I had had enough, but no one was going to scare me out, so I went back out the gate and up the road into town. Every step of the way, I thought I was going to be shot, but I just took my time and went back to where the rest of the men were. Some of them had a crap game going on a blanket on the ground in the backyard of a house. I watched for a while, then went past them and sat down with my back to a small fruit tree. I put my head down and in a few minutes I was asleep.

It seemed as if I had just closed my eyes when right behind me there was a rifle shot. Then Billy Roberts, one of my men, was hollering, "Look out, Kipp! Get outta there!" He kept firing and I yelled, "What's the matter? Are you crazy?" He yelled, "Get outta there! There's a German in the house!" Up in the gable end of the house was a vent behind which there was some movement. I got behind the tree and hid. Billy had been shooting craps when he just happened to look up as a German put a rifle out of the vent about 20 feet from me and was getting a bead on my head. Billy kept firing until the German backed away from the vent, and then I got up and got out of there.

A section from one of the other platoons came in from the far side of the house. They threw several grenades in and called for the German to come out, but there was no answer, so they said they would go in and get him. Off to the side of us about 100 yards away was a Sherman tank. They called for us to stand back and they would get him, so we got out of the way. They turned their 6-pounder around and blew out the side of the house. After the dust had settled, we again called for the German to come out. For an answer, there were three rifle shots up in the attic of the house. Some of our men went in, and there they found not one German, but three of them, all shot through the head. They had shot themselves rather than surrender.

If Billy Roberts had not looked up when he did, they would have got me, too. Our men had been sitting in that backyard for at least an hour, and the Germans had been watching them for all of that time. By the time the dust and excitement had settled, it was getting late in the afternoon. Very shortly, Dick, the "A" Coy. cook, came rolling in with supper. By the time supper was over, it was starting to get dark. As usual, we were told nothing of what was going on. Major Gilles had disappeared and had left no orders. He had also taken the platoon commanders with him.

As it got dark, the men just lay down right where they were and went to sleep, which was contrary to all of our training. When it got dark, why did we not put sentries out? I was the only one who knew that there were Germans not more than 200 yards away. They could come through that small woods and be on us before we knew it. We were only about 30 yards from the bush across an open field. There was no way they did not know we were there.

I got Billy Roberts and a Bren gun, told my men where we would be and told them to send someone out for us if we were needed. Then we went out almost to the edge of the woods and set up a listening post. If anyone came through the woods, we would hear them and could give an alarm.

I decided I would let Billy sleep for an hour while I watched. Then I would wake him up and he could watch while I got some sleep. Billy very promptly went to sleep, and I very nearly did as well. In fact, I could not say that I did not sleep a bit. My head would drop down and I could not keep my eyes open, but just at the right time, I would catch myself and rouse up. I fought sleep for an hour. I don't know how, but I did. Then I woke Billy up for his turn.

I shook him and said, "Are you awake, Billy?" After a while he said, "Yeah." "Are you awake, Billy?" "Yeah." "Are you sure?" "Yeah." We changed places. He got behind the gun, and I lay down beside him and tried to go to sleep. Before I could get to sleep, Billy was already snoring, so I raised up again and gave him a shake. "You awake, Billy?" "Yeah," he said. "You OK?" "Yeah." "You sure?" "Yeah, I'm all right." "Well, keep your eyes open. I'm going to sleep now." But it was no use, Billy was snoring again. I tried again, and again had the same results, so I just pushed him out of the way and took over the gun myself once more.

Again I fought sleep. My eyes would close in spite of everything. My face would drop down and when it hit the gun, I would wake up. I tried everything I could to stay awake. I did not want to stand up because I would show myself. If there were Germans in the woods, I wanted to see them, not them to see me. If I stood up, I would be a silhouette on the skyline and they would see me easily. If they attacked through the woods, I was in a position to break up their attack and send them back. There is nothing more discouraging than to attack in the face of a Bren gun. The Germans had a lot of respect for a Bren gun.

I was nearly in a trance when I realized something was moving. I could hear it. *Swish, swish, swish.* I was immediately wide awake. Whatever it was, it was too late to wake Billy. I listened, trying to pinpoint the sound. *Swish, swish, swish.* It was men walking through the grass.

And then I got it! It was coming from the right and behind me. Off to my right about 10 yards was a hedge. It came down the edge of the field from the back of the houses. Whatever it was, it was coming down that hedge. It could not be our own men. But who else could it be?

No one but my own men knew I was out there. If I made a noise, whoever it was would shoot. I listened as they came down the hedge. When they came to the end of the hedge, they stopped. They were about five yards away. I strained my eyes to see in the dark. Then I could make out the shape of their helmets. They were Canadians. Now I had to make contact with them, and I just prayed to God Billy wouldn't snore. They would not ask any questions; they would just shoot.

Very carefully, I started to crawl towards them until I got about six feet from them. Then I went, "Pssst!" They looked around, and I quickly said, "Don't shoot," this time loud enough so they could hear me. One of them said, "Who is it?" I answered, "Lincoln and Welland. Who are you guys?" "Argylls. Come on in." I crawled up to them and asked them if they had seen any Lincs. They said no. They had come right straight through "A" Coy. and no one had even seen them.

They said they were going through the woods and up on top of a hill they called 195. That was the hill I had seen in the afternoon. I told them I had been there in the afternoon and that it should be all clear to the top of the hill. We visited for about fifteen or twenty minutes. Then the word came up the line for them to move on. I wished them luck and went back out in the field to Billy, who was still sleeping.

I thought that now the Argylls were out in front I might as well get some sleep, too, so I lay down beside Billy and was soon asleep.

I had just gotten to sleep when one of my men was shaking me awake. "Come on. Quick. We're moving." We woke Billy, picked up our Bren gun and ran back in. The tail end of our column was just moving, and we latched onto the end. It was pitch-dark and we did not know where we were going, but we were glad to see the end of Grainville-Langannerie and to know that we had survived another day. Little did we realize, the day was not yet over. It was only about nine o'clock at night, and, before the day was over, there were some of us who would not make it.

7

HILL 195, "BUTCHER HILL"

ON AUGUST 9, 1944, about nine o'clock at night, we were stumbling across a field in single file. No idea where we were going, or why. A couple of my men and I had nearly been left behind, and I wanted to catch up to the rest of my platoon.

We stretched our legs and headed out past the column of men, all the while trying to find out what was up. There were a lot of rumours, but no one seemed to know. We crossed the field and came out onto a road. Turning left, we followed the road. I had caught up with Company Headquarters and my platoon was right in front. There I learned we were following after "D" Coy., who were out ahead of us somewhere. "C" and "B" Companies were behind us, and we were going to Hill 195.

About this time, I noticed a trail off the road heading south up the hill. But with "D" Coy. in the lead, we followed the road. We had only gone about another 300 yards when there was a shot in front of us. Everyone stopped and stood milling around in the road, asking each other, "What's going on?" I was still close enough to Major Gilles and his second-in-command, Johnnie Baldwin, to hear them talking. They seemed very agitated about something. They seemed to think something was not right. Just about this time, we could hear machine guns starting to fire behind and to the right of us. Shooting from behind as well as in front was enough to make anyone nervous.

Immediately, we found ourselves in what was like a swarm of bees—bullets, hundreds of them. We could hear them in the air and hitting the ground around us. There were bullets all over the place. Men were screaming and going down. It took a few seconds to realize we were being fired on. I hit the ground by the side of the road and there were bullets zinging all around me. Major Gilles hollered, "Follow me, men!" He sped past me on the run, heading for the field to the left of the road, and hit a fence, one of the only wire fences I ever saw in France. It picked him up in the air and threw him back onto the ground. I heard him hit with a thump. As well as knocking the breath out of him, it knocked the fight right out of him, too. And that took a lot of doing. He went into what we later termed "battle shock"—the shock of kill or be killed, the result of being in so much shelling and just the horror of war. I know I went through it several times. A person just went into a "funk"; you lost your nerve, and the cold would set in. The only thing you could do was wrap yourself up in a blanket to keep warm and let it wear off, sometimes in a few hours, or maybe it would take all day.

Baldwin took over command of the company. He said, "There are some buildings up ahead. Get into them." The machine guns were still firing. We crawled or ran, just anyway we could. About two or three hundred yards up the road, we came into the small village of Saint-Germain-le-Vasson. (There were two towns called Saint-Germain: Saint-Germain proper and Saint-Germain-le-Vasson. Saint-Germain-le-Vasson was a farm headquarters.) Captain Baldwin and Lieutenant Armstrong picked up Major Gilles and took him along. Other men picked up the dead and wounded and took them into the village. No. 7 and No. 8 Plts. went into some sheds on the right side of the road while No. 9 Plt. went into a house on the left side.

It was a very devastating experience to hear the shot up ahead of us, but then to be fired on by our own MGs! I believe it was the New Brunswick Rangers, a heavy machine gun regiment, that fired on us. They had orders to shoot across that particular road at an appointed time, and they did not know we were there.

It was dark and cold in that house. I lay down on the floor to try to get some sleep; and then the shock set in. This was the first time I had gone through it. It was a hot summer's night, but I shivered and shivered. My nerves were completely gone. I shivered and froze all night long. There was no sleep for me that night. I think it was one of the longest nights in my life. After a very long time, I could see it was getting light out. The boys started to wake up and someone got a fire going in the stove. They got water out of their water bottles and boiled it up. Someone had some tea, and before long they were passing out hot tea. I heard someone say, "Here, give this to the corporal." I was handed a mess tin half full of hot tea. I think it was the best drink I ever had in my life; in fact, it was a lifesaver. It started to warm me up, and already I was beginning to feel better.

Baldwin said, "Someone better go outside and have a look around." It was my place to go, but if he had said, "Corporal Kipp, you go out," I would have refused. I was not ready yet. He looked at me, but I must have looked pretty sick, as he sent someone else.

I was picking up all the time. The tea had done wonders, and soon I was beginning to feel bad about someone else having to go out in my place. About ten minutes later, I was ready to go. I just wanted to get out of that house and see what was out there. I opened the door just a crack and looked out. The sun was just coming up and there was no one in sight. I lay down on the floor, opened the door a bit and slithered out on my belly just like a snake, down the steps and around the corner to the south side of the house, out of sight.

There was an alleyway about four feet wide between the house and a hedge. The sun was shining and it was warm right there. I was feeling better, but I was still cold, so I lay up against the side of the house and went to sleep. In about ten minutes, I was awake again. I was warm and ready to go out and find a fight. I would make my own reconnaissance.

I rolled over to the hedge, found a hole in it and looked through. About 150 yards out in an open field, there were some Germans crossing in front of me, going from west to east. They were too far away for me to do anything about it with a Sten gun, so all I could do was watch them go.

The open field stretched up the hill for nearly half a mile. Up there were some trees, and as I watched, Germans came out of them and advanced across the open field in an extended line in an attack formation. They were firing as they advanced, and someone was firing back at them. I had a grandstand seat to watch a German attack.

I could see some of them going down. Whoever they were attacking was giving a good account of themselves. About half of them reached the west side of the field, but the firing picked up. They disappeared in the trees on the west side of the field. There was obviously a real battle going on just out of my sight. A few Germans came back out and retreated back across the field from where they had come, leaving more than half of their men dead on the field.

I had had a good view of the battle, but I did not know who they had attacked. Later, I learned they had attacked the support company of the Lincoln and Welland Regiment, who had gotten to their position on Hill 195 the night before. This attack by the Germans had overrun one of our anti-tank guns and killed the crew before they were beaten back by one of our infantry companies, who had also gotten to their position.

I went back to the main road. Farther on down there was a corner, and I went down and turned around it. There were a few old farm buildings on the right side of the road. On the left side was an orchard, and farther down the road was a German army hut.

I went over to check it out. I opened the door and went in. What a mess! Equipment was all over the place. There were clothes, gas masks and all kinds of equipment. Whoever had been there had left in a hurry. They must have been in bed when the shooting started. Their blankets were thrown back, and clothes and shoes were all over everywhere, just as they had taken them off the night before. I thought there must be some bare-naked Germans out there somewhere. The door at the far end of the building was wide open where they had gone out. They had taken nothing with them.

I looked out the back door. There was nothing and no one in sight, so I returned to the main house where we had spent the night. By this time, Baldwin and Armstrong had figured out what had happened.

The night before as we lay outside of Grainville-Langannerie, we had gotten orders to proceed to Hill 195. Our route was to follow the road until we came to a trail that would take us through the German lines and up to the top of the hill. *That* was the trail we had missed! "D" Coy. was to lead the way. They were to be led by a scout, who did not have a map or clear orders as to how to get there. "A" Coy. would be second in line, followed by "C" and "B" Companies and a support company.

To make a long story short, the scout got lost. When the commander of "D" Coy. came into some buildings, he knew something was wrong. He stopped, but he had no time to do anything. Just then, a platoon of Germans came down the street. They saw each other and everyone scattered. The Germans ran, and the Canadians ran. Some of the Canadians went on through the orchard, where they picked up thirteen German prisoners. The rest of "D" Coy. scattered all over. I was told that they did not get back together again until the next day. When they got up to Hill 195, I don't know.

When "A" Coy. came into the village, they decided something was wrong and stopped. The man in the front was carrying a Bren gun. When he stopped, he dropped the butt of the gun on the ground. The gun fired, hitting him in the chest with a bullet, and he died right there by the muzzle blast of his own gun. The other men saw two Germans setting up a machine gun in the road right in front of them, and again everyone ran.

As no one was to be on that road, and they knew there were Germans in there, the machine gun regiment, in the town of Saint-Germain behind us, was to open fire and make sure no Germans attacked us as we went up the trail.

When we heard the shot in front of us and were stopped in the road, that was also just the time they were to start firing. We got caught in it. Instead of turning and going up the trail, we had gone into Saint-Germain-le-Vasson. Now, in the morning, we would go back to the trail and try to find out what had happened to the rest of the Lincoln and Welland Regiment.

Major Gilles had still not come out of shock and was in a very bad way. We went east out of Saint-Germain-le-Vasson, back to the trail and up Hill 195. I again fell in at the end of the column. As I went past the sheds, I could see that we had had to leave some dead and wounded men there, with the promise to send help when we could.

We came back to the fork in the road and went into a small copse of woods. It was just a few trees and bushes about 40 by 60 feet in size. I picked up my men and took them straight through to the other side. Stepping out into the open to get a look around, I could see it was just like a big park. There were several copses of bushes around us and one larger woods out in front. As I watched, a Sherman tank came in sight and went behind the bush out of sight, heading up to Hill 195. Then I heard a shot. Up went a big plume of thick, black smoke. The tank was on fire. Off to the right about 40 yards was a copse of trees just like the one we were in. As I stood looking around, two German soldiers came to the edge of it and stood looking out at me. We looked each other over good, then they went back in their bushes, and I went back in mine. The men in the company were all going to sleep, all but the crap players who were getting a game going. I rounded up my men, put a Bren gun out to watch the bushes where I had just seen the Germans and gave orders that there were to be two men on guard until otherwise ordered. They grumbled and asked why they should be on guard—no one else was. I did not tell them about the Germans. They were probably the ones I had seen coming this way in the morning.

All of this time, there were tanks moving in on all sides of us. There was a big tank battle going on all around us and tanks were burning in all directions. A Sherman tank moved in about 50 yards from us and started firing at something up ahead of us. Soon we could see another Sherman tank up there, and they were shooting at each other. This was an awful mistake! Our own tanks were fighting each other and did not know it! I ran out in the field to the tank. If I had known anything about tanks, I would have gone under it. There is an escape hatch on the bottom of the tank. Since I did not know this, I climbed up over the side of the thing. I got up on top, where I could see that the turret was open. I started from the back end of the tank towards the turret. Just two more steps and I would have been on my knees looking down the turret. All of a sudden, exactly in the spot where I was heading, there was a big clang and a streak of fire as an armour-piercing shell bounced off the turret. It zinged by me and did not miss me by much more than a foot. Just two more steps and it would have cut me in two. Right then and there, I decided if these guys wanted to fight, let them go to it. I jumped off the tank and ran back into the bushes. From there, I watched as the two tanks manoeuvred to get a good shot at each other. The tank in front of us moved in behind the copse of trees where the Germans were and out of our sight. Apparently, this is what had happened. The Canadians in Sherman tanks had come in from one way, the Polish men came in from another direction. Neither one knew the others were there. Our men heard the different language and thought they were Germans. They fought each other most of the day and many Canadian and Polish tanks were knocked out—and many men were killed from that mistake. But I was not going to climb up on that tank again.

Scattered all around us were clumps of trees like the one we were in, and it soon became apparent that there were Germans in most of them. But they were keeping quiet. Every once in a while, someone would say there was a German up there. They would look out of the bushes, then go back in out of sight. We just left them alone.

Up on Hill 195, we saw one of our men come out and start down towards us. We watched as he came down past each clump of bushes, but the Germans let him come. No one bothered him. When he got almost to us, I could see it was an old friend of mine, Lieutenant Dickie, and I went out to meet him. The first thing he said was, "Your pal, Jim Bell, was killed last night." What a shock that news was! But much to my relief and joy, this eventually proved to be wrong. Jim had gotten lost in Saint-Germain and had not gotten back in yet.

Dickie had brought orders to us that we were to wait until it got dark. Then we were to proceed up to the positions where we were to have gone the night before. This cheered the company commander up a bit, but he had still not come out of his shock yet.

Although we had had nothing to eat since the night before and our water was all gone, we were doing very well. Later, when a couple of tanks came in, they left us all their water, but I did not get a drink of it. They had been up on Hill 195 and they said it was very bad up there. They did not call it Hill 195; they called it "Butcher Hill," because there were so many dead there already. The fighting was very heavy, and, at times, hand-to-hand. Our men were dug in, and the Germans were attacking not only our regiment but the Argylls and the Algonquins as well. All along the hilltop, they were sending in everything they had, including their heavy Tiger tanks. From where we were, we could hear the noise and see the smoke.

As the afternoon wore on, we were isolated. As it was apparent that the Germans were going to leave us alone, a lot of the guys went to sleep. Along about two or three o'clock, we saw movement back by Saint-Germain. Three or four tanks had moved out in front of the town, and infantrymen came out and climbed up on top of them. We all wondered who they were and where they were going. They came rumbling across the open field towards us. When they were about 150 yards from us, they stopped, the tanks all lined up in a row. As well as being armed with a 6-pound gun, each tank was also armed with two .30-calibre machine guns.

As the infantry got off the tanks and formed up to attack, the tanks opened fire on our position with their machine guns. By the time we recovered from our shock, they must have fired several thousand rounds at us. As soon as the infantry was in line, they all started to advance on us. By this time, the infantry was firing at us with rifles and Bren guns, and they were coming in on us with fixed bayonets.

The bullets were coming so thick we could not get our heads up to let them know who we were. Some of the boys were screaming and crying. Someone was hollering, "They're going to kill us! They're going to kill us!" But all we could do was get as close to the ground as we could. I found a depression in the ground and got in it. The bullets were bouncing off trees in all directions. Branches of trees were falling on us, and I guess all of us thought, "This is it! Killed by our own men!" There was a shallow ditch that ran through the north side of our bush. Most of the men managed to get in there, but the attack was coming straight in to this ditch. If the tanks came in, they would run right through there and over a lot of our men. I was back on the south side of our little bush watching it all, and wondering which way to run when I got the chance. I was not going to stay there and let a tank run over me. A bullet might just wound me, but a tank would kill me. I was going to get out of there even if I had to go in with the Germans in the next bush.

When the attack was about 50 yards in front of us, my platoon officer, Lieutenant Armstrong, jumped to his feet and ran out waving his arms and hollering. Why he was not killed, I will never know. He ran straight out into a hail of bullets and never got a scratch. The advancing men saw him and held their fire. They were as surprised to see us as we had been surprised by their action.

Some of their officers came forward to find out what we were doing there. They had been fighting Germans who were behind us. They did not know that we had taken Langannerie the day before. When they came into the town, they looked south and saw movement. As far as they knew, there was no one there but Germans.

They had no idea how we had gotten there, as we were completely surrounded by Germans. They formed up again and went to the west into Saint-Germain-le-Vasson, where we still had dead and wounded men. At this time we found out that the whole Canadian army was lost. Regiment commanders had lost their regiments, brigade commanders had lost their brigades, and divisional commanders were driving around in their jeeps trying to find their divisions. The Polish and Canadian tanks were fighting each other, and, as in our case, our own infantry had attacked us.

By the time this excitement was over, it was late in the afternoon. Our water was gone and we still had nothing to eat. Major Gilles was finally on his feet. Although he had not yet taken command of the company, he was very much better. All he would need now was a bit of action and he would be all right.

The second-in-command, Captain Baldwin, was getting things organized to move. As soon as it was dark, we would move off. I got my orders. I was to be last man in the column. It would be my job to see that there were no stragglers, and to see that we were not attacked from the rear by any of the Germans, as we were going to pass right through them. Finally, we moved off, Company Headquarters in the lead. I followed back just far enough so I could keep track of everything. We would be a day late finally getting up on Butcher Hill.

Night fighting was a bit different from daytime fighting. The daytime fighting was attack here, and when they were beaten back, attack somewhere else. If they could punch a hole through and get behind us, they would have us. After dark, it was mostly harassment. A rifle shot here or a burst of machine gun fire there. Maybe a grenade tossed in at you—anything to keep us up and tire us out.

As we neared the top of the hill, we could hear that was what was going on. Our lines must have stretched nearly a mile along the top of the hill. The whole hill was lit up by gunfire, and they must have been driving tanks all up and down the line, just on the other side, to bother us. They made an awful noise as they went up and down the line, and we did not know if they would try to break through or not.

We came into the position. A sunken road ran east and west, and our men were dug in, in the south bank just short of the brow of the hill. There was a wheat field right in front of us. This gave the Germans a good chance to crawl right in on top of us in the dark.

As I was the last man in, I had to hunt up my men in the dark. Someone told me they were down to the left somewhere, so I went to the left and passed a burnt-out scout car, and that is where I found them. They were digging into the bank for cover. I found a hole and sat in it to watch. All of the men were paired off, except for me. I was the odd man. Tonight, I would get no sleep, as there was no one to watch while I slept.

The Germans knew there was something going on in our part of the line, so they kept banging away at us. Our men kept firing just to let them know we were ready for them. They would crawl up through the wheat and throw grenades in at us, or get as close as they could and fire their guns right in our faces. This kept up for a while and then quieted down. I went out several times and made sure my men were not all sleeping, but they were doing all right. There was a man awake in every hole. It must have been three o'clock in the morning and I could not keep my eyes open, so I decided it would be all right to sleep for a bit. The men were doing a good job and they were not far away from me, only about six feet on either side of me. But I was very rudely awakened by a Schmeisser firing right over my hole. A German had crawled right up to me. The boys started firing on each side of me and I threw out a No. 36 grenade, but he got away. That was how close the fighting was all night long. When daylight came and we took stock, we had lost a few men, but we still held the position.

We had had nothing to eat now since the night we left Langannerie, and I had had nothing to drink since the morning before in Saint-Germain-le-Vasson. It was beginning to tell, as I was getting weak and a bit light-headed.

Everything was quiet now, so I decided to go for a walk and look the position over. I went down to the right, past the scout car. On it, I could see a jerry can. "It should have water in it," I thought, and I pried the cap off and took a taste. The can was so burned that the water was black and very bitter. I could not drink it. "So much for that," I thought, and moved on. Away down at the end of the line, I came out into an open field. I looked down to the right, where I could see into Saint-Germain-le-Vasson and make out the house and the hedge I had looked through the morning before. I was on the spot where I had watched the Germans attack. I looked up on the top of the hill, and my eyes came to rest on a smashed 6-pounder anti-tank gun. It was one of ours, and all around it were dead Germans. In fact, there were dead Germans all over the place. They had attacked our gun and killed the crew before being driven off by more of our men. That was the fight I had watched the morning before.

I went back to where one of our other platoons was located. The Germans were concentrating in front of them and doing a lot of firing over our heads. I teamed up with another corporal, Fred Storey, from No. 7 Plt., and waited for their attack. They were just a few feet out in front of us. We stood it as long as we could. We finally decided that if they were not coming to us, we would go to them. We each had a Sten gun, very good for a job like this. We got ready, jumped over the top and went out after them. We went out spraying bullets all over the place, firing from the hip as we ran, each of us emptying a magazine. Whether we hit anything or not, I don't know. By that time, the enemy fire was so heavy we had to draw back. We put on new magazines and charged the Germans once more, again emptying our guns. We were lucky to get back in without being killed, but we did break up the Germans; they moved out of there. I went back to my men, who were getting weak from no food or water but were still taking turns at sleeping and watching. This day went on just like the night before. The stretcher-bearers were picking up the dead and wounded and putting them in a field behind us. There was no way to get the wounded out because vehicles could not get to us. The stink of the dead was terrible.

Sometime during the day, a couple of men from the Algonquins came into our position. They were just to the left of us. They said they were taking an awful beating and were looking for water. They had lost a lot of men and they said the Argylls were in trouble, too. But we were all hanging on. We were completely surrounded by Germans. That day, Canadian tanks came in and cleared the Germans out from behind us again. And that night after it got dark, one of our sergeants, Sergeant Winterford, and another man gathered up all the water bottles they could carry and went back to Langannerie and brought back water. I managed to get a cupful. It would not have been so bad if it had not been so hot. The temperature went up very near one hundred degrees in the daytime. By this time, the smell of the dead was almost unbearable. That night, some of our wounded were taken out and that certainly helped. But to make matters worse, our commanding officer, the colonel, got down in a hole and refused to come out. Someone else, one of the company commanders, had to take over control of the regiment. After we got off Butcher Hill, we never saw that colonel again. After Paris was freed, he was sent there and given a staff job as the head Canadian in Paris. I guess it paid to be yellow.

That night and the next day were very much the same. The Germans kept up their attack without a break. Several times, Tiger tanks came in on us. They were either knocked out or chased back, but all the time they roared back and forth just over the brow of the hill. When they did that at nighttime, it sure woke everyone up.

About six o'clock that night, I was told to report to the company commander. There I was told that we were to be relieved. Another regiment was to take over our position and we were to go back out. I was to go back, but I didn't know where. I was taken out in a carrier and I was never so glad to get out of somewhere in all my life. When

I got back, the cook gave me food and water. I had had one cup of water and no food in three days. By that time, I was so weak I could hardly stand up.

When the rest of the company came down, I directed them to get their food and water. They lay down right where they ate and went to sleep. Ever since that time, our brigade, the 10th Canadian Infantry Brigade, has referred to Hill 195 as Butcher Hill. A name well earned, and never to be forgotten.

8

CLOSING THE FALAISE GAP

I HAD GONE INTO BATTLE on July 28, 1944. It was now August 13, just sixteen days later. It seemed like sixteen years. The Lincoln and Welland Regiment had taken 162 casualties: 34 killed, 91 wounded, 30 taken prisoner, 5 dead from wounds and 2 presumed killed in action. Even though I had been in the fighting for sixteen days, the regiment had been in it for only thirteen.

Even though we had done our best, we had taken a dreadful beating. Everything we did, something went wrong. Bad luck followed us wherever we went: we got lost, our attacks failed, other regiments had to come in and finish jobs that we had started. Only thirteen days, and already we were known as a "lost regiment." But a regiment is only as good as its leaders, and our leader, Colonel McQueen, was simply no good. A good peacetime soldier and a disciplinarian, but he didn't have the guts of a rabbit. And he could not plan a battle and carry it out. At Butcher Hill, he got down in a hole and would not come out. One of our company commanders took over leading the regiment. When we came down off the hill, he kept right on going, and we were all glad to see the end of him.

After we left Bourguébus, we had been through a lot of terrible fighting. Much of that I had put right out of my mind. If I had thought about it, I'm sure I would have just gone crazy. Also, much of the time I was in shock from the shelling and the fighting. There are four or five days of that time I have little recollection of at all, though our regiment history book gives the names and dates of where we were.

It was August 12, 1944. We had been pulled back from the front and were sitting up on the side of a hill somewhere between the towns of Cintheaux and Saint-Sylvain. The sky was full of bombers. As I sat on the side of the hill watching them come closer, I saw the bomb bay doors were opening. The 3rd Canadian Infantry Division was just across the valley from us, maybe only four or five hundred yards away. I watched as the bombs rained down on top of them and many Canadians were killed. In about two minutes, it was all over—just a big cloud of smoke and dust.

That night after supper, we were told we were moving. We were to take part in a big push to close the Falaise Gap. We were also told that when the Gap was closed, the war would be all over and we would be sent home. Imagine, just a few more days and it would all be over. By now, most of us had seen all the war we wanted. All we had to do was stay alive for a few more days. Very few of the infantrymen who were there at that time survived the war.

After dark that night, we formed up in single file and away we went across country, stumbling around in the dark. Soon we came out on a road and the line stopped. We were told we would be here for a while, so we all lay down to try to get some sleep, but there was really not much use. The sky was filled with planes. They were just stacked up, up there—hundreds of them. The noise was almost indescribable. Someone brought cotton batting to put in our ears. There would be one layer of planes at one level going out, with another layer up above them coming back. How many layers there were, I have no idea. The ground shook—even the air trembled. It felt as if there was an earthquake. I tried to sleep, but the noise and everything about it was making me sick. I just went into cold shock. I lay on the ground, freezing and shaking. In our company we had a man named Kelsey. He was a scrounger. For that reason, they had put him in the company quartermaster's store. His job was to scrounge everything he could get his hands on. Kelsey was the last man in Canada to be hanged, I am told. He was convicted of murder in Toronto after the war, and hanged.

That night as I lay on the ground hoping to die, someone came up the road. It was Kelsey. He said, "I've got something for you." He undid his tunic and pulled out a bottle of beer. It was a very warm night and the beer was very warm, and since I wanted a warm drink, I drank it. Shortly, my stomach began to roll; and then, was I sick. I think I brought up food I had eaten even before I left Canada eleven months earlier, but it did straighten me up. After a while, I stood up and walked around a bit, then lay down and went to sleep. After we had breakfast in the morning, we lined up again and moved out.

There was no hurry. We just took our time. As a rule, when the company moved like this, No. 7 Plt. was in the lead, followed by No. 8 Plt., while No. 9 Plt. brought up the rear. As I was in No. 9 Section, my section was last, and very often in cases such as this, I brought up the rear. That way, I could make sure no one lagged behind and everything was all right. We went up through the valley until we came out at the top of the hill, and there waiting for us were our TCVs.

On this day, August 13, we got a new commanding officer, Lt. Col. William Taylor Cromb. He had served with the Loyal Edmonton Regiment in Sicily and Italy, then as second-in-command of the Argyll and Sutherland Regiment in France. He had also served in Norway and was a very experienced soldier. I'll never forget the first time I saw him. Our platoon commander, Lieutenant Armstrong, had come up and loaded us in our vehicles. Very shortly, Colonel Cromb put in his appearance. We were all ready to go when he drove up in his jeep and stopped to look us over. That was the first time any of us had seen him. He was a wild-looking man with short grey hair that stood straight up. He had lost his hat and consequently was bare headed. As it happened, I had lost my hat also, so I, too, was bare headed. He looked at me, but as he told me later, he couldn't very well say anything to me because he didn't have a hat either. He singled me out and we looked right straight at each other. Eventually we would become very good friends. From that time on, things changed. Our attacks succeeded, our morale picked up and we soon lost the reputation of being a "lost regiment."

As usual, we were told very little of what we were to do, but we knew it was going to be big. Most of the fighting force of the Canadian army was here on this hill and lined up for battle. On the left was the 4th Canadian Armoured Brigade, who would lead, followed by the 8th Canadian Infantry Brigade from the 3rd Division, then the 10th Canadian Infantry Brigade from the 4th Canadian Armoured Division, then us, the 10th Infantry Brigade.

On the right, the 2nd Canadian Armoured Brigade would lead, followed by the two remaining brigades from the 3rd Division. The 10th Canadian Infantry Brigade was drawn up so that in the advance, the South Alberta Regiment would be in the lead, its three squadrons of tanks side by side. Behind the tanks would be three infantry regiments, the Algonquins on the left, the Argylls in the centre and the Lincoln and Welland on the right.

Each regiment had a front seven vehicles wide and ten vehicles deep. At two o'clock, we started and moved east for half a mile. Then each vehicle made a right turn. This made a front ten vehicles wide and seven vehicles deep. The plan was to go at top speed, crash through the enemy defenses, and go as far into their lines as possible. There was to be a smoke screen put down to keep the enemy from seeing us as we advanced, but as our vehicles picked up speed, we kicked up such a cloud of dust that the smoke screen could not be seen.

Our formation was soon broken up and became a mass of vehicles heading south across country at full speed. Completely disregarding all roads, we crashed through ditches, fences and all other obstacles but hedges. Each time we came to a hedge, all vehicles pressed close together to pass through a narrow gap made by tanks out in front of us. It was a race of all kinds of vehicles—TCVs, carriers, half-tracks, anti-tank guns and flails—all trying to go through a small opening at the same time. What a ride that was! We all hung on tight and hollered with all our might. What a racket!

Eventually, we came out on a main road and fell into place, Algonquins in front, Argylls behind them, and then the Lincoln and Welland. The tanks had already taken their objectives. The Algonquins passed through at full speed to their objectives, followed by the Argylls. The Germans could not believe what had happened. They were just sitting by the side of the road, watching. We had slowed down, and, at times, we even stopped. The Germans wondered where all the tanks had come from. They had never seen anything like it. Some of them had fires going and were cooking their supper. They came over and asked where they could surrender. They said the war was over. We unloaded from our TCVs and went into a field to wait our turn, when some Germans back on a hill decided to shell us. Another man, named Atkinson, and I were digging a hole to get in. We had made a hole about a foot deep in white chalk when the mortar shells started coming. We dived in. About 30 yards from us was a loaded ammunition carrier. I watched two men dive under it as a shell made a direct hit on it. There was a big explosion and it burst into flames. They never knew what hit them. Atkinson and I lay in the hole as the shells came down all around us, one hitting just on the edge of our hole. There was a pain right in the centre of my back. I said to Atkinson, "I'm hit." He said, "Is it bad?" We kept still for a minute, but it was hurting more all the time. Finally, I got up enough nerve to reach around and feel it. Right against the centre of my back lay a piece of steel about eight inches long and about one and a half inches wide, red hot and burning right through my clothes. That was the first time I had been hit. I didn't go to the doctor, but I should have. It was a bad burn that left a scar that is still there. The Germans were surrendering now by the hundreds. Our TCVs were picking them up and taking them back and they were darn glad to be out of it.

That night, we took up a position with the Argyll and South Alberta Regiments just outside the town of Olendon. We moved into a field that was surrounded by trees. I could see that this was farmland and I decided to go for a walk down the road, where I could see some farm buildings. I felt I would be quite safe, as there were a lot of our men around. I walked to the farm and went in just to look at the buildings, as they were all very old. Just as I got to them, a Frenchman and his wife came out to meet me. Shortly, we were joined by a girl who was about fifteen years old. They were the first civilians we had seen since we left the coast of France. They waved their hands around just like many French people do when they talk. They all talked French and I talked English, but we had a very good visit anyway. I wandered around looking things over while they followed me. I looked out across this field, which was full of mushrooms, so I started to gather the mushrooms and the girl came to help me. When we reached the end of the field by the road, I had all the mushrooms I could carry. The girl looked back to see if we were being watched, but the man and woman were too far away to hear us talking. Then she asked me if I had any chocolate. I told her to wait there until I came back. I had a couple of bars in my bag back at our bivouac, so I went and got them for her. She was still waiting when I came back and was all smiles when I gave them to her. The last I saw of her, she was shovelling them in her mouth as fast as she could.

I took the mushrooms to the cook, Dick Smith, who said he would cook them for me. That night I had mushrooms for supper. I offered some to some of the other guys, but no one would eat them. They all said, "Those things will kill you." In the morning, they said, "You still alive yet?" It seems no one else knew what they were.

The next day we did not move until about one o'clock. Then the companies started to move off. My company moved off in single file just to the south of Olendon. I can remember a road sign with the name Olendon on it. After we crossed the road, we formed up for an attack. No. 7 and No. 8 Plts. in the front, side by side, with No. 9 Plt. behind in reserve. I couldn't see much in front of us. Maybe 200 yards up was a hedgerow. Off to the right was a hill, and, at the top of this hill, I could see there was a road and a small woods. The hedge in front of us ran all the way up to the woods. Out in front of us on the other side of the hedge was an open field. This was where we were going. I was thinking to myself, "This is stupid. There's nothing here." All of a sudden the hedge in front of us erupted with machine gun fire, and an 88-millimetre gun opened up on us from the right in the hedge somewhere. We were out in the open—no cover for anyone. I saw several men in front of us go down. If we had been told what was going on, we would have been ready for it and known what to do, but this was a complete shock! Everyone went to ground. They had let our forward platoons get almost right to the hedge. Our company commander was in the very front. He called for the men to come on, then he jumped to his feet and managed to get into the hedge with some of the men. Then a bullet hit him in the upper part of his leg, travelling straight through and into his stomach. I was back about 80 yards behind him with my section out on either side of me in an extended line. He started to scream the most awful scream I've ever heard. It would start out, "Eeee-oooo-ooo-ooo," grow increasingly higher, then recede down to a groan and start all over again. There were wounded men all over everywhere and we couldn't get to any of them to help. If anyone moved, the guns started to fire again.

We lay there for about fifteen or twenty minutes, then up behind us came the South Alberta tanks. There must have been about eight or ten of them. The 88 in front of us roared to life, and hit a tank with every shot. Five or six tanks were put out in about a minute and a half. I looked back and there were tanks on fire all over the place. Any tank that had not yet been hit had stopped about 300 yards behind us. The 88 gun was camouflaged in the hedge and they couldn't see it, but I had it spotted. There was just a heavier and darker spot in the hedge where it was. Something had to be done. The company commander had died. He had lived only about fifteen minutes after being shot. He had let out one last awful scream and then died. I jumped to my feet and started back to the closest tank. I ran in a hail of bullets as the machine guns opened up on me. I managed a few feet at a time, then hit the ground. When they stopped, I would jump up and run another 15 or 20 feet. In this manner, I managed to get back to the first tank. I lay down beside it and they dropped out a telephone to me and informed me they couldn't do anything because it was a command tank and didn't have a gun on it. All they had was an imitation gun made out of wood. They told me to go to the next tank about 200 yards away, so I had to do the run all over again. But this time, the Germans only fired a few shots and quit. I made it to the next tank and lay down on the far side of it. They put out a phone for me to talk on and I told them I knew where the gun was. I gave them a point right in front of us for twelve o'clock and another point at about half past two, where the gun was. In a moment, they said, "We see it. Keep your head down. We're going to shoot." I got tight to the ground and put my hands over my ears, and they fired. The muzzle blast from their gun picked me up about two feet, then slammed me down on the ground. My nose hit the ground and started to bleed. I thought every rib in my body was broken. It felt as if there were sparks flying, and my head felt as if it had exploded. Even though I had had my hands over my ears, they were ringing. If they had not been covered, the sound would have burst my eardrums. They had told me they would probably fire twice, which they did. But by the time they fired the second shot, I was gone.

About halfway up the hill was a copse of trees, and I headed for it as fast as I could run. And at a time like this, I could run pretty fast! The trees were about 400 yards away and as I got closer to them, I could see another tank coming in on my right to hide in these trees. I got there about two jumps before it did. There, hiding in the trees, was another Lincoln and Welland man from Support Coy. His platoon commander had spotted the 88 in front of us and had sent him to direct the fire from the tanks. He was one of the biggest cowards in the regiment. He was in very little danger and could have made it to the tanks, but he hid in the trees instead. Later, he was given a medal for directing the fire from the tanks and knocking out the gun.

As the other tank was getting in amongst the trees, I was cleaning the blood off my face. When the tank was finally in position, the driver climbed out, walked around to the front of his tank, leaned back on it with his legs apart, and started to roll a cigarette. We all heard a clang—metal hitting metal. He dropped his cigarette and looked down. An armour-piercing shell had gone between his legs and made a hole right through the front of his tank. No one could believe it, but we all went and had a look. And sure enough, there was the hole in the tank. He and all the crew took off on the run. They thought it was great luck! They wouldn't be able to get another tank for at least three weeks, and now they would have nothing to do but have a good time until they got another tank.

By this time, I had gotten the blood off my face and gotten cleaned up a bit, but my whole body was sore. One of the men from "A" Coy. came in looking for me. He said Lt. John Martin had taken over command of the company, and that as soon as I got back, we were to make a frontal assault on the machine guns. I went back and rejoined my men. As soon as I got there, I hollered at him that we were ready. The Germans had never fired a shot at me while I was going back in.

Lieutenant Martin gave the order to move. Everyone jumped to their feet and in we went. The Germans opened up with everything they had, including the 88-millimetre we thought was knocked out. Our forward platoons had only a few feet to go, and they were through the hedge and onto the Germans in no time. No prisoners were taken. As soon as they were through the hedge, they turned right and went straight up the hedge, clearing everything in their path as they went.

As soon as we got to our feet, we were on the run. The 88 fired two or three shells. A man by the name of Berger was on my right about four feet from me. He was carrying our wireless set on his back. One of those shells made a direct hit on him. There was a big explosion, and he disappeared in a cloud of black smoke. I was about halfway to the hedge when I could see the men in front of me had turned right, so I took my men in that direction also. The men going up the hedge finally reached the 88. When the tank had fired on it, all the German gun crew had been killed except for one man, a German NCO. He had both legs broken but was still firing the gun all alone. Our men bayonetted him and finished him off. My platoon officer, Lieutenant Armstrong, came and told me to take the platoon up to the top of the hill and wait for further orders. As we were going up the hill, one of the other company commanders came up in his carrier. He tossed out our wireless set that he had picked up. Amazingly, it still worked. All they had found of Berger were his shoes, his feet still in them.

When we got to the top of the hill, we came to a sunken road where a company of the Canadian Scottish Regiment was dug in. We turned left and followed the road up to the hedge, which had grown wild and very thick. There were some good-sized trees in it. It was almost like a small woodlot. Up against the hedge were five or six tanks, camouflaged into the hedge. I don't know what regiment they were; they may have been 3rd Division. I stopped the men and told them to wait there while I went to one of the tanks. A man was lying on top of it, looking out in front through a small hole. I asked him what he could see and he said, "Come on up and have a look. But be very careful." I crawled up on my belly and over to him. He said, "Be very careful and look out this hole," and I looked very carefully. There was a valley running down into the open field we had seen before. Then he told me where to look. What a shock! That field was half full of German tanks. He showed me seven of them and said there were more. When I had finished looking, I climbed down, and no one had to tell me to be careful.

I went back to the platoon, but didn't tell them what I had seen. Very shortly, Lieutenant Armstrong came back and said we were to move down to the far end of the hedge and wait to see what we were going to do next. I led off with my section. After about 300 yards, I came upon another company of Canadian Scots. I could look down into a deep valley. About 700 yards away was a large farmhouse, and maybe a mile or so in the distance was a town. This was Falaise. Off to our right across the valley was another hill with a lot of small trees and brush. Our side of the valley was bare, open land. No cover at all. I walked over to the Canadian Scots and I could hear men calling for help. I looked down the side of the hill where they had made an attack and saw they had not gotten far. When they had come out over the brow of the hill, the Germans had opened up on them with machine guns from across the valley. They had managed to get back, but had left about twenty men, dead or wounded, out on the hill. Now, the Germans would not let them go out to pick up their wounded, who were pitifully calling for help. They would have to leave them there until after dark, and it was somewhere around three o'clock in the aftenoon then.

I saw Armstrong coming, so I went to meet him. He said our second-in-command, Capt. John Baldwin, had come up and taken command of the company. We were to prepare to go to the farmhouse in the valley. We were going to be in Falaise before dark. No. 7 and No. 8 Plts. would be on our left; "A" Coy. would lead the way. I was to go right down through the dead and wounded Canadian Scots. As soon as I was ready, we were to go. I could see the rest of the company forming up in an extended line for a frontal attack, and I knew they would never make it. I decided I would do it a little differently. I put my men, all seven of them, into a big arrowhead formation, with me in the centre. I spread them out, a good 10 yards between men. When we were ready, I signalled Armstrong that we were going, and then moved off, straight through the Canadian Scots.

As soon as we went over the brow of the hill, the Germans let us have it. The bullets came through like a swarm of bees. We could hear them and feel them as they went through. I had picked up someone's rifle. I felt a tug on the sling, and I could feel bullets going through my clothes, but we kept on going at a good smart trot. As soon as we came under fire, I called to my men to make a right turn. We went down the hill to the right instead of going straight down, and, in just a few yards, we were out of the line of fire. We proceeded nearly to the bottom of the hill, then swung to the left and went straight to the farmhouse. We were underneath the machine gun fire and they couldn't get down to us.

We came to a road and stopped in a hedge about 50 yards from the house. I had been so busy I didn't know how the rest of the company had made out. I looked back up the hill and could see them carrying wounded men back. They hadn't gone far before being chased back. We were down in there all alone. On our left, I could look right into the field where all the German tanks were. I knew there were tanks not 200 yards away, but I still did not tell the men. We took stock of what had happened to us. Most of the men had bullet holes through their clothing. I had five different bullet holes through mine and a piece of my rifle sling had been shot right out. There were two bullet holes in my right pant leg, one in the front and one in the back, and another in my left pant leg. My left leg must have been right in line behind my right leg when they went through. We must have been moving at just the right speed to get through them.

I didn't want to go into the house. That was an artillery target, or they could bring in a plane and bomb it, so I told the boys to dig in. We could only dig about six inches deep before we were into white chalk, but it kept them busy anyway. We had been there for only about fifteen minutes when in came Fred Storey and another man. He had seen that I had made it to the farmhouse, so he had come down through some trees to help me. Every once in a while, a German would come down the road from the right. We could not be bothered with prisoners, so we would shoot them, then drag their bodies off the road and hide them. I asked Fred if the rest of the company was coming, but he said they couldn't get through and we couldn't get back. I decided we would wait until dark. Then I would send a man back with a message. All we could do now was wait until it got dark. It was a long wait. But as soon as it started, it came fast. I got Braiden Henry ready to go. He was to tell Baldwin that if we didn't hear from him in a reasonable time, we would all come back. When it was dark enough that the Germans couldn't see him, he left on the run. He had no sooner left than a tank out behind the house started up and began to come our way. It rumbled up like a great big dragon, the fire shooting out the exhaust about 15 feet. It sounded like an airplane coming. We could hear the steel tracks rattling and banging. This made everything look different, and I decided we would have to get out of there. I told the men to leave two at a time. They didn't need to be told twice. And very shortly, I was left there all alone. The tank came out to the front of the house and stopped about 60 yards in front of me. I had stayed long enough, so I leaped to my feet and ran. This was definitely a time when discretion was the better part of valour. Before I got to the top of the hill, it was so dark I couldn't see anything. I got a little too far to the left, and instead of coming into our own lines, I came into the Canadian Scots. By looking up I could see the skyline, and when I got nearly there, I started to call out. After calling several times, I finally got an answer. I told them who I was and said, "Don't shoot." They called me right straight in to them. There were two men together and one of them took me back to their platoon officer.

He and his batman had dug a hole and covered it over with groundsheets. They were down the hole having tea and cake, so they gave me some. I asked them if they knew Bill Nicholson, who was in that regiment. The batman said, "Yes, he's over by the road, where you came up the hill." I decided as I was on my own now until morning, I would go over and find Bill. It was so dark I couldn't see anything. Suddenly, there was a crash of thunder and a big flash of lightning. Right in front of me sat a Bren gun carrier. If it hadn't been for the lightning, I would have run right into it. The rain started to come down, so I dived under the carrier and went to sleep. It rained hard all night. In the morning when I crawled out, I was the only man in the regiment who was dry. I could see the carrier was out in a field all by itself and I wondered why, so I looked inside. It was full of ammunition. I knew then why it was alone.

Our kitchen was about 150 yards away and the men were all having breakfast. I went in, got my mess tins and had breakfast. Baldwin came along, and all he said was, "Oh, you got back, did you?" We had come close to Falaise, but it would be a few more days before we got there. After everyone was dried out, our TCVs came up. We climbed in and left the hilltop to the Canadian Scots. I never did get to see Bill.

9

TRUN

O**N AUGUST** 18, 1944, at ten o'clock in the morning, we received orders to advance on and capture the city of Trun. This was one of the final stages in closing the Falaise Gap. To aid in the completion of this job, "A" Squadron of the South Alberta Tank Regiment, one troop of self-propelled 17-pounder anti-tank guns and a platoon of machine guns from the New Brunswick Rangers were to be under the command of the Lincoln and Welland Regiment and were to go with us as support.

The rifle companies were to be moved in armoured infantry vehicles known as "Priests." At about three o'clock that afternoon, I was ordered to enter the town with my section. I was the first one into Trun. I led my section down a small hill from the north into the main part of the city. The air force had attacked just ahead of us, and the whole city was aflame. The road into town was littered with dead Germans and horses. It was almost completely blocked with upset wagons on fire and German equipment scattered all over everywhere. Out at the south side of the city, our air force fighters had stopped a couple of Tiger tanks and were going after them with rockets.

I sent back word that I was in the town before proceeding farther to the south side. We were on a main road out of town heading for a bridge across the Dives River. No. 7 and No. 8 Plts. came in on my left, and we proceeded to make our way towards the river. About 500 yards down the road was a house and a horse barn. In front of the house, mounted on a big, heavy trailer, was a huge gun with a barrel about 30 feet long. During the First World War, this kind of gun was called "Big Bertha." I could have crawled right down into the barrel. We followed the road past the house and barn until we came to the river where No. 7 and No. 8 Plts. took up positions on my left. Just across the river on my side of the road, maybe 50 yards in front of me, were the remains of an old house. Just the perfect spot for a sniper. He could get us all from there.

I decided to move my men back behind the first house where there were some slit trenches. There was a hedge that went about halfway between the house and barn, and across the field to our right were more buildings. It was nearly five o'clock by this time, so we settled down to wait for our supper and to watch the Germans down the road from us. Some of the men went into the slit trenches to have a sleep, and I was out on watch by myself. Shortly, out of the buildings on my right, I noticed about a dozen Germans emerge, creeping stealthily along. They were moving in to attack No. 7 and No. 8 Plts. from behind. The platoons did not know they were there. I called to my men to follow me. They all came out of the slit trenches, and I, expecting my men to follow me, was off and on my way. Just then, someone, I don't know who, fired two mortar shells right on our position. They wounded two of my men and chased the rest of them back into the slit trenches. I was already gone on the run and thought my men were right behind me. The Germans were headed my way and would cross at the end of the hedge. When I got there, I discovered I was all alone, and it was too late to go back.

I had brought a Sten gun with me, and I poked it through the hedge and waited. When they were about 10 yards from me, I fired a burst into them. They were taken by complete surprise. Three Germans went down and the rest put up their hands and surrendered. One German who had been behind came out of one of the buildings. Why he was lagging behind, I don't know, but he was coming across the field on the run now. Just at that time, Braiden Henry dropped down beside me. He said, "Will I get him?" I said, "Let him have it." He fired, hitting the German in the leg. His leg went out from under him and he just rolled. He was one surprised man. I chased the rest of the Germans out onto the road and called for someone to come and help. Some other men came and took the prisoners away and later sent some stretcher-bearers to take care of the wounded. There were four of them. One was wounded in the leg, another had a slight wound, and the third we looked at and decided he would live if he got help. The fourth had two bullet holes low in the left of his chest. They had just missed his heart and had lodged in his lungs. There was no doubt he was dying.

They took the first three away. One was put in an ambulance with one of our men, who was also badly wounded, and they rushed them both to a hospital. I was later told that when they arrived, our man was on top of the German, whom he had choked to death, and they were both dead.

Meanwhile, I had stayed with the mortally wounded German. I sat down beside him. He had a few words of English, and I had a few words of German and French. He got it across to me that he was twenty-two years old. He was a very good-looking boy. He showed me pictures of his parents and his girlfriend. He gave me his parents' address and asked me to go and see them when we got to Germany. He knew he was dying. He began to cry, and clasping my hands tight with his, he pulled them down onto his chest. I would have given anything to save his life, but I was helpless. And to make matters worse, I was the one who had shot him. He did not have much more time to live. A few minutes later, he started to choke and cough. He was weakening fast and there was red froth coming out of his mouth and nose when he breathed. He held both of my hands in his and cried. Then, pulling them both up tight under his chin, he coughed up blood all over my hands, and died. I had killed him. I threw the things he had given me away, went back to my men and washed the blood from my hands. I can truthfully say it was one of the hardest things I did in all the war. It is something you do not forget. There is not a day of my life I do not think of him.

By this time in the war, I had earned the name of being "kill crazy." I was not! I did not enjoy it any more than anyone else. But I had learned that you could not give them a chance. When I came onto them, if they did not have their hands up, then they were not going to surrender. And if I was going to survive, I had to be hard. And I was! I was very aggressive and good with a gun. It had already been said that I alone accounted for more Germans than any platoon in the regiment. If I wanted to survive, I had to get them before they got me. It was the kind of life that if you hesitated for even a moment, you died. But every day of my life, I think about that German.

We went back into town, where we were told to expect a German attack to try to take the bridge. We knew there were German tanks out there because we had seen them. I took a PIAT (Projector, Infantry, Anti-Tank) gun and got Braiden Henry to come with me. We went to the horse barn and spent the evening taking turns watching and sleeping. The attack didn't come, but by that night, we were covered with lice—just crawling away with them—and no way to get rid of them.

Although this had been a very quiet evening, it could have been otherwise. Several times we heard the sound of German tanks out in front of us. All that evening, we had kept our PIAT gun trained on that bridge, and if any tanks had come up there, we would have had a real fight on our hands to stop them.

I hadn't seen my platoon officer, Lieutenant Armstrong, or the sergeant of my platoon since we had come into Trun. I didn't even know where they or the other two sections were. Just before dark that night, Lieutenant Armstrong came into my position. He told me that the engineers were coming up to mine the bridge and to get it ready to blow up should an attack come. I was to send two men out in front of them to protect them, and one of the other sections would also send two men to watch the other side of the road. I said I would go myself rather than send my men. I rounded up Braiden Henry again, and he and I went out. On the way, we caught up with Corporal Thorne, another section leader, and one of his men. Braiden and I went to the right side of the road into a corner of the old house. Thorne and his man went to the left side of the road. When the engineers finished their job, they were to come out and tell us and we would all go back into town. The job shouldn't have taken too long. We waited for a couple of hours and didn't hear a word from them.

Thorne said he would go back and see what was going on and then send his man back to us with word. When they got back to the bridge, the engineers were gone, so Thorne and his man went back in and left us out there with no word as to what was going on. Of all the men in my regiment, Thorne was the one man I had absolutely no use for. To put it plainly, he was nothing but a miserable bastard!

Braiden and I stayed out for a while longer. We were just about ready to go back in when we heard someone coming up the road from the German lines. We got to our feet and, keeping in the shadows, crept to the edge of the road. It was not too dark yet, so we could see pretty well, and, shortly, two German soldiers came in sight. When they were almost to us, we stepped out with our guns on them. It was a German officer and his batman. I asked him where he was going, and he replied that he was trying to escape and get back to Germany. I told him, "Well, you've made a mistake. You're now going to Canada." We took his gun from him, but he asked if he could keep his gun belt, so we gave it back to him and Braiden took them back into town. It was a nice warm night, so I stayed out by myself for a while before going back to my section position to check on my men. I had some really good men. Some of them were awake and watching, so everything was all right.

I don't remember much about that night. I guess it was uneventful. All around us there was heavy fighting, but my position was quiet. The next morning, August 19, 1944, I could hear screaming out in front of us. All night long, we had heard it. I could not even begin to describe how it sounded; whatever it was, it was in terrible pain. I decided I would go and find out what it was. I went down the road, over the bridge and past the old house. Farther down the road to the left was a farmhouse. The road was a sunken road, with the field to the right behind the old house being about six feet higher than the road itself. If I could have seen the field, I certainly wouldn't have gone. It was an open field filled with thousands of Germans. They had gotten this far trying to escape and were now caught in the Falaise Pocket. But fortunately, they could not see me, either. I strode past the farmhouse and out into an orchard, where I discovered a horse whose back was broken. It looked up at me. The look in its eyes was terrible. Then, raising itself up on its front legs, it tried to get up. But it could do no more than that. Then it screamed. Unless you have heard a scream like that, you can't even begin to imagine it. I was going to shoot it, but thought I had better check the house first. If there were any Germans inside and they heard a shot, then they would get me, so I went inside the house. While I was in the house, I heard a shot outside. Stepping cautiously back outside, I found one of my men, Billy Roberts, had also come to find out what it was, and it was he who had shot the horse. Billy just loved horses, and he was crying when I went out to him. He said he had been sure it was a horse out there, and he just had to come out and see. We went back into town together.

Ever since we had been in Trun, we had noticed there were Frenchmen in white helmets going in and out of the German lines with horses and wagons. We were told that they were the free French army, but we didn't trust them. Why could they go through the Germans just like that? We sure couldn't. They told us a story about a German general out there who wanted to surrender. Supposedly, all we had to do was go out and pick him up.

On the morning of August 19, our company commander, Maj. John Baldwin, came to my position in the company carrier. With him were Lieutenant Armstrong and several men. I was told to get three or four men and go out and see if we could find this general and bring him in. Armstrong didn't know that I had been out to the farmhouse earlier that day. We all climbed aboard the carrier and went out there again; down the road, over the bridge and into the farmyard. The carrier unloaded us and returned to town. Armstrong said he would take half the men and go back down the lane and have a look, while I was to take the rest of the men and go down the road and have a look. He went one way and I went the other, back out onto the road and south. We had only gone about 500 yards down the road when we heard the most awful racket. It sounded just like an airplane right on top of us. We stopped and waited to see what was coming, and, boy, we soon found out! About 100 yards in front of us, two Tiger tanks rumbled out of the field on our right and crossed the road in front of us. We dropped in the ditch in a hurry and they didn't see us. They continued into the field to our left. As far as we could see, there was no one there who wanted to surrender! The best thing we could do was to get out of there, so we turned around and went back to the farmhouse. We had no sooner made it back when a German car came up the road and headed towards the bridge. I said, "Come on, we'll get them," and we ran out to the road. The car was stopped a little way up the road and the men were getting out of it. We called to them to surrender, but they had other ideas! One of them turned to us with a Schmeisser machine gun and started to fire. Just at that time, I also realized that we had come out there in such a hurry I had brought only one magazine of ammo for my Sten gun. No matter, we were way outgunned anyway. The German gun was good for 100 yards, my Sten gun was good for only about 30 yards, and the Germans were about 50 yards from us. Walter Balfour was with me, and I hollered "Run!" and we sure did, back down the road from whence we had come, just as fast as we could go, and in a hail of bullets.

Walter yelled, "I'm hit!" but I hollered, "Don't stop! Run!" We were getting out of range by this time. We turned in at the farmhouse, hoofed 'er up the lane and disappeared around the house, out of sight of the Germans. I grabbed Balfour's Bren gun, told him to stay there and ran around the house into the orchard where the horse was. The Germans were still out on the road, but they had climbed back into their car and were almost to the bridge. If I could get into the corner of the orchard, I'd have a good shot at them.

I was just running under a tree when something zinged through about four feet over my head, cutting off branches and limbs, which fell down on top of me. I stopped in a hurry! But before I could move again, another shot whizzed through. Maybe I didn't want to chase Germans as much as I thought I did! I did an immediate about-face and scurried back to the house. Apparently, that morning the anti-tank platoon of my regiment had installed a 6-pound gun in there. They had it all set up and ready to go when they saw me out in the orchard, and, mistaking me for a German soldier, thought this would be good target practice. Fortunately, the sergeant on the gun got excited, and instead of putting in high-explosive shells, he put in armour-piercing shells. If he had used high-explosive shells, they would have killed me. The German car had sat on the road 200 yards in front of them, and they never even saw it. However, the Germans stayed there long enough to shoot Sergeant Wilson from No. 7 Plt. right between the eyes. He never knew what hit him.

I got back to the house just as Armstrong came running up the farm lane, white as a sheet and so excited he could hardly talk. He said they were working their way down the lane when he decided to have a look through the hedge on the right side of the lane. He stuck his head through the hedge, and never got such a shock in his life! He couldn't believe what he saw! There in the field right in front of him were thousands of Germans. The field was just black with them! He turned, and he and his men raced back to the house just as fast as they could run. He said, "We're not safe. Let's get back to town as fast as we can." I hollered, "Follow me! And don't bunch up. Keep well apart." We couldn't go up the road because the Germans were still there. But at the back of the house, I had noticed a ditch about eight feet deep that was all grown up with brush. We could stay on the right side of this ditch and the Germans would never see us. So away we went, me in the lead, with Armstrong bringing up the tail end.

We had only gone a very short way when, all of a sudden, in the ditch right beside me, someone started to holler "Kamerad! Kamerad!" the German word for "comrade" (used to mean "surrender"). My Sten gun was cocked and my finger was on the trigger. I just whirled around and jumped into the ditch, ready to shoot; and there, screaming for me not to shoot, were two women, an old man and a newborn baby. Why I didn't shoot them, I don't know. They were very surprised to see I was a Canadian. They all started to talk to me at once in French, of which I couldn't understand a word. However, I got them out of the ditch and sent a man back to bring up Armstrong, who spoke a bit of French. We got their story from them. They had fled the town on August 18 when our planes attacked and had hidden themselves in the ditch. That night, in the din of battle and under fire from the Germans to the south and Canadians to the north, one of the women had had a baby out there. Her husband had been with the free French army. He knew she was going to have the baby and he had come in to be with her. The Germans caught him that night and shot him. The rest of them had been out there in the ditch all this time, in between the Germans and the Canadians, too scared to come in for help, and all this time they had had no food or water. I put them right behind me in the line and took them back into town. It was there we learned that the Germans had shot Sergeant Wilson. When we got back, we went right into his platoon, only to find they were just carrying him away. I did not know it then, but my revenge on those Germans was coming soon. They had killed Wilson, wounded Balfour and very nearly got me.

The old man, the baby's grandfather, asked me to come with him. I wondered what he had in mind and I soon found out. He was going to take me to his home and give me a drink of wine, but when we got there, his wine was all gone. Some of our men had gone into his house and stolen it. For years, I wondered about this baby—is it a boy or a girl, and is it still alive? In 1986, when I was in Trun, I had hoped to find this person, but as I could not speak French and could find no one who could speak English, I could find out nothing about it.

I went back to my section position. The Germans had now started to come in to surrender. They came in twos, or threes, or maybe more. They just wandered into town, some of them being carried or helped, as many of them were wounded. Two Germans came into my position, carrying a man who had been burned. He didn't have any skin left on him. His eyes were gone; his nose and ears were burned off; moisture was oozing out all over him, and he was mumbling away to himself, right out of his mind. He was an awful-looking sight! They asked where they could get some help for him and I sent them back into town. A German officer came in and wanted to see our commanding officer. He asked him if he would stop the shooting and give him a chance to take care of his wounded men. There were several thousand dead and wounded men out in front of our regiment. Our colonel told him no, but said if he would surrender with his men, we would take care of them. One of our men in "D" Coy. told me later that the Germans had tried to break through their lines and escape. They had formed up in three ranks and refused to stop.

They were going back to Germany. Our men shot them. He said there were piles of dead Germans out there on the road in front of them. We lost a lot of men there, too.

Very shortly, Lieutenant Armstrong came in and told me we were being relieved by the Stormont, Dundas and Glengarry Highlanders, and I was to take my section back to the hill north of Trun to a small place called Le Ménil. I was glad to be out of there.

It was in this battle at Trun that Major Currie was awarded the Victoria Cross. He was leading "C" Coy. of the Lincoln and Welland Regiment and "B" Coy. of the Argylls at a town called Saint-Lambert.

IO

WE GO TO CHURCH

AUGUST 20, 1944: We had been fighting for two days in what the Germans called the "Corridor of Death." This was a strip of land in Normandy that had the Americans on one side and the Canadians on the other. The Germans were trying to escape through the Canadian lines. They were funnelled into a small corridor from Trun, Falaise, Saint-Lambert-sur-Dives and into Vimoutiers. This was what we called the Falaise and Argentan Pocket or Gap. On August 18, "A" Coy. of the Lincoln and Welland Regiment had been the first to enter the city of Trun. I had led the way with my No. 9 Section of No. 9 Plt. And now on August 20, we had been relieved by the Stormont, Dundas and Glengarry Highlanders Regiment, and were we glad to be leaving! We had taken several thousand prisoners and left two to three thousand dead and wounded Germans in the fields out in front of us. We were now on the top of a hill near the town of Le Ménil, just a short way north of Trun.

I was dead tired and covered with lice. As there was nowhere to have a bath and get rid of the lice, I decided to spread a blanket and go to sleep. I had just settled down when the padre came through and said, "I am going to hold a church service and communion. Come if you wish. Everyone is welcome!"

Although our chaplain, Padre Kennedy, had had church services every Sunday back in England, very few of us ever attended. Some of the boys said they did not believe in it, and as they had never gone to church before, there was no reason for them to start. But now, it was different. We had been in the fighting for three weeks and many of our men had been killed, and though back in England they could claim to be an atheist, there were no atheists in the slit trenches. In the last three days, I had lost three men. I had five men left. I looked at them and said, "If anyone wants to go to church, bring your guns and come on." We carried our guns wherever we went.

We were at the edge of an escarpment on a large plateau and could look right down on my old position in Trun about three-quarters of a mile away. We could also look down the road, across the bridge over the Dives River and right into the Germans.

The padre had put up his table, laid out his things and was now in the process of getting the men seated in place. About half of the Canadian army was up on that hill, and they all wanted to come to church. And all had to bring their weapons. There were infantrymen, tank men, flame-throwers, machine-gunners and Bren gun carriers. Just name them, and they were there. They all crowded in, the infantry in rows at the front, Bren gun carriers close behind, the tanks right behind them with their crews sitting on top, and around us were the anti-aircraft guns, the gunners sitting on them ready for action. We were sitting on the ground in front of a tank with its gun out over our heads. On our right sat an anti-aircraft gun, and us hanging on tight to our weapons. Everyone was armed to the teeth and ready for action. The padre could not believe the turnout. He figured if he got twenty-five men there, that would be a crowd. My guess would be close to two hundred. He could not keep that many men together like that for more than a few moments. What a target that would be for the Germans!

He opened his service with a hymn, "God Our Help in Ages Past," said a prayer and then launched right into his sermon.

Down the other side of Trun across the Dives River, we could see a dust cloud coming fast. It was coming our way, up the road, over the bridge and into town right through my old position. We could make it out now—a German scout car. What I wouldn't give to be there! Just the day before, I had tangled with those guys in that car. They had wounded one of my men and killed one of our sergeants. The padre had his back to it, but he could see he had lost his congregation. He stopped and turned around to watch as the car came through the town, out on the road and straight up to us. It was out of sight when it got to the hill, but we could hear it coming, the motor wide open. Then it roared over the top of the hill 75 yards in front of us, streaked straight through our camp and on down the road. But the road was full of tanks and the fields on either side were full of vehicles of all kinds. There was nowhere for them to go. We watched as they swung to the left looking for a way through, but there was no way out. Circling to the left until they came back to the top of the hill, they soon found there was no other way out and were now coming straight back to us. They were about 400 yards from us when the anti-aircraft gun on my right went into action. The gunners lowered it into a horizontal position and fired. *Phom! Phom! Phom!* One shot hit the car. The Germans jumped out while the car went on across the field a short way before it stopped. The shell had phosphorus in it and some of the Germans were on fire.

I jumped to my feet, hollered, "No. 9 Section, follow me!" and we took off on the run to capture them. There were four or five of them. Three of them were on fire. When we got to them, two of them had already put their fires out; it was just their clothing that had been on fire. The third man was *really* on fire. One of his comrades had pulled what was left of his clothing off, but it was no use. He was on fire *inside*. We just stood there, frozen with shock and horror, and watched as he burned to death. He was rolling and writhing on the ground, screaming. We could see the fire going through his body. It was puffing and bubbling under his skin as he was turning black. We watched as his private parts just shrivelled up and disappeared. The fire rippled up under his skin like worms. His feet burned off. His hair just shrivelled up and was gone. His eyelids and his nose were gone. His mouth drew up into a round "O," and then his lips, still working, just burned off. There were little vapours of steam or smoke coming from him. He lay on the ground and screamed until he died. Why we did not shoot him, I don't know. When he finally stopped moving, we gathered up the other Germans, took them back to our camp and turned them over to our regimental police to look after. I was very glad to be in on their capture, as, the day before, they had killed one of our sergeants, wounded one of my men and very nearly got me.

The church service was all over, but the padre came over to where we were. He said, "I have waited in case you and some of your men would like to be served communion. If so, you are welcome to come." What we had just seen was just starting to get to us. I looked at my five men and I never said a word. We simply followed him back to his table. In my section at that time there were three Protestants, two Catholics and one Jew. All of us got down on our knees in front of the padre. He said a few words; I don't know just what. Then he passed us the wine, one after the other. "This is the blood of Christ." And then the wafer. "This is the body of Christ." And so on. After it was done, I thanked him for waiting for us and we left.

I never see a communion service without thinking of that day. It is all so vivid in my mind.

11

THE PURSUIT INTO BELGIUM

N ow that we had what we were told was the whole German
army bottled up at Falaise, the war should have been all over.
General Montgomery had told us that when we closed the Falaise
Gap, the war would be over. Germany would have to capitulate, and
we would all be home by the next Christmas. The battle was won and
there was just a bit of mopping up to do, but this was a case where the
mopping up was a lot worse than the battle. It soon became apparent
that much of the German army had escaped and that the next month
would be a very hard part of the war. So far, although we had had a
lot of heavy fighting, it had been mostly individual battles and we had
had a chance to rest in between. Now, we were chasing the escaped
Germans and for the next month, there was very little rest.

After Sergeant Wilson was killed at Trun, I was promoted to a
sergeant. No. 9 Plt. was changed over to become No. 8 Plt., which
meant I had the same men I had in No. 9 Plt. However, my platoon
officer, Lieutenant Armstrong, stayed in the new No. 9 Plt., as by this
time, we were short an officer in "A" Coy. We didn't have an officer in
No. 8 Plt. Instead, we had two sergeants. Art Winterford, who had
been my sergeant and was my senior, was to lead No. 8 Plt.

At this time, Art was sent back on LOOB (left out of battle), and I
was put in charge of No. 8 Plt. An officer and a sergeant worked by
taking turns; when one was on, the other was off. That way, they

managed to get some rest. At night, one would look after the platoon through half the night and then they changed over. The men were getting tired and someone had to check them all the time or they would go to sleep. As I did not have an officer to share this responsibility, I had to do it all myself. This meant that I didn't sleep at night, and I got very little sleep during the day. And it soon started to tell.

About this time we heard a rumour that the Polish division had not been heard from for three or four days. They were lost and it was suspected that they had been surrounded by the Germans and possibly exterminated. The 4th Division was to go in and rescue them. They were thought to be somewhere around Vimoutiers. At dusk, on the night of August 21, 1944, we were loaded onto the tanks of the Sherbrooke Fusiliers of the 2nd Canadian Armoured Brigade. We had been shuffled around all day and were tired out. In our regimental history book, that night is described as the most miserable night we had spent since we had been in France, but to me, it was one of the best. As we climbed onto the tanks, it was starting to rain. This was a French Canadian regiment from Quebec and they were a good bunch of guys. They had some big tarps that they unrolled on top of the tanks so we could get underneath where it was warm and dry. We all went to sleep. The tanks moved a short way down the road and stopped. All night long, they would move and stop, and then move and stop again. It didn't matter; we slept through it all.

By morning, we had not gone very far, but the rain had stopped, so we crawled out into the sunshine. It was then we could see why we hadn't gone very far. As far as the eye could see were long lines of German prisoners. The road was plugged with them and the tanks couldn't move. Instead of the Germans capturing the Poles, the Poles had captured the Germans. They had hundreds of them, and after what the Germans had done to Poland, they were enjoying every minute of it. The Poles were now in charge and the Germans were scared to death, and I couldn't blame them. The Poles were all drunk; everyone had a bottle and was celebrating. They came down the road handing out bottles of Calvados, swearing at the Germans and letting them know who was the boss now. What they did with them all, I don't know, but they killed a lot of them. If a German made a wrong move, they just shot him.

That afternoon I took my men into a field where I was told that we were to be for several days for a rest. We also found some air force fellows who had been shot down. The French people in the farmhouse there had hidden them for most of the summer and they were glad now to be free.

I had also lost one of my men, a fellow by the name of Slater. I went to look for him, and when I found him, he was so drunk he couldn't even stand up, and he had been eating leeks. You could smell him a mile away! I tried to get him back to our area, but he couldn't stand up, and I couldn't carry him as he weighed about 200 pounds. He fell down and passed out, and by that time, I was so mad I just left him there. He was there all night. When he came back the next morning, he said he had met up with some Polish men and had had a drink with them, and that he was very sorry. He was actually a good man.

On August 23, our rest was over and we were ordered in pursuit of the Germans, first east, and then north to the Seine River. The fighting was a bit different now. The Germans were fighting a rearguard action and were in full retreat, but not licked, not by a long shot. There were a lot of rumours as to just where we were going, but it turned out that we were in a race to beat the Americans to Paris. We loaded into our TCVS and headed east with the tanks of the 4th Division out in front of us. There would be a few tanks out in front, followed by a company of infantry, and then more tanks and infantry behind them. The Germans fought in several different ways. Maybe they would leave an 88 sitting on a corner or out in a field. When we would come down the road, they would knock out one of our tanks and everyone would have to stop. Sometimes, it would be several hours before we could move again. Other times, it developed into a small tank battle, or maybe the infantry would have to unload and move in. Generally, by the time the infantry got to where the 88 had been, it was gone anyway. The Germans would retreat up the road a ways and do it all over again; or maybe they would leave a platoon of infantry or just a machine gun.

I remember one day when we were going up the road. It was raining and we had the side curtains down. All of a sudden, bullets started whining over our heads. Some of the men were sleeping, their guns on the floor or in a corner. I always hung onto mine. When the bullets started coming through, I jumped out over the back tailgate and hollered to the men to come on. The TCV stopped and I rolled into the ditch. The men all dropped to the floor, and no one could find a rifle or anything while I was hollering at them to get out there. A corporal from the TCV in front of us got a few men out, and they charged up the hill by the side of the road. There were two Germans up there about 40 yards from us with a machine gun. The corporal captured them and brought them down. Luckily, no one was hurt.

One day we came to a small town and our TCV stopped right in front of a church where they were having a wedding. The bride came out on the church steps to see what was going on, so I ordered my whole platoon out of the TCV. We lined up and we all kissed the bride, then climbed back in our TCV and went on our way.

We had started this push on August 23. It was now the next day and we had been constantly on the move. There had been a bit of fighting, but "A" Coy. had not been in it. In fact, we had hardly been out of our TCVs, and, by this time, we were getting pretty tired. We had had very little to eat and what sleep we had was on the move. Believe me, those seats were pretty hard. This night, it started to rain. It just poured down, buckets full of it. The convoy was moving very slowly: move a ways, then stop, then do it all over again. Every time we stopped, we had to put a guard out in the rain, mostly to see that the trucks ahead of us didn't start up and leave us behind. About two o'clock in the morning, I couldn't sit on that seat any longer, so I got out to take a turn. The rain was coming down in a torrential downpour. I walked up and down the road for a while in the rain. Then I found a small building of some sort, so I opened the door and stepped inside. It was not much bigger than a telephone booth, but at least I was out of the rain. Soon, I started to get sleepy. Another guard came along and I talked to him for a while. He had just come out, so I said to him, "You know where I am. If anything happens, let me know. I'm going to sleep." I stretched out as best as I could in such a confined space and was soon asleep. I should have learned my lesson at Trun—don't sleep in places like that. In the morning, I was crawling away with lice, but again, they only stayed a couple of days.

The next morning we moved on. I had picked up a mouth organ and I would play it most of the day. Mostly, I played "Danny Boy." Bill Thorne didn't like it, and I guess after three or four hours of it, it was enough to make anyone mad, but the more he hollered, the more I played.

The Germans had started to use air burst shells. They would first stop the convoy and then fire them over our heads. They would explode about 30 feet above us and send shrapnel flying all over. They were bad. Every time they fired one, it would get two or three men and there was no way to get away. All we could do was jump out and run, and then we had to stay away from our TCVs until our side either silenced or chased out the gun that was firing the shells. Then we'd head down the road a ways; they would start shelling all over again. It was not only bad for us, it was killing a lot of cows as well. We saw a lot of dead cows. They didn't know enough to get out of the way.

We were stopped one day when I saw a French girl out in the field milking her cows. I went over to her and asked to buy her pail of milk. Just about that time, the convoy started to move again. I threw her some money and ran with her pail. We drank all her milk and kept the pail. Now that we had a pail, whenever we saw cows out in the field, I went out and milked them, so we had milk right regular.

About four o'clock on August 25, we rolled into the town of Fontaine-la-Soret. We were starting to see quite a few people now, and they were glad to see us. They came out to meet us with flowers, wine and women. The stores were open, so some of the men went shopping, while others went visiting. And some of us just lay down on the sidewalk and went to sleep.

After a while it started to get dark. The engineers were going to build a Bailey bridge over the River Risle, and "A" Coy. was to go with them to protect them while they worked. We were supposed to meet them there. It was a march of about seven miles. After we had marched for about three hours, we came into a town. There was not supposed to be a town on this march. We had circled around and

were back in the town of Fontaine-la-Soret, so we started all over
again. In about another three hours, we came into another town, and
again, this town turned out to be Fontaine-la-Soret. Nothing to do
but start again. The third time we came into Fontaine-la-Soret, we
just gave up. We lay down on the sidewalk and slept until morning.
By this time the engineers had the bridge up, so we got in our TCVs
and crossed the river. We must have walked 20 miles that night, and
in the morning, we were right back where we started. Up all night,
and tired out.

We spent most of August 26, 1944, riding in TCVs, going through
several small towns—Le Neubourg, Crosville-la-Vieille, Criquebeuf-
la-Campagne, Daubeuf-la-Campagne and into La Haye Malherbe,
where we met men from the U.S. army. At half past six that night, we
congregated in a field on the outskirts of La Haye Malherbe with the
South Alberta Regiment (tanks), the New Brunswick Rangers (machine guns) and a troop of 20-millimetre Oerlikons from the 8th
Light Anti-Aircraft Battery. We had our supper and then settled
down for the night. A patrol from the scout platoon was sent out to
find a route to the River Seine. They returned sometime in the night,
and the next day around noon we climbed into our TCVs and started
to move. We went through several more small towns with names I
can't even say, let alone write. About two o'clock, we came out of a
woods onto an open road. We had seen our fighter planes working on
something up ahead of us, and now we could see what they had been
after. They had caught a German convoy on the same road we were
on about half an hour ahead of us. What a mess they made of them!
This was a horse-drawn convoy and there was German equipment all
over the place—wagons on fire, dead horses and dead Germans all
over. There were wounded horses, teams with one horse dead and the
other not able to get away. They just stood there and looked very re-
signed to their fate. There was a wire fence that one horse had
crossed while the other had not; it was dead. We wanted to stop and
do something for them, but we couldn't. A tank cleared the road in
front of us and we went on through.

Just a short way up the road we stopped. About half a mile to our
right was a small town, Criquebeuf-sur-Seine. Our road turned and

went down into that town. We got orders to unload and prepare to attack, "A" Coy. in the lead; No. 8 Plt. was to lead off when ready. This was one time when I would like to have said to one of my corporals, "You go first," but as platoon leader, I had to go first. I strung my men out in single file and moved off down the road. It was one of the hardest roads I've ever travelled. Like always, I was told nothing; just go. The road sloped down to the town and there was not even a ditch to hide in or a thing to get behind. It was just as open as a new-mown hayfield. At the edge of town on the left, there were some old factory buildings. If I remember right, there were three of them. I can see them yet—two storeys high, with a row of open windows in each storey. Big black windows. And I knew there was a machine gun or a sniper in every one of them. When I was about 300 yards from them, I started to pick a spot in front of me. *That* was where I would get it. After I passed *that* spot, I would pick another spot. I was slowing down. I sure did not want to go on. I knew I would never make it. I watched every window for movement. Then picked another spot. I was getting closer to the town all the time. Then I began to think, "Maybe I will make it." Then I was at the edge of town. My hair had started to lay back down by this time. Then I was going down the main street, and I began to think that maybe there was life ahead.

Across the town square to the right stood a bunch of men all in a line, and I wondered why. I soon found out. The Germans had lined up all the men in town and were preparing to shoot them, when they saw us coming down the road. They just left the men standing there and ran out the other end of town and across the Seine River. I soon saw there were no Germans left. I went on down the street until I came to a bridge over what I thought was the Seine River. I crossed the bridge just so I could say I was the first Allied soldier to cross the Seine. After hearing all my life about the Seine River, I was very disappointed with it. It wasn't much more than a big creek. Then later I discovered it was just a branch of the Seine and I had crossed over to an island. I sent a man back with word that I was at the river, and then deployed my men in a hedgerow about 30 feet back from the river. A short time later, the South Albertas moved in and took up a position right with us. I was glad to see them. I knew that as long as they were there with their tanks, the Germans would not attack. Then a military policeman came up and took up a position on the bridge. Years later, I was in the Tillsonburg Legion talking to a friend of mine, Russell Heath, and he told me about going into that town and being put on that bridge. I didn't know at the time that it was him. When we compared stories, he remembered seeing me, but he also didn't know it was me.

The Seine River was down in a valley. On the far side of the river, maybe six or seven hundred yards away, there was a big hill. As I stood looking over there, I saw a group of Germans run up from the river and head for the top of the hill. There must have been half a dozen of them. I ran to the tank and pointed them out to the tank men. I can hear them yet, "Oh boy! Let's get 'em!" I got back and they fired a shot right into the group of Germans. Down they went, every one of them. In a minute, a couple of them jumped up and started to run again. The tank men fired again and down they went. The next morning, I counted them and they were all still there. We had gotten every one of them.

The Oerlikon guns started to fire over our heads onto the hill across the river. When they fired those guns, they never knew whether their shells were going to hit 20 miles or 20 feet in front of the gun. When they fired, the barrel went around in a circle, spewing shells in all directions. The shells exploded on impact and flew into small pieces of shrapnel. The sound of those shells going over was devastating. They made a kind of hollow bang and you didn't know whether it had gone over or exploded. I dived into the hedge and looked back over the town. The shells were hitting all over town; windows were breaking, pieces of roof were flying in all directions. Shells were even hitting the hedge where I was and I realized I couldn't stay there. I looked over at the bridge and Russ Heath was still standing there. He had to stay there all through the shelling. Something had to be done. They had to be stopped, but no one could go back and stop them. I jumped up and ran as hard as I could run to the right and down the hedge, with shells flying all around me. I circled around to the right side of the town and went back. When I got back to the far side of town, I could see the guns, about

100 yards out of town, in the open field where I had come in. Our support company was right in front of them. Already they had killed two of our own men and wounded several others. Our men were all on the ground trying to get out of the way and they could not get out to stop them. I picked up a Bren gun and went out and hollered at them. I told them to stop or I would open fire. They stopped and came in to see what the trouble was. When they saw what they had done, they were a pretty sick bunch of men. They never, ever tried firing over our heads again. I went back to find my men. Some of the houses were all shot up; roofs and windows demolished. We hadn't been in that town two hours, and yet, we had done far more damage to it than the Germans had done throughout the entire war.

When I arrived back to my position at the bridge, an old Frenchman came out of a house and told me by sign language not to eat supper. They were going to feed us. When the Oerlikon had started to fire, my men had all run into a shed to get away from it, so I joined them there now. Several times the old man came out to make sure we weren't eating. Finally, both he and his wife came out together. He was carrying a huge platter of eggs fried in homemade butter—just swimming in it, in fact. She served a big platter of homemade bread, fresh out of the oven. We started to eat and I can say, without a doubt, it was one of the best suppers I have ever eaten. Before we had that gone, they came out with more. We ate eggs and bread and butter until we could hardly move. It was dark when we finally finished, so the men all crawled back into the shed and went to sleep. Someone had to be outside, so I took a Bren gun and crawled into the hedge and went to sleep. I didn't wake up all night. In the morning, the company runner came up and told me the rest of the regiment had crossed the river in the night. I was to take my platoon down the river, where there was a boat waiting to take us across. We were going to attack Hill 88 on the other side of the river.

As "A" Coy. had led the way into Criquebeuf-sur-Seine, we would now be the reserve company in the attack on Hill 88, and since I had led the way the day before, No. 8 Plt. was now the reserve platoon. The rest of the regiment was across the river and was even at that time fighting over there. We had a very leisurely breakfast, then moved down to the river, where we crossed in a good-sized boat. The first company had crossed in the night in a small boat using shovels for paddles. We landed on the far side of the river (I never did know if it was the north or south side) and followed a road up the hill. The Argyll Regiment had gone up ahead of us. As I understood it, the plan was for the Argylls to go one way and the Lincoln and Welland Regiment to go another at the top of the hill. I had sent my platoon on ahead in single file. They were moving very slowly as there was fighting up on the hill. I had stopped to relieve myself of a bit of excess water, so I was left behind. It was a very nice day and I was going to enjoy it all I could. I was looking the land over and just taking my time when I heard something in the bushes along the road. It sounded about like a sheep bleating. Then I could see movement in there. I had thought I was all alone, but, evidently, I was not. I took the safety off my Bren gun, set it on my hip and got ready to shoot. Whatever was in there was coming out. I hollered in German to get their hands up, and up went a very dirty white handkerchief on the end of an arm and I could hear a very weak voice saying, "Schießen Sie nicht" (Don't shoot). The bushes were quite thick and the man was really having a hard time getting through them, but he finally made it. And out stepped the most sickly-looking German I had ever seen. Most of them were in good condition, but this one was skinny and very pale. He didn't look as if he could go much farther. I threw his rifle back in the bushes and told him to empty his pockets. His handkerchief was filthy and looked as if he had used it to clean his boots. He didn't have much of anything—just a lump of black bread wrapped in a very dirty cloth, and the bread was mouldy. I threw it in the bushes after the rifle. Then I told him to go back down the road. Our echelon was back there. I would let them capture him; he didn't look very dangerous, and I had to catch up to the rest of the company. I went around a curve in the hill and came upon a small German tank by the side of the road. It was a kind of scout tank, with very light armament and a crew of two. I walked over to it and looked in to find two Germans in it. One looked as if he was just sitting there, but the other one only had half a head. The top from the nose up was gone. I didn't linger, as it was not a very pretty sight, and continued up the hill.

When I got there, Major Baldwin had come back to find me. Our second-in-command, Captain Snelgrove, had only just taken over the lead of "C" Coy. (who had lost their company commander), in time to be killed himself. Baldwin had gone up in his carrier to help Snelgrove, but he had been fired upon and had to come back. On the way back, he had run over and dragged to death a sergeant from the Canadian Scottish Regiment, which had moved up and attacked through our position. So far, I had been very lucky in this battle. The fighting had been very heavy and there had been a lot of casualties, but I was at the very tail end of the line and was so far back, I didn't know what was going on. I had just been enjoying the day, but now that was over. When Snelgrove was killed, everyone had been pushed back.

Now, I was ordered to take my platoon and go through the rest of the company to retake the position. There was a big flat field up there—just a wide open space. I put my men in an extended line and advanced. I didn't know just what to expect, but I knew by now we had lost a lot of men. I advanced until we came to a road, then I stopped. We had not been fired upon. I stopped right where Snelgrove had been killed, but there was no one there. The Germans had pulled out and were gone. Now there was nothing to do but wait for more orders, so we sat there for about fifteen or twenty minutes.

There were the remains of some old buildings nearby, and one of the men went down to an old shed about 50 yards away. He found something and hollered at me to come and have a look. I was sitting on the ground beside my Bren gun. Without thinking, I just got up and started over to him, leaving my Bren gun on the ground where I had been sitting. I was almost over to him when he said, "Look there." I turned to look and got the shock of my life! A German soldier had come out of the woods on the far side of the road and was standing right beside my Bren gun. Cold chills raced up and down my back. My first thought was to run to the gun, but what was the use? He was right there. I carried a pistol in a shoulder holster under my arm, and I pulled it out now and walked back towards the German. He was carrying the barrel of a German MG-42 machine gun in his hands. He handed it over to me and said he wanted to surrender, so I started to breathe again. I asked him where the rest of the gun was and he pointed across the road. I went across the road and there it was behind a tree. He had been there waiting for a chance to come out all the time we had been there. I asked him if he had shot our captain, but he said no, that it had been his partner. His partner had shot the captain and then run, but he had stayed behind to surrender. He wanted no more war. I left my men there and searched up and down the road both ways, but there were no more Germans. Just a barn full of rabbits down the road a ways. But I had learned another good lesson. I never again walked away and left my gun. I kept it in my hands all the time.

Hill 88 had been a pretty tough place to crack. It had been defended by many 88-millimetre guns, so we had all thought that was why it was called Hill 88, but it was not; eighty-eight was just a number on a grid map. Just to the right of it was a hill called Hill 95 where the Argylls and the Algonquins had had a hard fight all day. The Canadian Scottish Regiment now passed through the Lincoln and Welland Regiment on their way to attack to the north. Baldwin came back through and ordered me to take the platoon, follow the road we were on and rendezvous with the rest of the regiment by the town of Igoville. We followed the road down the hill and around a curve where we found "A" Coy. waiting. I went over to Baldwin, who was talking to a strange officer with a red band on his hat. By this, I knew he was a staff officer from Brigade Headquarters. Baldwin introduced me to him and said he was to take command of No. 8 Plt. I was glad to see him; now I would have a bit of help. The new officer, I never did know his name, told me to take the platoon over in the field at the edge of town, and, as it was thought there were still Germans in the town, to be prepared to attack. I went to the edge of town. We were right out in the open. One sniper there could pick off the whole platoon. The boys all said, "Hey, this isn't right. We don't have a chance." And we didn't, but that was the place we had been told to go. While we were arguing over it, we could see a horse convoy of Germans going out the far end of town. We fired at them, but they were too far away. We now knew there *were* Germans in there and the men didn't want to stay in this open place. There was one house by itself out from the edge of town and I decided to take the men in there. That would give us a place from which to fight. We had just nicely installed ourselves in the house when a Frenchman and his son came in. They told us the Germans had all gone. He asked us if we would like some steak. "Boy, would we!" I grabbed a butcher knife out of a drawer and handed it to him and away he went. We got a fire going and got everything ready to cook. He came back in about twenty minutes with the nicest steak I ever saw. We cooked it up and never ate better. That was the first time I had ever eaten horse steak.

About this time, in came the new officer. Did he go after me! He had told me where to take the platoon and he expected his orders to be followed. In this, he was right, so I couldn't say anything, but I had led the platoon long enough that I knew how to do it. You do not put men in the position we had been put in, and I could see this man was pretty green at the job.

We had had an easy day of it, so I wasn't surprised when he told me that No. 8 Plt. would do the guard duty that night. He made it plain I was to look after it and do as he ordered. I expected that as a platoon officer he would share the night with me. I watched him get into his sleeping bag just as it was getting dark. I already had the guards out and I changed them every hour on the hour all night long. I had already had a month of fighting and was very tired. This was his first night on the line and he was fresh. By the time the last watch came, every man had had a turn. I told the last man to get some sleep, and I would stand the last watch. I picked a position where I could watch the whole camp and sat down with the Bren gun. And then I fought sleep—for an hour I fought it. My head would go down and I would nearly lose the fight, but, at the last second, I would rouse up. There were times that I did go to sleep, but just for seconds, and then I would come out of it. Finally, the sun began to come up.

Dick, the cook, got up and started breakfast. The cookhouse was about 100 yards behind me, while down to my left about another 100 yards, was the rest of the company. They started to get up also, grabbing their mess tins and heading for the cookhouse. I watched my new officer get out of his sleeping bag and head for his breakfast. My line of vision was like a triangle with the kitchen on one point, the officer on another and me on the third point. He started on an angle for the kitchen. It was daylight now with no chance of a surprise attack. If I was going to get some sleep, I had to get it now. I put my head down and was gone that fast.

About a minute later, I woke up to someone shaking me. Instead of going to the kitchen, my officer had come over to me. He went up and down my back for being asleep. He said I was asleep on guard duty and he was going to report me to Baldwin. I was so mad at the injustice of it all, I couldn't even talk. If I had said anything to him at all, I think I would have shot him. After all, life was very cheap. I just rolled over with my back to him and went back to sleep, and he left me there. A bit later, one of the boys brought me some breakfast. That night, I had had only about fifteen minutes of sleep. But sleep was over now, so I finished my breakfast and decided to go for a walk.

There were some farm buildings about 200 yards in front of me, and I decided I would go and look them over. As I walked across the field, I noticed it had a nice shady drive that was full of German equipment—gas masks, packs, just about everything. The packs were really beautiful. They were all made of spotted-pony skin. It had been what was called an Alpine Regiment—very elite. Caught off guard by our air force just the day before, they had just dropped everything and run. I wanted one of those packs in the worst way, but while I was looking them over, I saw something out in the field. I went out to see what it was and discovered it was the body of a little girl about seven or eight years old. She was wearing a white dress with small pink and blue flowers on it and had a doll in her arms. She had been out in the field when the planes strafed the place and didn't make it back to the house. The people in the house had left, and she was all alone. I went back to our camp and sent one of the men to tell Padre Kennedy she was there and to ask if he would look after her. He took out a work party and they buried her. Later, he sent word to me that he had taken care of her and thanked me.

Baldwin came and told me that the new officer had been returned to Brigade Headquarters and that I was in charge of No. 8 Plt. Nothing else was said. For as long as Baldwin was my company commander, he never, ever questioned my judgement or what I did.

At eight o'clock in the morning of August 29, 1944, the rest of the regiment had been ordered to move and they had already gone. They were on the road to a town called Ymare and then on to Boos. "A" Coy. was the last to go. We stopped at a place called Franquevillette for the night.

On August 30, we started out again to chase the Germans, and after passing through several small towns, we stopped and set up camp in a small woods to the southeast of Buchy. Orders were given to settle down. We would be there for four days to rest and refit. Then, only two hours later, we received orders to move and were off to the Somme River.

I remember September 1, 1944, as the day we made the longest advance of any day during the war. From one o'clock until seven o'clock in the morning, we advanced 46 miles. We left everything behind and were way ahead of the rest of the Canadian army. That day was a day of short, sharp fights and going full speed ahead as Germans watched us from the roadside. As we sped through towns, Germans stood on the streets and watched us go. For the next week, it was nothing but push on. We lived in our TCVs, so what little sleep we got was done in them on the run. Most of that time is just a blur to me and I have very little recollection of it.

I do remember one place we came to, though. It was in the afternoon and we had stopped as we emerged from a woods. There before us was a huge wheat field, covering at least 50 acres, all cut and set up. To me, it was a very pretty sight. Out in the middle of the field sat a Sherman tank, all alone. About 250 yards in front of it was a small clump of trees. Our advance was to take us across the field, through a woods on the other side and into a valley where we were to stop. But that tank out there just didn't look right. We sat there for maybe half an hour. Finally, I was ordered to take No. 8 Plt. and go out there and look it over. I put the whole platoon into an extended line, with myself in the middle, and we began to advance across the field. When we got even with the tank, which was on our left, I stopped the men and went over myself to have a look at it. When I was almost to it, I could see a man sitting beside it. As I came nearer, he said, "Am I glad to see you!" And he sure was. He was badly wounded. He said he had been there since the day before. The tank had taken a hit from an anti-tank rifle, which was a heavy rifle used to knock out tanks at close range. He had been wounded when they were hit and the rest of the crew got out of the tank and ran, leaving him there for dead. He had gotten out of the tank but was unable to get back in to get food or water.

I sent one of my men back to get an ambulance for him while I approached the clump of trees. Once there, I could see where the Germans had been with the anti-tank rifle. There was one empty shell casing on the ground; everything else was gone. I took the platoon and continued through the woods and out into the valley. Shortly, the rest of the company came around by the road and into the valley where we settled down for the night. Again, without the help of an officer, I got very little sleep, keeping guards out and checking them every hour. It was beginning to tell on me. I was getting tired and very nervous. My nerves were on edge all the time. I had not had my shoes off since somewhere around August 20, and my socks had started to grow things. My shoes would get filled up with water that looked like very pale blood. I'd lie down on my back, put my feet up and let it run out the backs of my shoes.

That night about five o'clock we came into a small town at the edge of the valley. I was sent through with my platoon, but as I made my way through the town and out the far side, I didn't see even one German. We took up a position behind a hedge and waited. Out in front of us in the field was a large straw stack, and on our left was a house. While we were waiting for our supper, a German soldier came out of the house. He was very surprised to see us, and we were very surprised to see him! We went in the house to check things out. It was a German officers' mess—food was on a table all set with a white tablecloth. The German soldier had gone out of the house for a moment and when he returned, the German officers were gone. They heard us coming and ran. He had come out the front door to see what was going on, and there we were.

After we had our supper, we settled down for the night. We could hear Germans moving around out in front of us and we didn't like it.

The men were getting very nervous, and, about ten o'clock, I went out and set fire to the straw. It burned all night and gave us a good light.

We pushed on and the next afternoon we came to a river. I don't know if it was the Somme or not; all I know is that it was a river. Our regiment history book says we crossed the Somme River unopposed and congregated on an estate on the edge of town at quarter to six in the evening, but we crossed this river about nine o'clock at night. An officer had been sent to No. 8 Plt. that night to lead the platoon in the crossing and we crossed over on a log that stretched across the river. He went first and then I went right behind him. When he got to the far side, he said, "There, I'm the first Canadian to cross this river." Whether it was the Somme or not, I don't know. The officer disappeared in the dark and I never saw him again.

We came into a small town and discovered we were now in Belgium. When or where we got there, I don't know. Again, I was ordered to take No. 8 Plt. through the town. I advanced through the town until we came out the other side, and no Germans did we find. We were standing in a hayfield of about six acres and spied a hedge on the far side. We crossed the hayfield to the hedge, took up a defensive position and waited for orders.

Shortly, a man came out of the town to greet us. He identified himself as the burgomaster and said that now they were liberated, they were going to put on a big party. There would be wine, women and everything that went with them. As far as he was concerned, the war was over and there was no reason to go on. He could not understand why we could not just stop and have a party. He came out twice and begged me to bring the men back into town, but my job was to secure the town and that was what I was doing.

Out in the middle of the field was the town well. Everyone had to carry their water from there. I couldn't stand it any longer. I had taken a clean pair of socks out of my pack and was waiting for a chance to take my shoes off. I went over to the well and drew up a pail of water. Then, oh-so-carefully, I took my shoes off, one at a time. My feet had blistered and the skin had come off; my flesh had grown right into my socks. It all came off in pieces: socks, flesh, blood and everything.

Then I washed my feet in the pail of water and sat down by the well to dry them in the sun. I let the sun shine on them for about half an hour, but I was afraid they would burn. I took the laces out of my boots and opened them up to let the sun dry them out. It had been going on three weeks since I'd had my shoes off.

We moved on through Saint-Riquier, Marchéville, Hesdin and on to Saint-Omer. On the outskirts of Saint-Omer, a bridge had been blown up and we had to circle around the town. Whoever was leading the column got turned around, and we ended up going in circles. We went through Saint-Omer three times—and every time, the people came out and cheered. By this time, we were told to unload and walk. It had now started to rain, and we had walked 12 miles when, finally, our TCVs came up to us and we got back in—every one of us tired and ugly. This was the second time this had happened to us.

On the afternoon of September 7, we came into the town of Ochtezeele and stopped for the night. In the morning, we moved on again. We would go a little way, stop and clear out some German resistance and then move on. The night of September 8, we stopped just short of Oostcamp, where "A" Coy. was put in a barn to get some sleep in a straw mow. It felt very good there, but the stay was short. About ten o'clock that night, we were called out to attack the town of Moerbrugge, across the Ghent Canal.

12

GHENT CANAL

MOERBRUGGE WAS a small town on the north side of the Ghent Canal close to Bruges. In this part of Belgium, there are many small towns close to each other. Sometimes, it is hard to tell where one starts and the other ends. Moerbrugge consisted of a road running parallel to the canal, and another road at right angles to the first. A third road ran parallel to the first on to the town of Lekkerhoek.

In this attack, the Argylls went in just at dark. Two companies established themselves along the right-angled road, going straight across the canal and straight up the road. A third company went through their position to the next road, made a right turn and were on the second road that ran parallel to the canal.

"D" Coy. of the Lincoln and Welland Regiment followed, and took up a position ahead of the Argyll Coy. on the road inland that ran parallel to the canal. There they joined up with the Argylls, who were now fighting for their lives against a very determined enemy. (It was in this area where General Montgomery made his mistake when he planned his battle for the city of Arnhem. I think he got his intelligence reports from American news reporters, who told him the area was held by very poor German troops that consisted of old men and Polish soldiers who were fighting in the German army. And many of them were just that, but they were also led by some very good German troops, plus German marines. Any Canadian soldier who was there knew that the American report was just not right.)

"C" Coy. moved in behind our "D" Coy., while "B" Coy. was to the left of our crossing point. "A" Coy. was the last company to cross the canal. It must have been three o'clock in the morning when I brought my platoon down to the canal. I had been wondering why everything was going so slowly, and now I found out. Both the Argyll and the Lincoln and Welland Regiments had crossed the canal in one small rowboat. It carried only seven or eight men at a time. They climbed in and paddled across, then the boat was pulled back by a rope and another boatload went over. We crossed at the spot where there should have been a bridge, but the Germans had destroyed it. My platoon was reserve platoon. I saw to the crossing and crossed in the last boatload. "A" Coy. had turned right and were going down the first road parallel to the canal. I could hear them fighting down the street and I was very glad of my position. If all went well, I would not see much fighting. I was getting very tired by this time and my feet were still in bad shape. Just across the canal, the medical officer, Captain McKenzie, had set up a first aid post. My men had gathered there and were waiting to follow down the road. When I got there, the Germans were attacking the first aid post. Major Baldwin, the medical officer, Captain McKenzie and I lined up in a window with the Bren guns and fought them off. They were in some houses right in front of us. All the Germans finally left but one, who persisted in coming back. He got on the main street right where we had crossed the canal and came and fired around the corner at us. I slid down the bank of the canal and crawled back to our boat. The German was on the street in front of me about 15 feet away. It was dark and I could not see him, but I could see the flash of his gun as he fired. I laid my gun over the top of the canal bank and let go. We did not hear anymore from him. In the morning the German was gone, but there was blood on the street. We found an old man and his wife whom the Germans had beat up. They were in bad shape, but our medical officer took care of them.

"A" Coy.'s advance was moving a bit faster now. I got my men moving on a track along the deeply rutted canal used for horses and carts. Up at the front, a German MG-42 started to fire and the platoon sergeant of the lead platoon was killed and a couple of men were wounded. Bullets were coming right down the road at me. One was about knee-high, one a bit higher and to the right, and a third a bit higher yet and to the right. There may have been more, but I didn't stop to see. I dived into one of the ruts in the road and they strafed over top of me.

There was more firing up ahead and I could hear grenades going off. A good brisk fight was going on and I knew what was going to happen. Whenever trouble like that started, it always meant the reserve platoon would be called up. And sure enough, the order came back I was to bring up No. 8 Plt. and go through. It was starting to get light by now. I moved up to the front of my platoon and said, "All right, let's go." The fight had stopped and we moved up without incident. The forward platoon had dropped back by now. We went through and deployed in the open at the edge of town, and this put us right at the front. The Germans were in a small woodlot about 50 yards in front of us. Straight to the left of us across an open field, "D" Coy. had been stopped and could not move, their advance being held up by a house full of Germans next door. Baldwin told me to take a gun out in the field and lay down some fire, while he led an attack on the woods.

I took a man by the name of Atkinson and went out to the left. We had just gone about 40 yards into the open when a German anti-aircraft gun opened up on us from the side of the house where the Germans were holed up. That was a most devastating experience. Those were the kind of shells that exploded when they hit. All we could do was go to ground, and they sure laced us. We were both carrying entrenching tools, and we lay down side by side and started to scrape a hole in between us. And did we scratch! We got down about four inches and were into white chalk. That was as deep as we could go, so we got down as far as we could and lay there. At least we were safe—or so we thought.

There was a small tree maybe 20 feet high about 10 feet from us. These Germans were smart. They stopped firing at us and fired into the tree instead. That exploded the shells, and the shrapnel showered down on top of us. Atkinson said, "I'm hit," and I said, "So am I." I looked over at him. His face was covered with blood and I had some on my right shoulder. We could not stay there; they would kill us in a very few minutes. I said, "When they stop to reload, get up and run." They stopped briefly and we jumped up and ran in a hail of machine gun and anti-aircraft shells. Atkinson went around the house and I jumped into the canal. As I did, I could see a man sitting beside a tree. An anti-aircraft shell had hit him right in the face. Atkinson went to the medical officer and I never saw him again. He never came back. Meanwhile, I went in the house and upstairs to look out the window. There was a dead German at the foot of the stairs. I stepped over him and ascended the stairway cautiously, but there was no one else there. After a while, I decided I should go to the medical officer and have him look at my shoulder, so I went downstairs and again stepped over the dead man. It was about eight o'clock in the morning of September 9, 1944. The medical officer put a bandage on my shoulder and said he guessed I should go to the hospital for a few days. I went out and sat down for a while, then got up and went back to my platoon. For years to come, I would have cordite and shrapnel coming out of my shoulder.

All day long, the Germans went after us with everything they had—small arms, mortars, anti-aircraft guns, 88s and heavy artillery—but we hung on. Then some Germans advanced across a sugar beet field out in front of us in order to attack us. Four or five were shot down right in front of us, but one of them was just wounded. I watched him as he put his rifle up under his chin and shot the top of his head off.

About the middle of the afternoon, I went upstairs and over the dead man again. When I looked out the window, I could see the house where the Germans were. The sugar beet field was right behind it and came right down in front of us to the edge of the woodlot. As I watched, a group of Germans came out of the house and started for the woods. I let them get about halfway there before I started to shoot. They had no cover and after I had knocked down a couple of them, the rest turned and tried to get back to the house. Some on the ground got up again; I knocked them down again. One did get back and into the house. Another very nearly made it—about 15 more feet and he would have been there. Then down he went. He tried to get up, so I gave him another one. He lay still for a few minutes, then tried to crawl. I shot at him a couple more times, and, all the while, he was still trying to crawl. Meanwhile, another German came out of the house to help him, so I shot him, too. I would take one last careful shot and that would fix him. As I was taking close aim, I got an overwhelming urge to turn my head. I did not even stop to think about it, and there was absolutely no reason to do it. Something just said, "Turn your head," and so I did. I just snapped it right around. At the precise time I did so, a bullet zinged past my head right in the groove between my ear and my head. If I hadn't turned, that bullet would have hit me right above my left eye. This was the second time I had been saved by a sudden, unexplained urge. Someone was looking after me.

The crack of the bullet nearly deafened me. The shock of it knocked me across the room to the top of the stairs, so I kept on going. I had now become aware that something was going on outside the house. I ran out the front door. It was a wild place out there. The Germans were firing everything they had. At the same time, our own mortar platoon was firing heavy mortars on our position. Everything was just jumpin'! And in the middle of the yard stood Jim Alexander, one of my corporals, with a Bren gun on his hip, firing into the woods. The whole place was full of smoke. I yelled, "What the hell are you firing at?" He yelled back, "Germans! Can't you see 'em?" But there was so much smoke, I couldn't see anything. Some Germans had come out of the woods. I knew then that they had tried to get across the field to help their men stranded in the house. They had managed to get right up to the house, but Jim and all the mortar fire had been too much for them. Jim was wounded twice. While I had been upstairs, I did not know what had been happening down there. No one knew what I had done upstairs, and I never mentioned it. Jim was given the Military Medal for fighting off the attack. I had left eight Germans dead out in the beet field, but I didn't tell anyone about them. The next day, I was out in the field and they were still there.

It was pretty wild out there for a while. The Germans had very nearly entered the house. After things slowed down a bit, Baldwin came up to our position to talk it over. The Germans were still in the house across the field and "D" Coy. could not get them out. Baldwin said, "I think if someone took a PIAT gun out in the sugar beet field, they could blast the Germans out of the house." He did not know there were Germans still in the woods. To get out, they had to cross that field, and that they could not do. After nearly a day of fighting, there must have been at least a dozen dead Germans out there. I knew what he was getting at, and I wasn't about to volunteer, even if I did think I could do it. After a bit, he said, "If I send up a gun, will you go out and do it?" So I finally said yes, I would, and he went back to get a PIAT gun. This was a spring-fired gun that fired a bomb up to 300 yards or so. Mostly used on tanks at close range, but we also used it in house clearing. If one of these was fired into a house, *nothing* came out. While I was waiting for the gun, I went back into the house. I had seen a banjo in there. I got it and went outside by the side of the canal and sat there and played it for about half an hour. I did not know it at the time, but Battalion Headquarters was right behind us on the south side of the canal, and my playing made one of the great stories to tell of the regiment. I played, "We're Going to Hang Out Our Washing on the Siegfried Line," and everyone in Battalion Headquarters heard it.

There was still fighting going on all around me. Finally, Baldwin sent for me and I put the banjo down on the bank of the canal and left it there. He said he couldn't get a PIAT gun right then, but he would keep on trying. I wasn't disappointed. I went back into the house where we were and started upstairs. As I stepped over the dead German, he moved and tried to say something. I kneeled down beside him and took a look. He was in very bad condition but still alive. I quickly sent for a stretcher and took him to the medical officer, who shipped him back to the hospital. This had been a pretty rough day. The Germans had attacked our position three or four times. We had a kid with us, seventeen years old, whose name was Churchill. In one attack, he had been badly wounded and I had ordered him out and I thought he had left. A few minutes later, I heard a gun firing behind the house. I went to see who it was, and it was Churchill. That time, I took him out myself. He never came back.

When it started to get dark, everything quieted down. I put the men out all around the house, and then I went to sleep for a while. I checked the men three times that night. One man whose name I don't remember was out behind the house all alone. In the morning, I went out to bring him back in and I asked him how he had got on all alone. He said he had been alone only part of the time. "Oh," I said. "Who was with you?" He answered, "I don't know." A man had crawled in beside him and stayed for a couple of hours. This sure shocked me. I asked him what regiment the man was from, and he said a name. There wasn't even a regiment with that name in the Canadian army. It was a German soldier who had come in the dark and left before daylight. My man said, "I wondered why he was asking so many questions." He said he did not even hear him come in. All of a sudden, he was just there and talking to him.

Sometime during the night, "C" Coy. had cleared the Germans out of the houses on their street and had moved up to the end of the beet field. It was now safe to go out and check the Germans who were still out there. Two of them were still alive but were in bad condition. One of them had been there for twenty-four hours. I called for stretchers and a group of German prisoners came and picked them up. In the fighting at this position, there were four medals given for bravery. I was recommended for one but didn't get it. On that day, I was told that I had been recommended before and was to get a medal for that. It didn't materialize, either.

Ever since we had crossed the canal, the engineers had been trying to get a bridge across it so tanks could get over. They had made a couple of bridges, but the Germans were in a position where they could look straight down the street and see them. As soon as a bridge was up, they would blow it out. But now a bridge was up, and the Germans were gone, or so we thought. The first tank to come across just drove off the bridge and was knocked out. The driver of that tank was Chester Hotchkiss from Straffordville. But finally the tanks were across and we could see them going up the road towards Lekkerhoek. That road went east, there was a corner, and then it turned north again. Up almost to the corner was a large brick house, and we could see Germans moving around it. As I watched, one of the tanks fired a shot at it and blew the side of the house right out. Inside the house was a stairway that was now visible, and we could see the Germans running down the stairs and out of the house. Out in front of us, Germans were coming in to surrender, sometimes just a few and other times in groups of forty or fifty. One group of at least fifty came across the field with a white bedsheet on a long pole. That morning, we took more than four hundred prisoners, many of whom came in and said they were Polish and wanted to join the Canadian army and fight the Germans. They would come in with their hands up, saying, "Schießen Sie nicht, me Pole." (Don't shoot, I'm Polish.) Many of them did go to the Polish Division that was fighting in the Canadian army and did fight the Germans.

At noon on September 11, orders were received that we were to attack Lekkerhoek, so we moved off in single file down the road. As we were just moving to another position at that time, No. 8 Plt. was again at the rear of the column. It just happened that way. When we got down to the corner to turn north, we could see what was going on. Baldwin had stopped his carrier just around the corner. Down the road were several tanks that were also stopped. There were Germans down there. They had let two or three tanks go past and then knocked one out behind them. The tanks were trapped; if they moved, they would get it. The infantry would have to go in and take out the German gun, which was a bazooka. But this was not a small attack. We were to attack three small towns, all heavily defended, so it would take time to get in position. "A" Coy. would move down the right side of the road to Lekkerhoek. "B" Coy. would take the town of Veldkapel. "C" Coy. would go through Veldkapel and seize the road junction beyond. Then "A" Coy. would move from Lekkerhoek to the high ground. But for now, the tanks were stopped. Instead of turning the corner and going north, we went straight through and into a field on the right side of the road. As we went into the field, there was a house right there and we went about 15 yards behind it. There we sat down to wait.

As usual, we were told nothing. We only had one platoon officer and this was his first day in battle. I was not too far over in the field, so I could look back at Baldwin, who was standing by the carrier talking on the wireless telephone. Suddenly, there was a rifle shot just ahead and Baldwin went down. I jumped up and raced back to him. The bullet had hit him in the hand holding the phone up to his ear, and had taken off a couple of his fingers. It had barely missed his head. Both he and his company runner were on the ground behind the carrier. I asked them, "Where did that shot come from?" It had come from the backyard of the house right beside us, about 20 yards away. I got a rifle out of the carrier, crawled out from behind it on my belly and into the ditch. I went up the ditch on my belly until I was even with the house, then jumped up and made a dash for the yard at the side of the house. When we had gone into the field, we could not see in that yard because there was a small hedgerow. Now I could see that behind the hedge was a slit trench and I ran towards it. There was movement at the corner of the house. I did not stop running, but swung the rifle around and fired. A man went down, and I kept running for the slit trench. When I got there, I stuck the rifle down the hole and hollered. In the bottom of the hole was a German. He had blood all over his face and he was very scared. He looked up at me, and said, "Pretty grim, ain't it?" I said, "Where did you come from?" and he said, "New York City." I said, "I'll bet you wish you were back there," and he replied, "I sure do." I asked him what had happened to him and he said the other German had kicked out his teeth. I told him to get back down the road to Moerbrugge and he was sure glad to go.

I went and looked at the other German I had shot at and he was dead. Then I went back to the carrier. Baldwin was still there. He told me Major McCutcheon of "B" Coy. was to take over "A" Coy., and he and his runner went back. Later in the day, I saw the runner and he told me Baldwin had written out a citation for me for a medal, and that he, the runner, had personally delivered it to the adjutant. But again, that medal never materialized, either.

I went back to my platoon and told them what had happened. A man by the name of King came to me and we stood side by side talking. I never heard a shot, but then he said, "I'm hit." I said, "You're not," but he insisted he was. I asked, "Where?" and he answered, "Right in the chest." He opened his shirt and sure enough, there was a small blue hole in the right side of his chest, high up, nearly to his shoulder. He turned around and showed me his back, and there was a hole where the bullet had come out. One of my men hollered, "Get down, you damn fools!" and we realized that we were still standing there. Boy, did we get down in a hurry then. I told him that he had better go back, so he crawled over to the road and went back.

About that time McCutcheon from "B" Coy. on the left side of the road called over an order to move. "B" Coy. started forward, and I gave the order for "A" Coy. to move. Even though McCutcheon was in charge of "A" Coy., he was not there to lead us, so I took over and led the attack. Eighty yards in front of us was a hedgerow. We went in on the run, firing as we went. Behind the hedge was a big, long trench full of Germans. They fired a few shots, but we were on them so fast they could do nothing but surrender. They threw down their guns, and I left a man there to take them back while I took the rest of the company into the town.

Lekkerhoek was a row of houses down one side of the road. It was still about another 80 yards to the town, with yet another hedgerow. When we got to the town, all the men went to the right around the end of the hedge and in behind the houses. I saw an opening in the hedge to the front of the houses and went through it. There was a gravel walkway straight down in front of the houses, and what we would call the front yard was between the walkway and the road. Right there was a small hedge, parallel with the walkway and the road, with a path and gate through it to get to the road. I ran through this gateway into the yard. Behind the bigger hedge was an L-shaped trench full of Germans, but they were looking the wrong way. I was behind them and I started to shoot and holler at them. Down at the end on the right, a German started to bring his gun around. I fired one round from the hip and he just slid out of sight down in the trench. Some of my men realized that they had left me alone and came around the corner of the house to help me. There were about thirty-five or forty Germans who appeared to be glad to surrender. We had now taken around one hundred prisoners.

"B" Coy. had gone right on with their attack and were now three or four hundred yards in front of us in the town. I took the company up to meet them and asked McCutcheon where we were to go and what we were to do. He told me to turn to the left and take them down to the road junction where "C" Coy. was supposed to be. We could hear them coming, but they had lost a lot of men and did not get there. I put the men in a line and started across an open field about 300 yards from the road junction. I was out front in the lead. Shortly, I realized some of the men behind me had stopped. I looked back and saw Jim Alexander running across the field. Jim stopped and pointed his Bren gun down a hole and started firing. We had gone past a slit trench with a German in it. He had let us go past, then raised up and shot Jim's best friend in the back of the head and killed him. Our advance came to a complete stop. Some of the men went to help Jim, while the rest just milled around.

As I looked down to the road, I could see we were nearly there. But I could also see movement down in the ditch, and I hollered at the company to get moving. As they started to sort themselves out and move on, I ran to the road, firing as I went. When I got there, the Germans threw grenades out at me. There was a strong wire fence there, so I couldn't get at them. Meanwhile, they were crawling down the ditch as fast as they could go. By the time the rest of the men got there, the Germans had gotten away.

We took up a position for the night. No. 8 Plt. was on the corner out in the open, while No. 7 and No. 9 Plts. were on our right. There was a big straw stack there with a shelter underneath it for the pigs to sleep in. Both No. 7 and No. 9 Plts. slept in there that night and nothing eventful happened until morning. At last light the night before, some tanks had moved in behind us and were situated between "A" and "B" Companies. When daylight came, some of the men from No. 7 and No. 9 Plts. came out of the straw stack and started to move around. The tank men about 100 yards behind us spotted them and started to shoot at them with .30-calibre machine guns. Luckily, no one was hurt, but they set the straw stack on fire. Our men were very lucky to get out, but they lost a lot of equipment in the straw fire.

For the moment, all was quiet, so we sat around just resting a bit. Down the road was another hedgerow running at right angles to the road. As I watched, I could see a German going up and down the hedge. He would walk up a way and come back, and then he would do it all over again. We were in slit trenches that had been dug by the Germans and we were not moving around much. This German kept going up and down, up and down, so I got a rifle. He was only about 100 yards away and I said, "I'll get you." I took a shot at him, but he kept right on going. In a couple of minutes he came back, so I let another one go. He acted as if I hadn't even come close. I fired four or five times, but he was still there, so I got a Bren gun and sprayed the area. Still he didn't pay any attention. Just at that moment, a runner came in and said Major McCutcheon wanted me to come back to where he was. Sgt. Red Irwin was there, so I said, "Red, see what you can do about this German. I have to go back." He came over to me and I pointed the German out to him, and he said he would try a shot at him. I jumped up and ran to the road, which was about 20 feet away. I would have to crawl up the ditch until it was safe to stand up. As I rolled in the ditch, I heard a crack behind me and I knew it was a bullet hitting something. I looked back and Red was as white as a sheet. I hollered, "Are you all right?" but he couldn't say a word. As he had been getting a bead on the German, another German had been getting a bead on him, and the bullet had hit the stock of his rifle on the side opposite his cheek. He decided that was enough of that and didn't shoot again.

I went back to "B" Coy., where McCutcheon informed me that there were some light tanks coming up and that they were going to clear out the Germans. He was also sending up an officer to take command of "A" Coy. The tanks were soon there. They came up through "B" Coy., passed my position and turned right at the corner where I was. They were armed with heavy machine guns, and as soon as they went down the road, the Germans started to surrender and came back up the road to us. I wanted very much to see down the road, but it was not safe for me to go out and look. On the opposite corner across the road from me was a house, and behind the house was a backyard surrounded by a big hedge with a good-sized tree growing right in it. The tree was about eight or ten inches around and about 30 feet high. I thought, "I could get behind that tree, no one could see me behind the hedge, and the tree would be good protection." So away I went—across the road, around the house and in behind the tree. The hedge was just high enough for me to look over the top of it from behind the tree. I had no sooner raised up to have a look than a shell of some kind whined up the road and hit the tree about a foot above my head. It cut the tree right off—it just jumped straight up in the air. I wasn't long deciding I didn't want to look anymore, and I was around the other side of the house by the time the tree came down right where I had been standing.

On September 12, "A" Coy. was to stay and hold the town of Lekkerhoek. "B" Coy. would pass through us and attack the town of Veldkapel. "B" Coy.'s sergeant major came up to our corner and turned left in the company carrier. He was to go down the road and see if there were any Germans in that direction. I watched him go around the corner and down the road. About two minutes later, there was a big bang. He had run over a bomb buried in the road.

"B" Coy. went on through and captured the town of Veldkapel. When all was secure, "A" Coy. lined up in single file and moved off to follow them down the road. We now had a new company commander, Major MacPherson, who sent Sergeant Winterford ahead to have a look with the "A" Coy. carrier. While he was gone, we sat down by the side of the road to wait. I sat down right beside the bombed-out "B" Coy. carrier. As I sat under a big tree with my feet in the ditch, I became aware of something dropping from the tree. Curious, I looked up. There, about 40 feet above me in the tree, was what was left of the "B" Coy. sergeant major, dripping on me as I sat there.

Winterford went down the road about half a mile and turned into a gateway where there was a house. He drove up to the house and there, hiding behind the house, was a German 88-millimetre gun. The Germans saw him and immediately ran and jumped into the vehicle used to pull the gun and took off across the field. Winterford turned around and came back, full speed. A tank regiment came up the road, and we climbed on and started towards the town of Sijsseele. I had picked up a bag full of handguns and for some reason I had them with me. The tanks stopped, we got off and made an attack on something—probably a farmhouse. The German 88 was there and it managed to fire one shot before the tanks got it. I had left my bag of guns on the top of the tank on which I had been riding. The tank was hit and burned, and I had to stand back and watch my bag of guns go up in smoke.

On the night of September 13, the Algonquin Regiment crossed the Leopold Canal at a place called Moerkerke. It was too much for one regiment and they took a terrible beating. They were driven back with a loss of 142, all ranks. On the night of September 14, I was sent out on a patrol towards the Leopold Canal. We were making our way up a side road, going along the ditch so we wouldn't make any noise on the road, and I was in the lead. Behind a hedgerow on my left, I heard someone about 10 feet from me coming our way. I called out, "Who goes there?" There was no answer, but someone took off on the run across the field. I was carrying a Bren gun and I sprayed bullets all over the field. The men behind me dived for cover. I never did find out who I was shooting at, or if I hit them or not.

I was tired out and my feet were so sore I could hardly walk. I had to lie down on my back every once in a while and let the watery blood run out of my shoes. I had to get out for a few days and get some rest. Sergeant Winterford, who was supposed to be the senior sergeant in No. 8 Plt., was still LOOB. One day, I was talking to him. He had been out for about a month now and I had not had a rest since we came into France. He was a pretty good fellow and we made a deal: the next battle we were in, he would lead the platoon and I would be LOOB. We would just not tell anyone until they were gone and I would be left behind. Boy, would I catch up on some sleep!

The time had come. The company loaded into the TCVs all ready to leave. I knew I would not see some of the men again. Some would be killed or wounded, so I went out to see them off. Major MacPherson came back to check things, and there I was on the ground, and Winterford was in the TCV. He said, "What's this? Why are you not in there?" So it all came out. We were going to change places for a few days. I was staying back and Winterford was going. MacPherson said, "Oh no, you're not. I'm not going without you." He stood right there until Winterford got out and I got in. That was the closest I had come to having a rest.

But now I had walked as far as I could go. Something had to be done about my feet. I got back to Company Headquarters from that patrol about three o'clock in the morning and went in and made my report. My platoon was in another area about a mile away and I was ready to stop and call it a day. I just made my report, then went outside, lay down and went to sleep. Morning came and I got some breakfast. Plans were under way to attack the city of Eekloo. They were now forming up to move, with "A" Coy. in the lead. But I was all done; my mind was made up. I was going to the doctor. "A" Coy. would have to get along without me. I did not even tell anyone I was going. The regiment was all in their vehicles ready to move. I went back down the road until I found the medical officer, who was all packed up and in his jeep. I asked him if he would have a look at my feet. He ordered me to go back to my company or he would have me court-martialled for leaving my platoon. I sat down by the side of the road. I was not going any farther. I said, "You will look at my feet or I will go and show them to the Colonel." He said, "All right, let's have a look." This was September 15 and it was only the second time I had had my shoes off since August 20. My feet had grown into my socks. I pulled my socks off, and flesh and skin came off with them. They just fell to pieces. The doctor took one look and said, "Get in. You better stay with me for a while." I climbed in and went to sleep. He told me to go to the cook and get some salt and water in a dish, and to soak them three times a day.

By ten o'clock that morning, the regiment had taken the town of Eekloo with very little fighting. That night, I slept in a very big house in a big bed with white sheets on it. I was so dirty I almost hated to get in it. All the next day, I slept on a stretcher on the top of a jeep. We were on the move, and that night, September 16, I slept under a table in a barroom. I think I spent three days and three nights doing this, and then, as we were short of men, I was sent back to my platoon.

All this time, the regiment had been fighting in and around Oost-Eekloo, Moerhuizen, Strooibrug, Kaprijke, Heuleken and several other small towns. This was very low land and the Germans had blown up some dams and let the water out. As a result, we tramped around in two feet of water. "B" Coy. had a brand new carrier, which was staying on the road by keeping between the fence posts. There was actually a small stream or a canal that had a bridge over it, but no one could see it because of the flooded conditions. The bridge had been blown, and down went the carrier right out of sight. A Sherman tank came along and ran right over it.

That night, I had my platoon in a farmhouse completely surrounded by water. I would see that everyone got some sleep. If the Germans came, we would hear them in the water. I put two men at the gate by the road and they were to change off every hour. One man at the back of the house was all that was needed, and the corporal and I would take turns. I would go to sleep and at one o'clock he was to wake me up. I went into the bedroom and went to sleep on the bed. At one o'clock, he came in. I had gone to sleep with a .38 revolver in my hand on my chest. When the corporal came in to wake me, he stood by the side of the bed and put his hand on me. He said he knew he'd done the wrong thing just as soon as he'd done it. He dropped to the floor as fast as he could, and I fired right over his head. I got up and changed the guards for the rest of the night, then I took the last watch out behind the house. The next morning, the company commander sent for me. He said, "What happened last night? You didn't have any guards out at the road." He said two German soldiers had come up the road in the night. There was a tank back behind us and they had pounded on the side of the tank to wake the tank men up. They wanted to surrender. I went to my platoon and lined them up and started to ask questions. Finally, two men said they had seen the Germans go past, but that they had just let them go.

It was quiet around there that morning, so Capt. Wallace Barkman and some of the men went out for a walk on some high ground that was above water. There was not supposed to be anything in the field, but there was a slit trench out there with a German in it. Wally, who was Russian and spoke several different languages, called to him to come out. He called in three or four different languages, but he still would not come out, so they threw a grenade in the hole and killed him.

The author in front of the former Luijten home at Bolwerk Zuid 50, where the battle of Bergen-op-Zoom was planned. After the battle, the Luijtens put Charles to bed in the living room (window at left).

*Top: The bombed-out factory where the "battle of madmen in the dark"
took place, Bergen-op-Zoom, Netherlands.*

COURTESY L.P. ROOSENBOOM

*The laundry building with the makeshift bridge across the zoom. The
small round window was Lt. Carl Holst's sniper position.*

COURTESY L.P. ROOSENBOOM

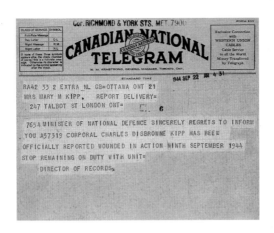

Telegram received by the author's wife in September 1944.
"Everybody around you was getting them too."
COURTESY MARGARET KIPP

A white arrow marks the green door from which Charles made his escape from
the gin factory out onto the street during the battle of Bergen-op-Zoom.
COURTESY L.P. ROOSENBOOM

*Hotel de Draak, headquarters of the Canadian army
during the battle of Bergen-op-Zoom.*

COURTESY L. P. ROOSENBOOM

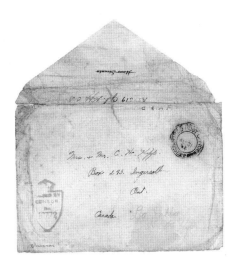

*This envelope contained Charles's letter to his parents of August 27, 1944
(see Appendix). Note the crossed-out German name on the flap.*

COURTESY ROSEMARY HOPPER

*Tank obstacles on the banks of the zoom that Charles hid behind after making his escape
from the gin factory, during the battle of Bergen-op-Zoom.*

COURTESY MARGARET KIPP

Preparing to go on leave to England, Cpl. Jim Marr (left) and the author sew clothes and do laundry, Germany, April 1945.
COURTESY MARGARET KIPP

Support Coy., No. 5 Plt., Lincoln and Welland Regiment, in Germany,
May 1945. Author in front row, second from right.

Cpl. Jim Marr (left) and Sgt. Charles D. Kipp at the
Holland–German border, March 1945.

On September 22, we returned to the city of Maldegem but did not stay there very long. "A" and "C" Companies, along with the Mortars Platoon, No. 4 Platoon (a carrier and machine gun platoon) and No. 5 Platoon (an anti-tank platoon), were sent to relieve the Lake Superior Regiment on the Leopold Canal. "A" Coy. was sent into the town of Strooibrug. This started a new phase of the war. We would now move into a holding position.

13

THE LEOPOLD CANAL

SOMEWHERE AROUND three o'clock on September 22, I received orders to take my No. 8 Plt. into Strooibrug and take over that position from the Lake Superior Regiment. Strooibrug was a small town in between two canals that came together at the west side of the town, putting it on a point of land. It had a network of First World War trenches and fortifications and a big air raid shelter deep in the ground. I had sent the platoon on ahead under the command of Cpl. Jim Alexander, and I was now on my way in. The main canal, the Leopold, was on the north with a dyke on each side of it. We were on the south side and the Germans were on the north. At this point, the canal was only about 14 feet wide. The other canal to the south, the Canal de Dérivation de la Lys, had a dyke on the north side of it. To get to Strooibrug, we followed behind the dyke of the south canal so we could not be seen by the Germans.

I was not in any hurry to get there. It was a nice sunny day and I was enjoying my walk all by myself. When I was about halfway there, I saw two men carrying a stretcher with something on it covered with a blanket. I thought, "Oh no, I've lost a man already." I asked them, "Who have you got there?" One of the men said, "Have a look." I turned back the blanket and there on the stretcher was a pig they had killed to eat. I was very relieved to see that it was not one of my men. I only had seven men left in my platoon, along with one signals man who was manning a telephone line from Company Headquarters to my headquarters in the air raid shelter. A full platoon strength was thirty men, all ranks; a section was nine men, all ranks. So, at that time, my platoon was less than a section in strength. By this time, the Canadian army was running out of volunteers, and we had taken so many casualties, we did not have the men to replace them. We were very much understrength. The company commander had told me before I went up to Strooibrug that we were to get some new men, and that he would send them up as soon as they arrived.

I arrived in Strooibrug somewhere around four o'clock and went to look the position over. At this point, the canals were somewhere around 100 yards apart. There was a pathway that led up to a trench. The trench was shaped something like the letter "t" or a cross, and about five feet deep. Straight up at the end, it came to the dyke, which was about eight feet high. It was here that Corporal Alexander had taken up his position with another man. It was about 16 feet straight across the canal to the German position. Farther back in the trench was an arm to the left, where he had positioned two men about 40 feet back. I went back to see how they were. With the dyke about eight feet high there, this part of the trench was shaped like a dog's hind leg, and at each crook, there was a place in the wall just big enough for a man to hide in and shoot from. I went back to look over the trench to the right. When nighttime came, I would have to man this trench myself. I went in to the right, then turned to the left, which led up to an observation post. There was a low wall across it and on the other side of it was a firing bay. I settled down to have a watch for a while to see if there was anything there.

There was. I saw movement and soon I could see a German about 16 feet in front of me. I had gone in very carefully, so he had not seen me yet. As I was watching him, I could hear movement on the other side of the dyke on my side of the canal. There was definitely something coming up the other side of the dyke, and there was no one there but Germans. I could hear it coming closer to the top. In just seconds, it would be over the top right above my head. I put the safety off my Sten gun and got ready. As soon as I could see, I would shoot. Then up it came. But it was white! I was squeezing the trigger, but stopped. A big white billy goat came out and stood on the top of the dyke, looking right down at me with its ears up. I knew the Germans would be watching it and would know I was there. It was not safe. I ducked down low and left and went back to where my platoon headquarters was to be.

By that time, supper had been sent up to us, and with it came our reinforcements—one new man. He was a steady-looking man, a bit older than the rest of us, but I didn't even bother to ask him his name as I knew he would not be with us very long. After we had our supper, I decided I would take him with me on the right branch of the trench. We went into the observation post and I told him to stay down. He was not to get out of there or stand up. I wanted to go the rest of the way down the left arm and see what was there. I told him I would be back by the time it got dark. I went to the left arm and made my way down it to find it opened up about 60 yards down right onto the canal. I could look straight across. I had just arrived when I heard a rifle go "pop." Then a grenade went off. I knew it was a rifle grenade, and it was in the right arm of the trench. I hurried back to find Jim Alexander just getting my new man out. He had climbed over into the firing bay; the German had seen him and fired over a grenade. He was dead. He had lasted somewhere between five and ten minutes, all because he did not listen to what he had been told.

I wondered how I was going to deploy my men for the night. Jim and his man would be on the point at the end of the trench. Two men would be in the left arm of the trench. Two more men would have to be back in the trench on the south canal. The seventh man would be with me in the right arm of the trench. The signals man would have to stay in the air raid shelter to man the telephone. I would get no sleep that night. In fact, no one did. The Germans were masters in the art of harassment, and they weren't long in starting. A blast of machine gun fire over our heads, then a rifle shot—*bang, bang, bang*—all up and down the canal. Silence for a few minutes, then *bang*. This went on for a while, just keeping us on edge, then maybe there'd be nothing for fifteen or twenty minutes. Then it would start all over again.

By nine o'clock, they were firing just like a full-scale attack, one machine gun firing straight down the trench just over our heads—sheets of flame. The trench was lit up until I could have read a letter from home. The bullets were going straight back, hitting the brick houses and then coming right back at us. The signals man came out and said I was wanted on the phone, so I had to leave my post and go to the phone. It was MacPherson. He said, "How're you making out? Just try and hang on. I'm going to send up some help." Then I had to go back. I could hear grenades going off, so I went to check on Jim. It would take more than grenades to get him. He said the Germans were swimming the canal, then shooting and dropping grenades. He said they'd wait until the Germans got right over top of them, then they would throw grenades at them and drive the Germans back across the canal. I checked the other men and they were doing the same, but they were soon going to run out of grenades.

I decided I had better check the right arm of the trench. There might be Germans in it, but I had to go. While there, I fired a few shots just to let them know there was someone there, and then went back to the phone to have grenades sent up. There were piles of grenades in the air raid shelter and I took all I could carry up to the front, and then went back for more. Soon, all of the grenades that were primed were gone. Men were sent from Company Headquarters with more, but they were not cleaned or primed, so I set the seventh man to cleaning them. They came packed in grease, but not everyone knew how to prime them, so I had to do that myself. I would prime all I could carry, then take them up to the front.

About eleven o'clock, I went to check on the men in the left arm. They had stopped firing and we were worried. I crept down their trench, but I couldn't see them. Then I found them. At first, I thought they were dead, but on examination, I found that they were just lying on the bottom of the trench with their arms around each other, so scared they could do nothing. They were petrified. And so was I. I put the boots to them and kicked them until they were on their feet. I called them everything I could lay my tongue to. They were good men, but this was just too much for them. I kept at them until they were more scared of me than they were of the Germans. Then I split them up. I sent one of them up with Jim and had Jim's man come back there.

The Germans kept up a continuous attack all night long. It was, without a doubt, the most terrible night of my war so far. It would soon be morning and we had managed to keep them out of our trenches all night long. I was on my way back to the air raid shelter. I got right to the door, when all of a sudden, everything let loose on the south canal. First, a blast from a Bren gun, then from machine guns, rifles, grenades and flares. The Germans always fired a lot of flares—just a *pop*, and then everything lit up. Men were hollering at each other in both German and English. We had no idea what it was all about.

One of my men, Corporal Arnold, came up to me. We stood at the door of the shelter looking at the gap in the hedge where the Germans had to come through. Suddenly, I could hear men running and saw movement at the gap. Arnold said, "We don't have a chance. What'll we do?" I said, "Get back in the air raid shelter." I knelt down on one knee so as not to be so big a target, and waited for them to come. I had a Sten gun and the range was less then 10 feet. Nothing was going to get past me. I waited, all ready to shoot. Then I realized, too late, that they were not coming through the gap in the hedge. They were going down the trench at the back of us, and they were getting away. They could go down that trench to an island where the two canals came together, then swim the canal back to their own side.

It was daylight by now and some men came in from No. 7 Plt. I did not know it, but they were in a position right behind us on the south canal. They had all been in a house asleep, with a guard posted outside. One of the men had had to go outside to relieve himself. He took the guard's Bren gun and told him to go in and get some sleep while he went around the house to relieve himself. He had just gotten started when he looked back down the canal and saw a whole line of Germans coming up the south canal. They were going to go right past the house, so he opened fire on them. They did not know anyone was there, and they were so surprised they ran straight past the gap in the hedge and down the trench for home.

Someone had called Major MacPherson and he was up there in just a few minutes. He climbed through the gap. I was still standing there. He said, "Are you all right?" I was in such shock, I couldn't talk to him. He took some men from No. 7 Plt. and went down the trench. There were several Germans sitting down there waiting for the chance to surrender. I don't think that MacPherson was aware until that time that there were only seven men in my platoon. The Germans had crossed the Leopold Canal to the right of us, then crossed to the south canal and come in behind us. According to some of the prisoners we had taken, there were about one hundred of them. Just five more minutes, and they would have had us. We held that position for two more nights, and at nighttime, MacPherson sent in some men from No. 7 Plt. to help man our positions.

That day there was nothing much doing, but I was so hyped up I could not sleep. I took a rifle and looked through some of the houses. There was one house right beside the air raid shelter, and we discovered someone had knocked a hole from the basement right into the air raid shelter. I decided to check it out upstairs. At the top of the stairs was a hall that opened into two rooms, and I could see there was a window to the north. This would give a view right into the German lines. I got down on the floor and crawled to the left side of the window. In this way, I could see the German positions to the right. All was quiet over there. I crawled over to the right side, and that way I could look to the left. There, right in front of Jim's position, stood a German in a slit trench. I could just see his face. I manoeuvred around and got the muzzle of the rifle on the window ledge. I could not put my head up too high. I had tried this before and very nearly died and I was not going to do it again. Finally, I got a bead on him and fired. As soon as I fired, though, I knew I had missed him. I had pulled it to the right when I squeezed the trigger. The bullet must have just grazed his face as it went past him. He sure disappeared in a hurry.

One of the corporals in No. 7 Plt. had been trained to set booby traps, and he decided to booby-trap the back door of the air raid shelter, which came in off the street down a set of stairs. He fixed it all up with flares and thunderflashes, which would be set off by trip wires. When he was done, he came in and warned us not to use the back door. We had a black man with us by the name of Leek, but we called him Kiska. He was really just a big boy, only nineteen years old. When it was dark, we could not see him unless he smiled, and then all we could see were white teeth. He liked to get out at night and wander around in the dark. He was not due to go on a watch for a while, so that night he went out for a prowl. When his time came to go on watch, he came back, but he came in the back door and set off the booby traps. When all of those things started to go off, he just jumped from one foot to the other. We could see him on the steps. There were flares and everything going off all around him. Then he made a dash down the rest of the stairs and into the shelter. His eyes were as big as plates, and I swear he was just as white as the rest of us. It sure was a good fireworks display! And that was the only excitement that night; all was quiet.

The next day Major MacPherson came back up and brought with him a new platoon officer who was to take charge of No. 8 Plt. This was fine with me. I showed him all around our positions and gave him a rundown as to what we were doing. Then I took him upstairs to have a look over the German positions. When we got to the top of the stairs, he was ahead of me and walked right out into the room in front of the window. A bullet burst through the window. It sounded just like a mortar shell. We both dived for the stairs and slid on our bellies down two flights of steps, through the hole in the wall and right into the air raid shelter. Later in the day, he went back to Company Headquarters and I never saw him again.

On September 24, "B" and "D" Companies took over our positions, and we went back to the town of Maldegem to rest and enjoy ourselves for three days. What a rest that was, though it started very well. First, we had a shower and then we moved into a German barracks, where we were told that we were to go to a Canadian army show that night. After supper, we got into our TCVs and away we went. It was in a big auditorium and there must have been about five hundred men there. It was a good show, but my nerves were in very bad shape. I sat in there as long as I could, but, eventually, I had to leave. I went out the door and sat on the steps and lit my pipe. It was a very nice evening and I could hear planes going over. Off in the distance, there was the rumble of guns and the sky would light up like lightning. Farther away, I could hear the "whoomph" of bombs going off, and, back up on the Leopold, every so often there would be a machine gun firing. They were German guns that we called "burp" guns, because when they fired, they just went "burrrrrr, burrrrrr."

The steps were in an alcove, and back behind me was an entryway into the building. After I had been there a while, I became aware that I was not alone. Someone was watching me. I slowly turned around and put my back to the side wall so I could see into the entryway. It was dark, but I knew someone was there. I just smoked my pipe and waited. Finally, a girl stepped out of the shadows and sat down beside me. She put her hand on my arm and said, "What's wrong?" She could see that I was all nerved up. I said, "Just nerves, I guess." She was with the show and her job was packing the costumes. We had a good visit, but I have forgotten her name. I would like to meet her again; she helped me a lot that night. I was almost a nervous wreck. When the show was over, up came the TCVs. Just as No. 8 Plt. was coming out the door, our TCV drove up and I took the platoon out to it. The girl walked with me to the back of the truck, said goodbye and good luck, and gave me a big kiss. All the boys hollered. When we got back to the barracks, the company runner was waiting for me. I was to report to Battalion Headquarters as fast as I could get there. So much for my three-day rest.

Plans had been made for a raid across the Leopold Canal. This was to be a large-scale raid. "C" Coy. with three platoons would make the raid. "A" Coy. was to provide covering fire from the direction of Saint-Laurent. "C" Coy. would cross the canal 700 yards east and advance into the town of Moershoofd and take prisoners. I did not know if "A" Coy. was still at the show or not. My job was to take a section of men from the carrier platoon and form a firm base on the south side of the canal. If "C" Coy. got in trouble, it was up to us to engage the enemy and let "C" Coy. escape. Supporting fire was to be supplied by all the field artillery in the 4th Canadian Division, plus our own mortar platoon and a troop of tanks from the British Columbia Regiment. Two Bofors guns from the 8th Light Anti-Aircraft Regiment would fire tracer ammunition for direction. I was taken directly to Saint-Laurent and, as usual, told nothing about what was going on. The section from No. 4 Plt. (Carrier Plt.) was already there, and a guide led us to our position.

At 5:15 A.M., "C" Coy. crossed the canal. Our artillery were already firing. "C" Coy. had three targets to fire at. One was directly to our left on a crossroad on the north side of the Leopold. The second was into the town of Moershoofd, and the third was directly across the canal from our position, about 50 yards in front of us. The artillery was to fire on one, then move on to the next, taking turns. I don't know how many guns were firing or how many shells they fired on each target, but there were a lot of them. Of all the guns that were firing, one gun was firing 50 yards short and right on our position. We could hear the shell coming—it just howled as it came in. They didn't just fire one salvo; they fired five or six at a time. They lit right in amongst us. There were about seven or eight of us there, and the men all said, "Let's get outta here!" But that was the spot we were to be in and I would not let them go. I spread them out and told them to keep their heads down. Every time those shells came in, they threw dirt all over us. We were soon in a dirty mess of dust and smoke. We stayed right there and they just pounded us. We could hear that short shell every time. The ones going over us were all right, but those that lit on us sure made a different sound. Some of the men screamed and swore at me because I would not let them move, but that was our spot. An officer came up to where we were and said he had been sent up to take charge. He tried to tell us it was German fire, but we knew better. It was an awful spot to be in. We were all shaking from nerves, and mine, already in bad shape, were getting worse. I wanted to get out of there, but could not. It was terrible.

At 6:15 A.M., Captain Dandy, "C" Coy. commander, sent back word: "Gathering in the harvest." We had surprised some Germans cooking bacon for their breakfast, so our men ate the Germans' breakfast. We heard "C" Coy. coming out in front of us. They had taken fifteen prisoners. By 8:00 A.M. "C" Coy. were back on our side of the canal and we were still being fired on. A runner came and told us to come fast. The Germans had started to shell the town. The officer led off on the run. I counted the men and looked around to make sure there were none left dead or wounded. Luckily, we had not lost a man, and that was a miracle. Why we were not all killed is more than I can say. I ran for town, and as I got there the TCV was moving, so I jumped and the men pulled me over the back. We were the last to leave and I was never so glad to get out of a place alive as I was then. I always was of the opinion that something or someone was looking after me. I can say that this was another time when I was saved by something more than good luck.

We got back to Maldegem and I went up to my room in the German barracks. It was over. I sat down on my bed and started to shake. My nerves were completely shattered. It was a warm day, but I got *so cold.* I shook, and the bed shook. I was a bit delirious and could not control myself. When we had come out of Strooibrug, some of our men had been given forty-eight-hour passes to go to Brussels, and they had just come back. One of them was Kiska, and he had brought back a bottle of liquor. He dug it out, and said, "Here, Sarge, you need this more than I do." I opened the bottle and started to gulp it down. In less than five minutes, I had drunk more than two-thirds of it. I thought I was still sober, but it had gotten the better of me. Why someone did not stop me, I don't know. I picked up a Bren gun, and, with the gun and the bottle, I went outside, but I still knew what I was doing. There was a TCV just leaving, loaded with men, and I tried to climb in the back. The men took my bottle and gun, and as we went out the gateway, they pushed me off the back. I remember that, but nothing more; I was out cold. That was somewhere near nine in the morning.

I was sick. My head was swimming; first, I could see, and then it was dark. If I could have thought, I would have thought I was dying. My head was in a pail; I was retching as if I would never stop. A man was holding me, then my head started to swim again, and I was gone. I came to several times, and each time, I was sicker than the time before. Finally, I came out of it enough to be able to see what was going on. I was sitting in a wicker chair in something that could be called a summer house or a closed-in patio. On my right, I could see there was a house. In front of me was a man sitting in a chair reading a paper. Every once in a while, he would lower his paper and look at me. A woman brought me some hot coffee. I drank it and it sure helped. Now, there was something to bring up, and up it came. The man grabbed the pail and held it for me. Then I passed out again. The next time I came to, I was much better, or at least I thought I was. That time, I kept the coffee down. I started to feel much better. The man said he had found me in the ditch in front of his house. He gave me a real talking-to. He told me I was lucky that it was him who had found me. There were a lot of German collaborators in Maldegem and they would have killed me if they had found me. By this time, I was quite rational, or so I thought. I thanked the man and said I would go on. He took me out to the road and headed me in the right direction. He asked me if I was all right, and I assured him that I was. I headed back to town, but didn't get very far. Up the road came a jeep going in the opposite direction. For some unknown reason, I put my thumb up for a ride, and it stopped. In it were an artillery major and a driver. I climbed in the back. They started to ask me a few questions, but what we did or what I told them, I have no recollection. I do not and never did remember the ride.

I came to several times, but all I knew was that I was still alive. Finally, I realized I was in a house, on a loveseat, being sick all over again. How long this went on, I don't know, but I eventually came out of it. There was a girl about sixteen years old taking care of me, holding the pail for me to be sick in, and then washing my face. I kept getting a little better all the time. I asked her where I was. She did not speak English and I did not speak Belgian, but I could speak and understand Flemish. She told me that I was in the town of Eekloo, and that she and her two sisters had found me on the street the day before. We had liberated Eekloo on September 15, and this girl said she had talked to me at that time, so when they had found me on the street, they recognized me. I was very sick, so they took me home with them. They had taken turns sitting up with me all night. When I came to this time, I knew I would now be all right. The girl took me out and put me on the road back to Maldegem. A truck came along, I put up my thumb, he stopped and I climbed in. He said, "Lincoln and Welland. I know where you guys are. I'm going right past there." In a short while, he stopped at the German barracks and I went in, but there was no one there; the company had gone.

I went around behind to where the kitchen had been. There was Dick, the cook, just packing up. He told me that the company had left early that morning and were now back up on the Leopold. He said I could ride up with him. While we were talking, a jeep came in. It was MacPherson. He said, "Oh, you got back, did you? I thought I could find you if I came back, so I did. I understand you were in pretty bad shape when you came back from the raid. You come with me." He took me up on the top floor of the barracks. Up there was a small room with a bed in it. He said, "You stay here and go to sleep. I'll come back for you." I lay down on the bed and went to sleep. He locked the door and left. That night, he came back, picked me up and took me up to the canal, but he kept me with him that night. The next morning, I went back to my platoon. I did not know what day it was, and I never, ever knew how long I had been gone. I now had control of my nerves again, but that had been a pretty rough time. The war was starting to tell on me.

Many of the men prayed when they thought their time had come or when there was heavy shelling. I was never a praying man; I thought I could look after myself. When the shelling got rough and they were coming down real heavy, I would start to count, "one-two-three-four, one-two-three-four, one-two-three-four," and keep it up until the shelling stopped. But now it was different: I was getting tired; my nerves were nearly shot from stress and too much war. Most men who prayed just prayed to stay alive. If it could be called praying, when we were preparing to go into battle, I prayed to be killed and get it over with. I would say, "God, make it today." I was not afraid of dying. I died nearly every day. It was the uncertainty of not knowing when or how, and preparing for death every day, that was more than most people could stand.

I did not ask new men their names or make friends. I could not send friends out to almost certain death. And many times I had to send men out, knowing there was not much chance of them ever coming back. For an infantryman, there were only two ways to get out: killed or wounded. All we could do was wait for it to happen, but we knew, one way or the other, it was surely coming.

After a battle, I did not look back to see what happened to Smith or Jones. I did not want to know. When a man disappeared, I promptly put him out of my mind and forgot about him. There never was a Smith or a Jones; they had never existed. Today I can look back, and the names and faces of those men are gone. I made myself forget for my own protection. If I had thought about those men and how they died, I would have gone crazy.

There was only one thing to look forward to—my time would come to die or be severely wounded—and each day brought it closer. It had now been more than two months of "kill or be killed," twenty-four hours a day. I needed a rest.

We were on a spot of the canal I did not know and have never found out. The platoon was in a farmhouse about 150 yards from the Leopold. Company Headquarters was back to our left. At the front left was a company of Dutch soldiers, and between them and us was a road to the canal. Our position was to the right of the road. Directly to the front was a haystack, nearly at the canal, maybe 130 yards in front of us. No. 7 Plt. was on our far right about 500 yards away from us. In front of No. 7 Plt. on the north side of the canal were more farm buildings occupied by the Germans. Sometime that day, a new platoon officer was sent to take charge of No. 8 Plt. What his name was, I do not know. When I went up to the front, the corporal in charge explained what we were to do. We were to put out listening posts every night just to watch for Germans coming across. Our listening post was about halfway between the house and the haystack. There was a hedge running parallel with the canal. The men were detailed for that night, so I stayed in the house. As soon as it got dark, the shooting started—machine guns and rifle fire—and it kept up all night. It was the Dutchmen, and they were shooting right at us. That night, they fired thousands of rounds at us. The new platoon officer had gone back to Company Headquarters for the night. There was not much sleep that night.

There was a chicken pen in a room behind the house that was home to some nice fat roosters. The next day, I went out with my pistol to shoot a few. It's not easy to shoot a chicken with a pistol. I think they can see a bullet coming because they would always duck at just the right time. They were all in there sitting on a roost and I finally got seven of them. We put them in a big pan and boiled them for supper. What a feast we had. That night, I took my turn to go on the watch with another man. I don't know who he was. We had to wait until it got dark to go down the road and get settled in. Soon the shooting started, but this time it was different. It was a German. He was out on the road only about 20 yards from us, and had seen us go into the hedge; he knew right where we were. We could not see him, but if he raised his head to get a shot at us, we would get him. He held up his gun and fired that way, but he could not get the gun up far enough to fire down on us. His bullets were going through the hedge right above our heads. The two of us lay there just waiting for him to stick up his head, but he was too smart for that. The hedge was too thick to get through or I would have gone back on the other side of the hedge and got him. He kept it up for several hours before he finally left. As he had us cornered, there was not much we could do except keep our heads down. Sometime in the night, a man crawled up on the other side of the hedge. We heard him coming and got ready. But when he got close, he said, "Hee, hee, hee, how ya doin'?" It was Corporal Corcoran from No. 7 Plt. He said he was just out looking around. He stayed with us for a few minutes, then away he went back to his own platoon.

The next day was rather uneventful. About three o'clock, the new officer came up to see how we were getting along. Up at the top of the stairs in the house, I had put two chairs with a board on them so I could stand on them and look out a vent in the roof right straight to the Germans' house across from No. 7 Plt. The Germans would bring out chairs and sit on the front porch. They would line up their chairs and tip them back against the side of the house and go to sleep in the sun. There was a red tile roof on the house, and the vent was half a tile with a hole about three inches by one and a half inches cut in the sheeting. The Germans were about 500 yards away. The officer stood at the bottom of the stairs while I climbed up to have a look out. Suddenly, there was a big crash. It knocked me backwards off the board onto the floor. My eyes and my hair were full of tile, and there was a bullet hole just an inch above where my head had been. A German sniper must have had a scope on that hole just as I looked through and probably saw a change of colour. I never looked through that hole again.

Sergeant Hill of No. 7 Plt. decided there were Germans in a nearby haystack. That night, he went down to set some booby traps. He ran a wire all the way around the stack, then loaded it up with flares and flashes. He worked on it for a couple of hours. I did not know much about those things, but, evidently, when they were all set up, he had to take pins out of them to arm them. He got everything ready, then pulled out all the pins. He went all the way around the stack. When he got back to where he had started, someone had put a nail in the first one. What a shock! The German had been watching him and he knew all about these things. Hill jumped up and started to run. He ran right into his trip wire and set everything off. I bet the German had a laugh. Hill was all tangled up in the wire and could not get out. The next day, we burned the haystack and the Germans did not bother us again.

One of those days while we were still at this position, a man from No. 7 Plt. came into our position with some messages. After delivering the messages, he started back to his own platoon. He had only been gone a short while when we heard some shots from that direction. I ran out to see what it was all about, and the man was coming back holding his arm. He had been shot through the wrist. He said a German had jumped out of the hedge and shot him, so I ran down to the hedge after the gunman, but there was no one there. The man had shot himself in the wrist, but it could not be proven. He's drawn a good pension ever since and is still living.

Our history book says that on September 27, "A" Coy. took over the town of Moerhuizen from the Lake Superior Regiment. Our position was now about one kilometre north of the town of Moerhuizen, once again on the Leopold Canal. Our Company Headquarters was on the main road out of Moerhuizen, just north of the Canal de Dérivation and just south of the Leopold. "A" Coy.'s position was on the Leopold just to the right of a road. On the left of the road was the small town of Strooibrug. We were in a cement bunker built into the dyke of the Leopold. To get to this position, we again had to go up behind the dyke of the Canal de Dérivation, but instead of crossing the road into Strooibrug, we turned right, went over that dyke and down onto low ground that we followed to the Leopold. Our work here was to put out sentries at night. We had listening posts set up about every 100 yards, and, again, the Germans were in positions about 15 yards from us, close enough that we could hear them talking, and they, no doubt, could hear us.

Most of our days were uneventful, but some days were memorable. Like the day the engineers came up to see about putting a bridge over the Canal de Dérivation, and one of their men, not knowing any better, walked up and stood looking out over the Leopold. There was a German just across the Leopold and he shot the engineer low down in the stomach. He fell to the ground in the centre of the road, and when our men tried to get him, the Germans wouldn't let them. He lay out in the road for about six hours. After dark, a man crawled out and dragged him back. The next morning, I said to Jim Alexander, "You better take care of that." Jim put his Bren gun over his shoulder and away he went. If there was anything the Germans liked to do, it was to lie out in the sun. We had watched this German before, as he would take off most of his clothes every morning and have a sleep. We could have shot him, but we didn't. But now he had shot one of ours, and he would pay with his life. When the sun was right, he took off his clothes and stretched out in it. Jim put his gun over the dyke and let go a good burst, then back he came with his gun on his shoulder. We watched as other Germans came with a stretcher and took the dead one away. They did not put a man back out there.

We heard rumours that the 3rd Division was to attack across the Leopold. One afternoon, in came a smart young corporal from one of their regiments. At least, he thought he was smart. He thought his regiment was the best in the army, and by his look, he thought ours was the worst. It hurt him to ask if he could scout out our position. I said, "Sure, go ahead," and told him I would send Jim with him. He let me know he did not need a guide, and especially one from our regiment. He was all dressed up in a German camouflage coat and a shiny pair of German jackboots. Away he went down the dyke and across the road into Strooibrug. We had men in there and they were watching him. With his German jacket, they thought he was a German. They watched as he worked his way down through the town. He went around a house right in front of them and crawled through a window. Then they saw his boots. As he kicked his way through the window, they opened fire—machine guns and rifle. I heard the shooting and I knew what it was all about. He had gotten into the house and all he could do was holler, which was what he did. Our men called for him to come out with his hands up and he did. They escorted him out of town and told him not to come back dressed like that.

On October 5, the Canadian Scots Regiment came up the road from Moerhuizen and attacked across the Leopold into what was known as the Breskens Pocket, an area between the Leopold and the sea. The area was strongly defended by Germans who were trapped in there. When the Scots got over there, Germans were on both flanks and in front. The Scots secured a small bridgehead and were lucky to hold it, for they could not advance.

Then the Germans pulled a very smart trick. They were trying to escape out of the pocket. At nighttime, we would hear them moving up the road on the north side of the canal. We would hear wagons moving, men hollering at their horses, cars and motorcycles. As soon as it was dark, they would start and keep it up all night long. Our artillery would fire at them—one hundred rounds of shells—yet the noise never stopped. This went on night after night. The Germans had made a recording, and they were playing it 100 yards in front of us. We told the artillery what it was, but they kept firing at it anyway. And all this time, the Germans were escaping across the water to the Scheldt estuary. The Germans left on the Leopold were putting up a fight long enough for their own men to escape, and most of them did.

The Canadian Scots were in big trouble on the north side of the Leopold right in front of us. This was Nick's regiment—my old pal

Bill Nicholson from Ingersoll, Ontario—and I was wondering how he was making out. Some of the boys had figured out an infantry-man's life expectancy was two and a half days. Nick had gone in on D-Day, so he was well over his allotted time. He had been in now for about four months and I worried his time was running out. They were trying to come down the north side of the canal and had to fight from one slit trench to the next. There was not much we could do to help because the Germans were in behind the dyke where we couldn't get at them.

One night, they decided they would bring our flame-throwers up and burn the Germans out. After dark, up they came right to our po-sition. We called in our sentries and we all went into our bunker. The flame-throwers were mounted on Bren gun carriers and had a 40-gallon drum of oil on them. They could fire about 60 yards. They stopped about 40 yards from our bunker and then opened fire on *us*. To get into the bunker, there was a tunnel in a U-shape. We went in one side and around the bottom or end, and back up the other side out into a big room. This was so no one could shoot into the bunker. We heard a big noise, and then fire rolled up into the tunnel. They kept firing and the fire came in around the U-turn and rolled into the room where we were. Some of the men screamed and cried. We won-dered how long the oxygen would last. They finally ran out of oil and stopped, but we had to wait until it all burned out before we could get out. It got very quiet in there while we were waiting. There was no other escape. By the time we got out, the carriers were gone, and it was a good thing, too. Some of them might have gotten shot, we were that mad.

The next night, it was decided to send a tank in there. Maybe it could help. So after dark, in came a Sherman tank. Again, we took in all of our men. The tank stopped in the same place the flame-throwers had been. Then it drove right up and sat on the top of the dyke. It was armed with a 6-pound gun and two .30-calibre machine guns. It sat there and fired all night long. In the morning just at day-light, the Germans put a bazooka over the dyke and fired a shell into the bottom of the tank. The crew was killed and the tank burst into flames. One man got halfway out of the turret and died. We came out, but there was nothing we could do but stand and watch him burn. First, his arms burned off; then he burned into the middle. The front part of his body rolled off the tank and onto the ground. It was just one big ball of roasted meat. We just left it there; we did not touch it. Someone would have to get into the tank and get anything that was left of the men for burial. The shells in the tank exploded, rocking the tank and making it look as if it was jumping around. But after a while, all was quiet and the only sound to be heard was the buzzing of the flies all around it.

14

THE DAY THAT CORKY DIED

N<small>O. 7 PLT. HAD</small> a corporal by the name of Corcoran. Everyone called him Corky. Corky was not too tall, and he had light-coloured, sandy hair and was covered all over with freckles. When he stood up straight, his hands hung down to his knees. He was homely and looked like an ape. He used to act like an ape, too. He would hunch over and grunt and squeal and walk just like an ape. And as bowlegged as he was, this was not hard to do. He was born and raised in the slums of New York. He had never gone to school a day in his life, but there wasn't a question on any subject he could not answer. He was, without a doubt, one of the smartest men I've ever known. Sometimes, when we were out on manoeuvre, at night in a bivouac after we were all in bed, Corky would give us Abe Lincoln's Gettysburg Address while mimicking the voice of our company commander to perfection. Then he would say, "Ask me a question. On anything." He knew the date of every battle that ever was fought. Ask him the capital of any country or state, and he could tell you. Sometimes he would say, "You'll have to give me a few days on this. I'll get back to you." In a few days or a week or so, he would say, "Remember that question?" and then he'd give you the answer. It would always be right. I never did have any idea how old he was, but he had fought in the Spanish Civil War. He was steady and very reliable. And more than once, when we were in a bad spot, he'd say, "Hee, hee, hee. Don't look good, does it?" Everyone loved him. He was one of the originals who had come into France with us, and there were not many left.

On the morning of October 9, word was sent up to us that the artillery was going to lay down a "stonck" right on our position. A stonck is an artillery term for a heavy concentration of shellfire on one position. As the Germans were only 10 or 15 yards in front of us, the artillery would shell the whole position. It would start about half past twelve that day. "A" Coy. would pull out at noon and go back to Company Headquarters, have dinner, and by dessert, it would all be over. Then, we would return to our bunker and take up our position again. At quarter to twelve, we lined up and headed for headquarters. I was the last to leave. I stayed behind to check on everything and make sure there was no one left there. The men had a habit of going to sleep in the sun on the dyke. By the time I left the position, everyone was out of sight over the Canal de Dérivation. I was in no hurry, so I took my time. The Germans were watching and knew something was up.

On the Canal de Dérivation was a bridge. For several days now, the Germans had been trying to knock it out. There were three big coastal guns up there: one was on the island of Walcheren; the second, I believe, was at Willamhaven just north of Bergen-op-Zoom; and the third, I don't know where it was. They fired them all at the same time, but they had never hit the bridge. However, our men had small boats they used to take supplies up to Strooibrug, and the Germans had managed to sink several of them that were tied beside the bridge. I had just reached this same bridge.

Company Headquarters was just across the road in a farmhouse. There was a small farmyard paved with brick and a barn about 15 feet from the house. The company kitchen was set up in the small area between the barn and the house. About forty "A" Coy. men were now in there getting their dinner.

I was just about to cross the road when I heard those guns fire— *Boom, boom, boom*—one right after the other. Then I heard the shells coming—*whoooooooeeeee*. They were big shells and made an awful howling noise. I was following the sound intently to see where they were going. I had been under so much shelling by this time, I could tell within a few feet where a shell would land. The first was going to go over, but it would be close. Then, with an awful howl, it went over and came down about 20 yards from the bridge, and about 50 yards from me. The second shell was coming in. It would go over also, and so it did, hitting about 100 yards past the bridge. I was lying in the ditch, thinking I had better run across the road, but instead thought better of it. This last shell was coming right in on us. It came over the house and right into the end of the barn, about 20 feet over the heads of all the "A" Coy. men, causing a huge explosion. I ran as fast as I could go. I knew I was going to be needed.

As I ran around the corner of the house, the whole yard was full of brick dust and black smoke. What a mess! The first thing I saw was Corky. The lower half of his body was gone. His guts were blown right out, and there was just an empty spot where they should have been. I could see right into his chest cavity, all red and white. His eyes were open—a very shocked look in them. He looked directly at me; and I know that he knew me. And then, as quick as that, the life went out of his eyes.

The door was blown off the house and I could see right inside. The company commander was flopping around on the floor like a chicken with its head cut off. One leg was flopping around at the side, still fastened to him by a piece of flesh. And he screamed and screamed and screamed. I can hear him and see him yet—with that leg flopping all over. A dead man lay in the open door of the house. There were arms, legs, pieces of human bodies all over the yard. The cooking utensils were splattered with blood. I could not do any-thing—I just stood there, looking.

The men who had escaped started to come back. Some came out of the barn, their faces black and their hair burned off. They didn't stand around; they just left. There was a threshing machine in the barn. One man had been blown so far into the back of it that he was trapped in it and could not get out. We had to pull him out by his feet. Men just wandered around in shock. The medical officer was there in just a few minutes and started to clean things up.

I went right into shock. I became very disoriented and could not concentrate on what I was doing. I, who had always known what to do and how to do it, could do nothing. I was helpless. I found myself walking down the road and over the bridge—no idea where I was going, or what I'd do if I got there. As I wandered up the road maybe about 300 yards or so, I noticed a small house to the side of the road. I was drawn into this house—why, I do not know—but I went in and walked down into the basement. There were several other men already there, sitting on the floor with their backs to the wall, knees drawn up in front of them, their heads on their knees, all crying. On the far wall were Red Irwin and Bert Thair, Corky's best friends, sitting side by side, crying. I sat and put my head down and cried. More men trickled in and sat down, until there were about a dozen of us. We all just sat and cried—not "boohooing," just sobbing and shaking. Tears were coming and we could not stop them. We cried until we could cry no more, and then we cried again.

I had gone into that house about half past one. Somewhere around five o'clock, I realized we had to get back up on the canal. It was my job to get the men back there. It was one of the hardest things I ever did in my life. I said, "All right, time's up. Everyone back to the canal. It's time to go." I had to speak several times, "All right, let's go." Finally, the men started to trickle out just as they had come in, maybe one at a time, or maybe a couple. As they got themselves in hand, they left. Soon there were only three of us left: Red, Bert and myself. I was weak and cried right out. I got up and left, but Red and Bert remained. They were good men and I knew they would come when they could.

It was dark when I got back up on the Leopold. I went in and went right to bed. The next morning, it was all put out of my mind. An infantryman could not dwell today on what happened yesterday. The men who were killed had never existed. In all these years, the memory of only a few of these men has ever come back. It was things like this that could drive a man crazy. And it always gives me a funny feeling when anyone talks about the Leopold Canal.

As for the artillery stonck they were going to fire—they fired two shells.

15

GOODBYE TO MORE THAN THE LEOPOLD

O N THE MORNING of October 16, when daylight came, we knew something had changed. All was quiet. In the night, the Germans had finished their escape from the Breskens Pocket and the battle was finally won.

That day I walked back to Company Headquarters. When I came out on the road, there was a man coming my way from the Leopold. He looked familiar, so I waited. When he got close enough, I could see he was crying. The tears were just rolling down his face in streams. It was my old friend Jim Bell. I said, "What's wrong, Jim?" He answered, "Nick got it." Our very good friend, Bill Nicholson, was one of the first across the Leopold. They had not been able to get the bodies out since the battle started on October 9. Jim just happened to be there this particular morning as one stretcher came out. The body was covered with a blanket, but some hair was sticking out. Jim saw it and recognized it as Nick's. He turned down the blanket to look. Nick had taken a burst of machine gun fire right in the stomach. He never even got to see his baby son. The prophecy of the coin toss did, indeed, come true. Each of us was to have saved the penny from home he had given us, and we were to have put them together when we all got back home after the war. Just as he had instructed me, I still have that very same Canadian penny my good friend gave to me so long ago.

In this battle of the Breskens, the Germans were in bad shape, too. For several days, they could not get their wounded out. They solved this by putting a small boat in the Leopold at the road to our left. Then they put a Red Cross flag up and came up the canal. As they went past our position, we came out and sat on the dyke to watch them. On the far side of the canal, the Germans did the same, and we sat and looked at each other. As the boat came back down, we all got back down out of sight. Most of the time all through the war, the Red Cross was respected.

On October 18, we moved off the canal and concentrated in another position. I do not know where it was. We moved into some houses late in the afternoon. That night we bedded down on the floor of a house. In the night, a British battery of "Long Toms" (big guns) moved in about 75 yards behind us. Just at dawn, they decided to fire their guns. I believe there were four of them. They all fired at the same time right over our heads. They blew all the windows out of the house and the shattered glass fell all over us. What a noise! We jumped and ran. They nearly blew in the side of the house. This ended another phase of the war. We would now take on a new phase—that of opening the way to the River Maas and clearing the Scheldt estuary. The powers that be were under the impression that they had a lot of Germans trapped in there and that they could not escape. They hadn't yet realized that the Germans had escaped from Breskens. But this was a piece of land the Germans wanted to keep. At one time, it was wide open and we could have gone right into Holland, but when we reached the city of Antwerp, there didn't seem to be any plan to go farther. While we sat and waited for orders, the Germans sent fresh troops back in there. They had retaken the land as far south as the main road into Antwerp. There were now at least sixty thousand German soldiers in there. The war was not over yet.

16

OBLIVION

O N OCTOBER 19 we moved into the town of Camp de Brass-chaet late in the afternoon. It was a very nice day. The chest-nuts had started to come down, and the first thing I did was go out and fill my pockets with them. We had our supper and went to bed early upstairs in a haymow. The roof had been blown off the barn and we could see right out and count the stars.

In the morning we got up, had breakfast and got ready for an at-tack. The Germans were holed up in a woods and in an old Belgian army camp they had used as an espionage training centre. About nine o'clock we headed out. "A" Coy. would attack on the far left of the camp. "B," "C" and "D" Companies would be on our right. The British Columbia tanks would be in an area to our left. We headed west out of town along a railroad track. As usual, we were not told anything. "A" Coy. was being led by a new company commander, Maj. Herbert Owen Lambert, a California native in a Canadian unit. My platoon, No. 8, was reserve platoon. I still had only seven men left in my platoon. We were in single file and I was the last man, with my platoon out ahead of me.

"A" Coy. was to go west to a certain point, then make a right turn, which would put them in an extended line. They would then attack in a northerly direction across the old rifle range and into the woods, then straight through the woods to the main road, which went from Antwerp to Breda.

All went well. The rest of the company, No. 7 and No. 9 Plts., went to the point, then made a right turn and started across the open field in front. I held my platoon back until the main force was well out in front. Then we made a right turn, and with me in the centre, followed the main force.

We had just started after them when they stopped. Something was wrong. We sat down to wait and see. We sat there for about fifteen minutes, until finally the main force made another right turn into single file and started back east. They had gone west about 200 yards too far and were way to the left of the rifle range. I turned my men to the right and started to go back east. The main force got about halfway back to where they should be when the Germans opened fire—rifle, machine gun, mortars, and even a Bofors anti-aircraft gun.

No. 7 and No. 9 Plts. made a run for it. Ahead of them was a hole in the ground about eight feet square, with a pile of dirt about eight feet high in front of it. The men all made a run for this hole. When the first man got into it, they could see a trench ahead of them and they went right straight through and into the trench. No. 8 Plt. had twice as far to go as they did. When we came under fire, we had to hit the dirt. Did the Germans ever go at us! I always kept my men well spread out and we started to move in short leaps and bounds. In this manner, we made our way across the field.

Most of us had gotten into the hole. The Germans were throwing everything they had at us. The machine gun fire was like a swarm of bees. I had just jumped in the hole when one of the men let out a yell, "I'm hit!" It was Slater. I could hear him flopping around on the ground, hollering, "Help me! I'm hit!" He was about 15 feet from the hole. I had to get him in there. The machine gun had stopped firing, so I jumped out and made a dash for him. I took about three steps and then rolled. As soon as I jumped out, the guns opened up at me. I dove down beside him as the bullets strafed about a foot over me. I said, "Where are you hurt?" and he said, "In the leg." Slater weighed about 200 pounds. The last time I had tried to carry him home, when he was drunk, I had gotten mad and left him. But this time I could not leave him; he would be killed if I did. There was no way I could carry him through that machine gun fire. It looks all very well in a movie—a man carrying a pal on his back through shot and shell. But it's not very practical. We did not dare stand up. I crawled around in front of him and told him to grab onto my ankles. Then I started to crawl to the hole, pulling him by my elbows six inches at a time. The guns had stopped firing while we were down. I had gone about three feet. Suddenly, he let go of me and jumped and ran. Apparently, he was not hurt very bad and had gotten over the shock. As soon as he jumped up, the guns started firing at him, but he made it to the hole. This left me out there all alone. As soon as the guns stopped momentarily, I dived and got into the hole. By this time, Slater was gone out the other side and into the trench.

There was still one man left in the hole with me—Kiska. The only way they could get us now was with mortars. They could drop shells right over the pile of dirt and into the hole. In the next two minutes, they must have dropped fifty shells onto us. What a barrage they put down! But they were just to the right of the hole, right on the edge of it. One shell in the hole would have gotten us. The shrapnel came into the hole, though. We could hear it buzzing and hitting the side. We crouched down close to the right side so the shrapnel would go over our heads, and it did. But before I could stop him, Kiska stuck his head up over the side. Why he did it, I don't know. But just as he did, a shell hit the edge of the hole about ten inches in front of his face. I had flattened myself on the bottom of the hole, and Kiska slid right down on top of me. For once in my life, I was glad to have a man on top of me. I did not move. I stayed right there until the shelling stopped. When I finally got up, I was covered with blood, but I was alive. Kiska was dead. I left him there, for there was nothing I could do for him.

I went into the trench. I knew Lambert was in deep trouble, and I would have to find him and help him if I could. The boys told me he was up at the far end of the trench and I ran up to where he was. I asked him, "What in the hell's wrong? What happened?" He said, "We're in the wrong spot. I've been waiting for you to come." No. 7 Plt. had climbed out of the trench and started for the woods about 100 yards in front. They had gone only about 30 feet and were now pinned down by heavy machine gun fire. While we were talking, No. 7 Plt.'s officer, Lieutenant Nightingale, jumped to his feet and hollered, "Get some artillery fire." A German sniper shot him in the stomach. We watched as he went down, but could do nothing. He lived about another five minutes, then died. Lambert said, "You're second-in-command of the company now. You take charge. I'll have to go back and get things straightened up." He got out of the trench and crawled away.

He was gone for about half or three-quarters of an hour before he came back. He said, "We're all right now. We're in the right place. And we'll attack into the woods." He had arranged for the British Columbia Regiment to send us a tank for a few minutes. Without some help, we would never make it into the woods. The Germans were just too strong for us. He said, "You get down and take charge down at the other end of the trench. As soon as the tank gets here, we'll go." By the time I got back to the end of the trench, I could hear the tank coming. The "B.C.s" were in a fight to the left of us and the tank had to get right back. It came across the field on the other side from where the hole was. It was just hitting the high spots—both guns blazing.

I kicked the men out of the trench and away we went. This time, I did not go in front; I chased them from behind. No one was going to stop. We went across the field on the run. As we went past the tank, it turned and left and was out of the field before we hit the woods, but it had put down such a devastating fire, the Germans never fired a shot. I led to the left and Lambert led to the right. He was running across the field, waving his hat and hollering, "Peanuts! Popcorn! Chewing gum!"

We hit the woods and went right straight in. There were a lot of Germans in there. Some of them had surrendered right away and the boys were rounding them up. I was standing by a hump in the ground when, suddenly, a grenade came out of the hump and landed not more than two feet from me and exploded. I saw it coming and jumped back. Luckily, it was a Bakelite grenade. They had to almost hit you to hurt you. I realized the hump was a cover over a slit trench. I swung my gun around to fire. My bullets would have gone right through and anyone in there would have been killed, but one of the other men had seen it, too. He stuck a rifle in the hole, and the Germans hollered "Kamerad" and came out. There were two of them and they were both older men, at least in their forties. Some of the men wanted to shoot them, but I said no. We sent them back as prisoners instead.

The battle was over now. We were standing in the woods looking around when someone said, "Look at that!" Down through the woods came a German, running as fast as he could go. He was not running in the usual way, but was going in great leaps. His left leg had been shot off at the knee but was still fastened to the upper part, and it was flopping all over the place. He was going on his good right leg and the stump of his left. We watched as he finally went out of sight, still running. There was nowhere for him to go. He was going to run right into both the British Columbia Regiment and the Argylls.

It had started to rain. Another German came through the woods and we sat and watched him as he advanced. He did not know we were there until he got right to us; he was one surprised German. He said he had been asleep. I noticed he had a lead pencil stuck in his rifle barrel to keep the rain out. We walked down through the woods to see where "C" Coy. was. In front of us was a big clump of what we thought were bushes about 30 feet high and all of 40 feet wide. We got right to it when, suddenly, a door opened in the side of it and out came a German. He asked if he could surrender. When we did not shoot him, he called back and out came at least fifty more Germans. We had not known they were there. They had made a big shelter out of branches and leaves and were living in it. It was so well camouflaged, we had not even seen it. We went on through the woods and out onto the highway, which was the main highway from Antwerp to Breda and right on through to Germany. It was about four o'clock by this time. The cook came up with our dinner and handed out the mail. It was October 20 and I got a Christmas card from a cousin in Michigan I did not even know.

We had lost quite a few men that day. The Germans had fought hard, but we had taken a lot of prisoners. That morning when we started, I had seven men in my platoon. I lost two of them, so that left me with only five. One platoon officer had been killed, and "A" Coy. was now down to somewhere around thirty to thirty-five men. There should have been one hundred, all ranks.

That night about eight o'clock, Lambert told me to get some men and take a patrol down the road to see if I could find the Argylls. It was pitch-dark and raining hard. We went through the woods until we found three men from No. 9 Plt. I ordered them to come with me. One of them was Corporal Irwin, but I did not know who the others were. It did not matter; I had my men. It was so dark we had to hang onto each other's belts to keep together, which made the going very slow. On top of that, we were right in a minefield. There were signs all over in German that said "Minen." We went down the road for more than a mile. The Argylls were to have a man out looking for us. We were getting tired, so we stopped to rest. Irwin was a darn good man, and he said, "Let me go on alone. If I don't find anyone right away, I'll come back." So I sent him on. He only went about half a mile and came back. We started back to our position, but how were we to find it in the dark?

When I thought we had gone far enough, I turned into the woods and walked right into "A" Coy. By the time I found our second-in-command, Captain Barkman, who had just come up a short while before, it was about half past three in the morning. I told Barkman we could not find the Argylls and that I was now going to go to sleep. The rain was coming straight down hard with no wind and the boys were lying on the ground with no cover. Everyone was soaking wet. There was a sand pit of some kind there, so I dug a hole in the side of it just long enough and deep enough for me to lie in out of the rain. I got into it and went to sleep. I woke up about seven o'clock in the morning and was very surprised to find that I was dried right out. The sand had acted like a blotter and had drawn the water all out of my clothes. It had stopped raining by now and everyone wondered why I was the only one there who was not wet.

I did not feel well and I was very light-headed, but I did not realize there was anything wrong with me, so after breakfast I went for a walk. Oblivious to the "Minen" signs, I walked right through them and down the road, where I came to a big house. I could see that there had been something buried in the ground and that there were buried wires running all over. I went up to the house and was going to go in, but I could feel danger, so I stopped. This was German territory. I looked around and could see what I had done. I walked very carefully back to our position in the woods and watched as a flail (a mine-clearing tank) came down the road exploding mines where I had just walked. It was only then that I realized there was something wrong with me, but I had no idea I was very sick. At last, the war had caught up to me. My nerves were at the breaking point and I was exhausted completely. Lambert came along and told me that we would have an early dinner and that we were to move. By noon, we were in our TCV and moving with no idea where we were going. Barkman was not there, so once again I was told I was second-in-command of the company even though a new platoon officer had been sent in to take charge of No. 7 Plt. Lambert considered me to be his second and did so as long as we were together in "A" Coy.

We headed north from Brasschaet. I have very little recollection of the trip. We had just moved off, and I was sitting at the back of our TCV, getting worse all the time. I had a feeling of indigestion and my chest was very sore and stiff. I was so weak I could not sit up. Soon my head was hanging down between my knees and my arms were hanging listlessly. I was not just light-headed; I was drifting in and out of consciousness. We would move a little way and then stop, and then do it again. Sometimes, I was aware of what was going on, but mostly not. I was so exhausted I did not care what happened. I was in the TCV in that condition for at least three hours. Finally, I became aware that we were stopped, but I just sat there. After a moment, I realized I should go and see why we were stopped and find out what was going on. It was a job in itself to get to my feet and climb out of the TCV. I dropped to the ground behind it and when I hit the ground, the shock of it was very painful. If I had not been holding on to the TCV, I would have gone right down. I thought everything in my chest was coming right out the bottom. I looked around and there was no one behind us. Lambert was in his jeep ahead of us, but everyone else was gone. We were all alone. When or where the rest of the company had gone, I had no idea. I plodded up to the jeep—every step was torture. Lambert sat in the jeep, looking up the road. He had been waiting for me to come.

Up the road about 400 yards was a T-intersection. The left went out into the country, while the right went into the small town of Foxmaat, which looked like a wide spot in the road. There was one row of houses on either side of the road. Neither Lambert nor I said anything; we both just looked. Finally, he spoke. "I'm sorry there's no help. They've taken my other two platoons away. Do you think you can do it?" I knew he was asking me to attack the town with my five men. There was only one thing now I had to look forward to, and that was dying. It was inevitable, and, I thought, the sooner now, the better. This job should have been a job for at least a full company, but by now, I was looking forward to being killed. I had faced it as long as I could; I could not take it anymore. The desperation to hang onto life and the fear of dying were gone. As I stood there, I thought all of these things. I just said, "Yes, I guess so," and went back to call my men out of the TCV. There was nothing more said. He would leave it to me to do it my way. He, like Baldwin, never questioned what I did.

We all hid in the ditch, which was about a foot and a half deep. The TCV backed up to a corner behind us and turned around. Lambert turned his jeep and they were gone. A frontal attack on this town could not succeed. I reasoned that if the Germans had been watching and saw our vehicles go back, they would think we had gone. We waited about twenty minutes, then started to crawl up the ditch on our bellies. It was a long way, and I was very sick. About 40 yards behind the houses was a hedge, running parallel with the town. By the time we got to the hedge, I had formed a plan. We turned up the hedge and every 50 yards I dropped off a man. When they were all in position, I waved my hand for them to get through the hedge. When they were all through, I hollered, "Let's go." We fired our guns and whooped and hollered like wild Indians. One shot was fired from the houses in front of me. I heard it sing as it went about 10 feet over my head. When I reached the houses, I made sure all the men were still there. Some went in the houses, while I went in between two houses and out onto the street. There was no one in sight, but I could see some of the house doors were open. When the men all came through, I ran across the road and between two houses. Out in the field, running for their lives, were thirty or forty Germans. We had taken them completely by surprise!

One of the men came down the street and said there was a woman in one of the houses having a baby. There was no one but her and her father, and he was asking for a doctor to help. There was no way we could get a doctor, so there wasn't much I could do. There was very little chance that the Germans would counterattack, so I sat down on the steps of a house. I guess the men went to deliver the baby.

About five o'clock, a jeep came up the road into town, going very slowly. I can imagine what Lambert was thinking. He did not know who was in there. When he got there, he told me the regiment would come in and stay there all night and he also ordered me to get to bed somewhere and rest. Soon, the other companies started to drift in. Where they came from, I don't know. Jim Bell came looking for me and we walked down the street, side by side, talking. From down the road beyond the T-intersection came a rifle shot. It whizzed right between our heads. This ended our visit. Jim went back to his own company and I went back to mine. I went into a house, lay down on a bed and went to sleep. I did not get anything to eat that night, and I had no idea where my men were.

I woke up about eight o'clock the next morning. When I went outside, they were all sitting on the steps waiting for me. One man got to his feet and went and got some breakfast for me. I was still very weak and light-headed, and in a bit of shock. As I ate my breakfast, I noticed it was very quiet. The town was empty. The men told me the whole regiment had left at seven o'clock the night before for an attack on the town of Esschen. Because I was sick, my platoon and I had been left behind. I suspect that they could not wake me up. I guess we were lucky; they lost a lot of men that night. I heard men talk of it later and they said it was the worst shelling they had ever seen. To make matters worse, it was our own artillery firing on them. In a letter, dated December 6, 1990, Walter Balfour wrote: "I recall you were sick at the time and we were glad you were able to miss the mess. Jim Monaghan and I were discussing you when Jim told me you were sick before the attack."

I was just finishing my breakfast when a jeep came into town. It was Lambert and he stopped to talk to me. I gave the mess tins to someone to wash and went over to the jeep. Lambert said, "I have a job for you," and then showed me a map. Down the road beyond the intersection, there was a side road to the right, and about half a mile up this road were some farm buildings. His orders were quite clear, "You will occupy and hold those buildings." The rest of "A" Coy. were putting in an attack somewhere else, but where, I don't know. He said, "Is that clear?" and I said, "Yes."

I called my men and we headed out of town in single file about five yards apart. We stayed on the road until we were nearly there. I was so tired and weak, we had to stop several times to rest. I was very short of wind and could not breathe. When we were nearly there, we got in the ditch, so if we came under fire, we could get down and get some sort of cover. We came to the driveway and turned in. We were in enemy territory and I could not believe we had gotten that far. The farmyard was paved with bricks, with the barn on the right and the house on the left. In the centre of the yard was a big water tank full of water. We got right to the water tank and then all hell broke loose. The only cover was behind the water tank. They were firing an 88-millimetre from a Tiger tank, machine gun and rifle fire, and the heaviest mortar fire I was ever under.

We had a French Canadian boy with us named Dorian. He got right down beside me, pounded me on the back, and said, "By damn, Kipp, I don't go wit you anymore. You get me killed." He lay down on the ground and started to cry. He was of no use to us like that, so when things eased up a bit, I said to him, "You go back and tell Dick, the cook, to give you a job for a couple of days." At this, a big smile came over his face and he jumped up and ran. At that movement, the Germans started to fire again and they continued to do so for over an hour. The tank was full of holes, there was water all over, and both the house and the barn were full of holes. My nerves gave way completely. I lay behind the tank counting, "one-two-three-four, one-two-three-four," louder and louder, until I was screaming and crying.

I could not hold on any longer. This was October 22, 1944. I had been in the fighting three months less three days, twenty-four hours a day. The only rest I had had was in September when I had sore feet—two days and three nights.

I got up and started to run around the yard. Why I wasn't killed, I don't know. I ran and screamed; I swore at the Germans and called for them to come in and get us. But they didn't come in—they had us right where they wanted us. After about an hour of heavy fire, they let off. There was a gateway out into the field. If they would not come in after us, I would go out after them. I went to the gate, looked out and saw there was a vehicle coming across the field. It was a truck pulling a howitzer. I watched as they stopped and set up their gun. Then they started to fire. On my left was a ridge of land, and the Germans were behind it. In my confused mind, the men out front were Germans and I went after them across the field at a trot. Luckily, before I got there, I got a bit of order back in my mind. Before I got close enough to shoot, I could see that they were British, so I went in and talked to them. They were just moving around. Whenever they saw something, they stopped and shot at it. How they ever got in there is more than I could understand. "A" Coy. was still fighting a mile behind them, and there were Germans all around them. The last I saw of them they were going deeper into the German lines.

I went back to the farm buildings. I wondered how I had gotten out there past the Germans, but they had not seen me. However, before I got back into the farmyard, they saw me and started to shoot. As soon as the shells started to come in again, I started to scream. I ran and screamed—around and around in circles. The circle kept getting smaller as I was getting weaker. I was gagging for breath. Then I couldn't even scream. I was just going, "Aahaa, aahaa, aahaa." I fell several times, but got up again. I did not know which direction I was going in. Two of my men ran out of the barn, right into the shellfire, to get me. Each one grabbed me by an arm, and we ran for the barn. I remember going through the barn door, then my legs gave out and I felt myself going down. They lowered me to the barn floor unconscious. I was completely gone.

The Lincoln and Welland Regiment diary for October 22, 1944, reads: "8 Plt. went up a side road, and were fired on by a German tank. Two men were wounded; one man was killed." They did not mention me. It continues: "'A' Coy. arrived on their objective at 1 o'clock. A troop of tanks from the British Columbia Regiment were sent to 8 Plt. position. But 8 Plt. could not be contacted." I had lost consciousness somewhere between half past ten and eleven o'clock. I was the only survivor of that battle, and I survived only because I was unconscious on the barn floor.

I came to, but then drifted in and out of consciousness. I had no idea where I was. Eventually, when I came out of it, I was in the back seat of a jeep and it was dark. I was in very deep shock. My whole body was numb. My chest was one big spot of pain and soreness. I was very short of breath and I felt like I was suffocating. Somehow or other, I had gotten my hands up underneath my tunic, and I was clawing at my chest and wondering what had happened to me. I had only eaten twice in the last forty-eight hours, breakfast both days. My stomach was very empty and I was very rundown—just skin and bones, a skeleton hunched over in the back seat. My chest felt as if there was a big lump of jelly in there. As I was clawing around my chest, I found I could let all my breath out and put my fingers up under my rib cage, and feel that there was a big lump there. It scared me and I was saying to myself, "What is it? What has happened to me?" I did not know what it was, but there was a sore spot on the end of it about as big as a quarter. I was rubbing it with my fingers, and then I pressed it. That knocked the breath right out of me, and I gasped for air. It felt as if I had been kicked by a mule. Later on, in 1960, I would have the very same thing again, which was diagnosed as a myocardial infarction—a heart attack—and determined to be caused by stress. In 1944, although I didn't realize it at the time, I was in the process of having a myocardial infarction, caused by both stress and exhaustion, by just being worked nonstop, without a break, until I had been pushed beyond the limits of human endurance.

I became aware there were some men sitting by the side of the jeep talking. Finally, I got out and went over to them. Every step was agony. I thought everything in my chest was going to drop out the bottom. I squatted down with the men, one of whom was Lambert.

He said, "Oh, you're going to join us, are you?" Then he sent someone to get something for me to eat. As I ate, I could hear them talking, but their voices sounded like echoes a long way away. It was just a hollow sound. When I was finished, Lambert said, "You're not to be evacuated. I have a job for you." I was beyond asking for help. I was just like a robot or a zombie. I could not think for myself. I just did as I was told. I knew what I was doing, but in the condition I was in, I could not speak up for myself or even ask for help. I could take orders, but I had no comprehension of my condition. I was too sick to even know how sick I was. No one asked me what had happened or what was wrong with me. Someone took my lanyard and put it around my neck and down my sleeves. They tied a revolver on each end and put them in my hands. I was told some of the men had gotten lost, that they were with someone else and I was to go and bring them back. I was taken out in a field and pointed in a direction and told to walk that way until I came to a fencerow, turn left and walk until I met some more men. It all sounded all right at that time, but since then, I have realized I could not have brought anyone back because I did not know where I was. I was put out into the darkness and told to go, so I went. I came to the fencerow, turned left, and eventually came into a group of men. If I had not been in such shock, I couldn't have done it.

One man was drinking tea from a mess tin. I figured he would be an officer, so I went to him and said, "I'm Sergeant Kipp from 'A' Coy. You have some 'A' Coy. men who got lost. I've come to take them back." He just looked at me, then handed me his mess tin of tea. I took it and drank it. I must have been an awful-looking sight. Finally, he said, "Those men are not here. They're out just now. You go to sleep and I will send for them." He gave me a blanket and I lay down at the foot of a tree and went to sleep.

In the morning, a man woke me up and gave me some breakfast. After breakfast, I went to the officer and asked for the men. He said, "They came in and I have sent them back. You come with me." He took me in his jeep to the headquarters of the South Alberta Regiment. There was another jeep there and he said, "That's Lambert's jeep. You get in there. He will take care of you." I got in the jeep and went to sleep. This was the morning of October 23. After dark, on the night of October 24, I woke up. I had been unconscious in the back seat of Lambert's jeep for nearly two days, with nothing but the will of God as to whether I lived or died. Lambert was taking me out of the jeep. He had his arm around my waist and my arm around his neck. He took me into a house and put me into a bed built under the stairs, then he handed me a loaded rifle with a bayonet on it and said, "Here, take this. You may need it before morning." I was still in severe shock and very light-headed. I thought that was a big joke and laughed about it. Then I went right back to sleep.

On October 25, I woke up and got out of bed. I had no idea where I was. I went and stood in the doorway, leaning up against the side of the door jamb. I looked out and there was our kitchen. Men were sitting around eating. It was morning to me and I thought they were eating breakfast, but it was actually one o'clock and they were eating their dinner. As I stood there, Lambert came around the corner of the house in his jeep. He jumped out and hollered, "Everyone on your feet! We're going to attack!" As he went past me, he said, "You stay here. You're going home." I wondered why, as I did not even know I was sick. I had "battle numbness," caused from the trauma of too much war, that rendered me incapable of realizing how sick I was.

The men were on their feet running. They dropped their mess tins, grabbed their guns and were off. I could hear bullets. I watched in dazed amazement as the pans on the stove bounced all over, full of bullet holes, and the cook and his helper dived under their truck. A bullet hit the door jamb about two inches from my head. I jumped and ran around the house, where I could see a town about 600 yards away. "A" Coy. was already halfway there. There was a road on my left and I could see flame-throwers going up it, firing as they went—great sheets of flame. My place was with "A" Coy., so I ran after them. About 80 yards out in the field, I came to some ditches and I went across two of them. The next one was full of dead Germans. I looked around and the ground was covered with dead men. There were piles of them. A German got up and came to me. He gave me his revolver, which I still have, and said he wanted to surrender. I told him to go back to the house and he went, very glad to be alive. I was told the rest of the Germans were buried in the ditch with a bulldozer. There were so many that was all they could do with them. There was a dead Canadian there by the name of Wagg, whom I knew well. I bent over to pick up his rifle, and as I bent over, a bullet snapped over my head. If I had not bent over at that time, I would have been hit. I ignored the bullet. I picked up the rifle and went on after "A" Coy. A hundred and fifty yards to my right there was another road into town. I could see English men coming down it, and they were having a real fight.

As there was no No. 8 Plt. at that time, No. 9 Plt. was going into town while No. 7 Plt. was moving off to the right. I came up to the edge of town where there was a small barn. I went to have a look and see if there were any Germans in it. At the far side of town, I could see a lot of Germans on the run across the field. Down at the other side of town, I could see flame-throwers on Churchill tanks coming our way. They were firing into a woods and the woods was a big mass of fire. I went to the barn and found a padlock on the door. I wanted to see in, so I broke a window. When I saw the broken glass, an awful thought came to me. Back in Chatham No. 12 training camp, I had a friend who tried to commit suicide twice: once by cutting his wrists with broken glass and another time by cutting them with a razor blade. I had never, ever thought of killing myself to end my war, but when I saw that broken glass, I thought about him. And I thought I could end it right then by cutting my wrists. Just at that time, I felt myself going down. I tried to hang onto the barn door, but I went to the ground unconscious. It was near 1:15 P.M., October 25.

When I regained consciousness, I found myself standing on the road. I felt different somehow. I had come out of the shock, and my chest, although very sore, no longer felt like it had a lump of jelly in it. It was as if I had been away and just come back. I looked up the road and saw stretcher-bearers coming with a man on the stretcher. I said, "Who have you got?" Someone answered, "Sergeant Brown." No. 7 Plt.'s Sergeant Brown was wounded at quarter past three. It was now about half past three, so I had been unconscious for more than two hours. While I was unconscious, the medical officer had set up a field dressing station about 75 yards from me. I was behind a hedge by the side of a barn. I had been told not to come and no one knew I was there, so no one looked for me. I followed the stretcher into the dressing station. The medical officer took one look at me and said, "Don't go away. I want to see you." I knew something had happened to me, but I had no idea what. I also didn't know that it was now four days later. From October 21 to October 25—all of that time—I had, to all intents, been unconscious. I could not tell anyone what was wrong or ask for help. It is my belief that on October 22, I had been taken to the doctor, but what he did or what he said, I have no idea. I had been unconscious, at that time, for at least ten hours. I have always wondered if I went from unconscious to asleep at that time.

The doctor looked after Sergeant Brown; they put him on a stretcher on top of a jeep, and the doctor said, "Get going. And take it easy. I don't think he's going to make it." (The next time I saw "Brownie" was in 1984 in St. Catharines, forty years later. He had made it.) The doctor came to me and said, "How do you feel?" I said, "Better." I had been conscious for only about ten minutes. "Take off your clothes. I want to look you over." I took my clothes off and he went over me, back and front. He checked my heart several times, but said nothing. I know now by his actions that there was something wrong with my heart. Finally, he said, "Put your clothes on. I want to think about this," and he left me. I put my clothes on. In a few minutes, he came back and said, "I have orders that only the seriously wounded are to be evacuated. You are not wounded and you are still on your feet. I can do nothing for you. Go back to your company." I did not tell him that I had just regained consciousness only fifteen minutes before, because I did not know it. And no one else knew it, either, because I had been all alone. Lambert was sitting in his jeep watching and I started over to him. The padre was there and he said, "You have had enough. I'll see if I can do anything for you." I went on to Lambert. He said, "I have to go to an 'O' group [orders meeting]. You take charge of the company and see to clearing the town."

The town was Wouwsche Plantage. I did as Lambert had ordered. I went into the town and took charge of the company, sending patrols through the town to search the houses. The last prisoner was taken about 9:15 P.M. He had been asleep in the basement of a house. When he woke up and came out to see what was going on, he walked right into two of our guards. They brought him into a house where there must have been about fifteen men in there asleep. I sat up all night and watched him. He was a fifteen-year-old ss man and spoke very good English, so we talked a bit. He said the war was a great adventure, but to me, by this time, the adventure was all gone. There were guns lying all over the house. There was no doubt if he could get his hands on one, he would kill us all. I fought sleep all night, and he watched me intently. He would say, "Go to sleep, Sergeant. It's all right. Go to sleep." I very nearly did. In the morning we put him in a jeep and sent him off to prison camp.

It was October 26, and "A" Coy. stayed in the town. I wandered around looking things over. I went out to the woods where the flame-throwers had been. What a mess! I looked in the slit trenches on the edge of the woods where there had been Germans. Their bodies had burned up, but their steel helmets were still there.

That afternoon we moved out of town and camped out in a field. At that time, we had wounded men still in the trenches. There were men with arms in slings and men on crutches still in the fighting. Although I wondered about it, I had no idea what had happened to me, and there was no one to ask. No. 8 Plt. was gone. I never saw any of those men again and they were now forgotten. On October 27, Lambert told me to go back to Battalion Headquarters to be examined by the doctor. Although I realized that *something* had happened to me, I did not know what. I did know that the doctor had examined me and that it was my heart that had caused his concern. Also, I remembered that, as they were starting the attack on Wouwsche Plantage on October 25, Lambert had said to me, "You stay here, you're going home," and I had wondered why.

As I was on my way to see the doctor, I put a lot of thought into what was happening. In my confused state of mind, I resolved that I would not leave my regiment as long as I was on my feet. I was experiencing survivor's guilt. After I had seen so many of my friends die, there was no way that I would *walk* away. After I had worked so hard to get into the service and get over there, I was not going to leave until either the war was over or I was carried out. So instead of going to see the doctor, I went back to Battalion Headquarters, where I found Sgt. Art Winterford, who was being sent home on compassionate leave. I visited with Art, then returned to "A" Coy. and told no one what I had done. There was no way I would walk out when there were so few fighting men left in the regiment. I could never have lived that down. Remember the poem "In Flanders Fields" by John McCrae: "If ye break faith with us who die / We shall not sleep." What would all the boys who had died think of me, if there was some way they could know I had walked away? Years later, I learned that I had suffered a heart attack of some kind and was to have been sent home. However, a few days later, the doctor was transferred out of the regiment, and it was all forgotten.

I had just gotten back to "A" Coy. on October 27 when up the road came two Churchill tanks—Englishmen. They went past our camp and turned the corner. Down the road a couple of hundred yards, they turned another corner to the left. Ahead of them was the city of Bergen-op-Zoom. We were only about a quarter of a mile from Bergen. The road to Bergen-op-Zoom was an endless succession of tripwires, teller mines and booby traps. They had only gone a short distance when there was a great explosion. The lead tank had hit a booby trap—a 500-pound bomb buried in the road. We sat and watched as a Churchill tank weighing 42 tons slowly rose 40 feet in the air, turned over, and landed on the side of the road upside down.

After supper, Lambert came to me and said, "Arm yourself with a Bren gun and meet me at my jeep." I got a gun and all the ammunition I could carry. When I got to the jeep, I saw they had a wireless set in the back seat. Lambert and his driver were in the front, so I got in the back and away we went. We stopped at the Churchill tanks and talked to the Englishmen. They told us they had not looked into the tank as yet, but they figured everyone in it was dead. It was about seven o'clock. We sat and waited until it got dark, then drove around the tank and up the road to Bergen-op-Zoom. After seeing that tank blow up, my hair stood right on end as we went up the road. If that 42-ton tank would go 40 feet in the air, how high would we go in a jeep? But nothing happened. We drove into the town. It was pitch-dark and starting to rain. We went just a short way into town, turned into the backyard of a big building, and stopped. I jumped out to do guard duty while Lambert and the driver carried the wireless set into the building. The driver then turned around and went back. Lambert went back inside to wait for orders while I stayed out on guard. In about half an hour, he came out and said, "Well, let's go look over the city."

In the next hour, we tramped all over town. There was a lot of German equipment there, but no Germans. We kicked bicycles to pieces, cut wires and did all the damage we could. At one house, there were a lot of wires going in a window—too many to cut, so we started to pull. We must have pulled the wires out at least 10 feet when there was a big crash inside. We dropped everything and ran. We came up into the town square, but there was nothing there, so we decided that the Germans had gone. We went back to where we had left our wireless set. Again, Lambert went in to report while I stood guard. About half past ten in the evening, he came out and said, "You might as well come in and get some sleep. They're in the town. 'C' Coy. came in on South Alberta tanks." There were no Germans and it was raining hard, so I decided to do just that. I slept on a brick floor that night.

In the morning, I looked the building all over. It was a German prison. This was a place where the Germans had held and tortured Dutch Resistance fighters. They had cleared everything out. All that was left was a bunch of whips. These were short-handled whips with leather lashes tipped with pieces of steel. About nine o'clock our jeep came and took us to "A" Coy. position.

I had breakfast and decided to look over the town. For the most part, the town was very quiet. Once in a while a shell would come in and everyone would run for cover. Many townsfolk were on the street, getting to know the Canadians. Bergen is a very old city and there is a lot to see there, including a sixteenth-century fort. During the Napoleonic Wars, an ancestor of mine, Sir George Disbrowe, a brother to my great-great-grandfather, Henry Sharp Disbrowe, and a great-great-grand uncle to me, was wounded in a battle at Bergen-op-Zoom in 1809, 135 years earlier. He later fought at the Battle of Waterloo in 1815.

The city of Bergen is divided in two by a "zoom," which is a drainage canal. We held the south side of the town and the Germans still held the north, including the town of Halstern. From the north, there was a railroad track coming into the liquor factories, of which there were two. The bridges across the zoom had been destroyed. I followed a main street north and came out on a street that ran parallel to the zoom. I knew the Germans were on the other side, so I went into a house. All of the window glass had been removed. If it got broken or shot up, they could not replace it. I crawled into a room upstairs on my hands and knees. These were very dangerous places. I got a look outside and I could see right over to the German positions. To my left front was the town of Halstern. The German headquarters was there. To my immediate front was an open field, and to my right front, I could see a large building. This was a gin factory. There was also a stove factory and a laundry building. I watched out of the window for about half an hour, but I didn't see very much, so I decided to go back to "A" Coy.

I went down the stairs and had just stepped out onto the street when I saw an officer coming my way. He was new and had just come up. I told him what I had seen and took him upstairs to have a look. Again, I was very careful and kept him back out of the way. We were to the left side of the window, looking towards the gin factory, when a German car full of Germans came down the street past the factory as far as the laundry building, turned right and came down a pathway towards us. When they were about 60 yards in front of us, I stuck up my rifle and fired. The officer stood up in the window and fired also. The car was hit and stopped in the open right in front of us. As they were on the other side of the zoom, we could not take them prisoner, and we couldn't let them get away, either. If we did, we would have to fight them later. A German opened a door in the back seat and tried to get out to hide behind the car. I got a bead on him, and as he slid out the door, I fired. He was about half in and half out. He never moved again. We kept firing until they all stopped moving. Up by the gin factory, a German came out with a Red Cross flag. When he was nearly there, we stopped firing. I said, "Let's get outta here." The officer wanted to stay, but I knew they would have a sniper after us any minute. We had been lucky so far, and by now, I had had too many close calls shooting out of windows, so we left. What the officer's name was, I do not know. I never saw him again. Later, I was told by a Dutchman who was nine years old at the time that we had killed eight Germans there. The Dutch people would not pick them up and they were left there for a week. I went back to "A" Coy. position and had dinner. I had seen so much war by this time that dead men did not bother me at all. I spent the rest of the day catching up on sleep. I just went into an empty house and went to bed.

It was also around this time that a good friend of mine, Lieutenant Armstrong from "D" Coy., went down to the canal with a Red Cross nurse and walked down the street with her in plain view of the Germans on the other side—a very dangerous thing to do. Although the Red Cross sign was respected by both sides most of the time during the war, it was not an absolute guarantee of safety by any means. Besides, she may have been Red Cross, but he was not, and it was a wonder a German sniper didn't pick him off. It was not until some of his men hollered at him to get out of there that he realized what a dangerous situation he was in, and he quickly got off the street and out of sight. Forty years later, I would learn that a German sniper did, indeed, have him sighted up.

After supper that day, I was in the basement of a house with a bunch of kids. They were singing and having a good time. There was a girl about fourteen or fifteen years old with us. The kids would all sing, and then they would stop and look at the girl. She would lift up her leg and let loose with two or three big farts. The kids would all laugh and clap their hands, and then they would do it all over again. They were sure having a lot of fun.

The company runner came after me and said Lambert wanted to see me, and he took me to a house at Bolwerk Zuid 50. The owner of the house, Mr. Luijten, was an English professor in Bergen-op-Zoom. Lambert and a corporal from No. 7 Plt., who was a stranger to me, had brought a Dutch underground man with them who had just come across the zoom from Halstern. We would interrogate him using Mr. Luijten as an interpreter. That night, October 28, we would attack across the zoom. We got all the information from him we could. He told us there was a footbridge across the zoom right where we had shot the Germans, and that it was protected by at least three machine guns. He advised us to stay away from it. When we had all the information he could give us, he left. The three of us, Lambert, the corporal and I, started to plan the attack. We had no idea how deep the zoom was and we had men who could not swim. We decided to try to get enough men across the bridge to take the machine guns out. It sounded like a good plan. We had one platoon officer in the company, but he was just new. I was to be second-in-command. I would assemble the men and get them ready to move while Lambert took our plan to Colonel Cromb.

We were now ready to leave the house. Mr. Luijten said, "Would you men drink a toast with me? To the success of your battle." We said we certainly would. He got out a bottle and some glasses, and as he was opening the bottle, he was talking to us. "Are you men not nervous?" He said that if he were going into battle like we were, he would be scared; he would run, he was not sure he could do it. He said even now, he was shaking so badly he did not know if he could pour the drinks. "Are you men not a little bit nervous?" We sure were, but we did not let on that we were. He filled our glasses level with the top. The corporal and I were sitting on the steps, side by side. We held our glasses high—there was not so much as a ripple on them. Mr. Luijten said, "I cannot believe this. How can you be so steady?" We both answered instantaneously in perfect unison, "Because we are Canadians." To that, he proposed a toast, and we had our drink and left.

Residents of Bolwerk Zuid, the street where the former Luijten home is located,
flocked out of their houses to meet Charles and have their picture taken with him,
November 1984.

COURTESY MARGARET KIPP

Reunion with the Luijten family in Bergen-op-Zoom, November 1984. Left to right: Professor Luijten, Toos Luijten (Hans's wife), the author and Hans Luijten.

*Charles and his "old enemy" Carl Holst meeting on the
Lincoln Memorial Bridge in Bergen-op-Zoom, May 1986.*
COURTESY MARGARET KIPP

Meeting Lt. Carl Heinz Holst (middle), 6th German Paratroop Regiment,
Bergen-op-Zoom, May 1986. On left is author's brother, William (Bill) Kipp.
COURTESY MARGARET KIPP

Canadian and German veterans meet on the Lincoln Memorial Bridge, named for the
Lincoln and Welland Regiment, Bergen-op-Zoom, Netherlands, May 1986.

COURTESY MARGARET KIPP

The author and Lt. Carl Heinz Holst (left) stand on the spot where they tried to kill each other 42 years before. On the right is Lieutenant Colonel LeCoutre, former company commander of the 6th German Paratroop Regiment.

COURTESY MARGARET KIPP

Laying a wreath at the cenotaph, Canadian war cemetery, Bergen-op-Zoom,
Netherlands, May 1986. Zaak Roosenboom is at the far right.

COURTESY MARGARET KIPP

This group photo taken in May 1986 includes the Luijten family and the Van Heren sisters, whose family billeted the author during the war.

COURTESY MARGARET KIPP

17

THE BATTLE AT BERGEN-OP-ZOOM

I WAS ORDERED TO GET the men ready—to make sure they had ammo and everything they would need. Lambert would take the plan to the colonel for approval. In about an hour he came back and said, "Let's go." I had everything ready and we moved off. However, we did not go in the direction I thought we should be going, so I said to Lambert, "Are you sure we're going the right way?" He said, "Yes. The plan has been changed." That is all I was told.

We came to the edge of town on the northeast corner and went through the inevitable hedge and out into an open field. We advanced into the field for about 80 to 100 yards and then turned left. It was very dark, but soon we could make out something in front of us. The skyline was up about 10 feet above our heads. It turned out to be a railroad track built on top of a dyke. Lambert was in the lead, I was right behind him, and the rest of the men were strung out behind us. We climbed up the dyke to the top and started over it. The men came up and spread out across the top of the dyke right behind us. Then everything broke loose. There were at least three German MG-42s that opened up on us from the front, along with rifle fire. It was devastating. It just swept the railroad track clean. I could see and hear men going down all around me, but for some reason, I was not hit. I dropped down between the rails. There was an iron post there about 10 inches high and I put my head right behind it. The bullets were hitting all over the place. They hit the post and they hit the steel rails. I could not stay there, for, eventually, I would be hit, so I just made a lunge over the rails and rolled down the side of the dyke.

Down by the side of the dyke was the zoom. When I stopped rolling, I was about 20 or 30 feet from where Lambert was. I could hear several men down in there with me. Why Lambert did not stop and reorganize, I will never know. I heard him holler, "Are you coming with me, or have I got to go alone?" Then there was a splash as he jumped into the water. I heard other men going into the water, but I have no idea how many. They were going west into the darkness. I called for the men who were with me, "Come on, let's go," and jumped into the zoom and started to swim. They tell me there was a skiff of ice on the water, but I didn't stop to find out. I climbed out on the far side and started to run. I heard some men on my left come out of the water and come after me. The sky over our heads was one big sheet of flame from the German guns. All I knew was that Lambert was somewhere ahead of me. They had all disappeared in the dark. I heard a crash to the left of me, and a man went down. A man said, "Are you all right?" and a voice answered, "I don't know yet." A bullet had hit him right in the front of his steel helmet. It had gone through, around his head and out the back. Miraculously, he was not hurt.

I just kept on going. I must have run about 100 yards until I came to a brick wall about eight feet high. Lambert and some men were already there. This was the wall around the liquor factory. A couple more men came running up. Two men put their hands together to make a step. We stepped onto their hands and they hoisted us to the top of the wall. I do not know if I was the first or second man to go over the wall. Then two men stopped on the top of the wall and pulled the last two men over. By the time the last man was over, I had them in a defensive position. We took a count of how many there were. Out of the entire company of about thirty strong, thirteen men had gotten into the factory. The rest of the company had been driven back with heavy casualties, and we did not know where they were.

Lambert told me "C" Coy. was coming right behind us. Then he told me the plan. "A" Coy. was to establish a position in the factory.

Five minutes later, "C" Coy. was to follow us into the factory. "D" Coy. would make a frontal attack across the zoom into a nearby laundry building. "C" Coy. and "D" Coy. would then advance and clear the factory. We could do nothing now until "C" Coy. came in, but they didn't come, and we did not know why. After it was all over, we learned why. They had formed up to follow us. Our artillery was to lay down shellfire on the factory at the same time we were to start our attack, but they missed the factory and shelled "C" Coy. 100 yards to the right instead. Their attack was effectively broken up, with many casualties, both killed and wounded. When that happened, "D" Coy.'s attack was called off until "C" Coy. could reform. This we did not know. That left us—thirteen men who did not know what was going on in a factory full of Germans.

We waited until it was very apparent no one was coming to help us. Lambert decided we would take over "C" Coy.'s job and clear the factory. This was easier said than done. The place was full of Germans. When we finally started to move, they were ready for us. We fought from room to room, up hallways and all over. For most of the night, we chased them up one alley and they chased us down another. We would chase them for a while and then they would turn around and chase us. They were blasting holes in the walls with bazookas and throwing in grenades. Lambert ordered the men to run all over the factory, shouting and yelling to make the Germans think we had a regiment. We never fired two bursts from the same spot. Actually, we fired very few bursts at all. Our Sten guns had clogged with mud so badly when we were crossing the canal that most of them wouldn't fire at all or would just go "pink!"—not enough snap even to detonate the cartridge. As a result, our Sten guns weren't much good to us. We were just running all over and shooting everything we could see. It was pitch-dark. The only light came from the muzzle flashes of the guns.

Gordon Sinclair used to have a CBC news radio program during the war that he always began with a little playlet, generally something regarding the war. Every night after supper, my parents used to sit by the radio to hear Mr. Sinclair's program. You can imagine their shock and surprise one evening when his playlet, "The Lost Patrol," was about Sgt. Charles Kipp and his part in the Battle of Bergen-op-Zoom in the gin factory, "a battle of madmen in the dark."

We were losing men and so were they, but we did not know how many. We were calling them every dirty name we could think of. Whenever we'd yell, "Come in and get killed! We ain't special troops, we're the Lincoln and Welland. Come on in, ya scum, and taste Canadian knives," a German would fire a grenade and give away his location, and then there'd be one less German. But eventually they were just too many for us, and we were pushed back to where we came over the wall. And there was no way for us to get out because there were now Germans on the outside of the wall. We hurled insults back and forth at each other. They called us Canadian pigs and said they were coming in to kill us. We laughed at them and dared them to come in and try it. "Come in over the wall . . . We're in here. Come and get us. We've got knives . . . Come in and see what our knives are like." We were completely surrounded by Germans and they kept calling to us to surrender. Two of the men came to me and said, "Sarge, we don't want to surrender. You're not going to surrender, are you? We came here to fight, and that's what we're gonna do." I told them that we had no intention of surrendering. After all, they could not get to us as long as we had ammo for our guns. After a bit, things slowed down. I guess they knew we could not get away. They would just wait until morning, when they would be able to see us.

All of a sudden, a German MG-42 opened up behind us. The bullets were flying all over the place. A man beside me went down, killed instantly by a bullet ricocheting off the brick wall around us. One was right in my face. The German who fired it must have been only a few feet from me and the muzzle blast blinded me. I hollered, "Get outta there, ya goddamned German bastard!" all the while firing wildly in his direction until someone else who could see came and took over. All I could see was a lot of bright spots in front of my eyes. It was five or ten minutes before I could see anything. Then I went after him, but, wisely, he was gone. There was a tower about 10 or 12 feet high with a platform on top of it, so I decided to climb up there. I thought that if he moved in there I would be able to see him, but I saw noth-

ing. After a while, someone came to me and said Lambert wanted
me, so I went to see him. We talked about our position and what we
should do. We knew we'd had it if we couldn't get reinforcements. We
had been gone so long, we knew we would have been crossed off as
dead or captured. Finally he said, "Something has gone very wrong.
Do you think you can escape and get back to the colonel and tell him
what's happening?" I had no other choice. At least by going, that
would be a try.

I took off all of my equipment and gave all the ammo I had to the
men. All I took was a .38 revolver and three rounds of ammunition for
it. When I was ready, I slipped down into their lines, going from one
dark spot to the next. I later learned that I had gone right through
their first aid station. I went very slowly and quietly, not making a
sound. I finally came to a driveway where they backed in trucks to
load. We had fought in there earlier, but now the moon was up and
I could see down the driveway to dark blue sky. The driveway was
maybe 30 or 40 yards long with a solid brick wall on the north side.
On the south side, there were several doorways opening into hallways
or rooms. That was the dark side of the driveway, so I moved down
there very carefully, not making a sound. Soon I reached a green door
at the end. I looked out and saw that it opened onto a street. I did not
know which way to go, but reasoned that I should go south because
down that way I could see the main part of town. I stepped out onto
the sidewalk and immediately spied a tall church steeple and decided
I should head for that. I knew there had to be Germans down that
street. If they saw me sneaking down there, they would shoot with no
questions asked. At least by coming from the direction that I was,
maybe I could fool them into thinking I was one of theirs. There
were steel cleats on the bottom of my shoes and the sidewalk was
brick. I just stepped out and started to walk—*bang, bang, bang,* the
cleats of my shoes resounding like rifle cracks on the sidewalk, loudly
proclaiming my presence with every step. I stepped right along, as
if I had every right to be there. Then I came to an open spot in a
driveway or an alley, and a German spied me and called out to me.
My first instinct was to shoot, but I couldn't see anything and it
would probably do nothing but stir up a hornet's nest. I did not even

hesitate—*bang, bang, bang.* Germans were calling to me from door-ways and windows. I just ignored them and kept right on going. Finally, I came to the laundry building and there was a German right there. I went past him only about six feet away. I guess he was so sur-prised, he didn't know what to do. Just a few more steps and I was in the zoom and swimming underwater. I went to the left about 30 feet before I came up on the south side of the zoom. If I came out of the water too fast, the Germans would hear the water dripping off me, so I just came out real slow, right tight to the ground, and crawled out and started up the bank. It was only about 8 or 10 feet to the top, but the Germans had put in a lot of tank obstacles—huge pieces of con-crete to keep the tanks from going down to the water. I got behind one as fast as I could. Now I was safe from the Germans, but there was another danger. I had to contact our own men, and not get killed doing it.

They were up at the top of the zoom. I moved from one obstacle to the next, going, "Hisst, hisst" every minute or two. I would say, "Hisst, Lincoln and Welland." No answer. So I moved up a little more and tried it again. Eventually, I got an answer, "Who's there?" I said, "Sergeant Kipp, 'A' Coy. Don't shoot." "Then come out where we can see you." It was really dark. I walked out and nearly walked into their rifles. They had them right on me. One of them said, "OK," and down went the rifles. I said, "Who's your officer?" and one of them said, "Armstrong." Good. I knew him well. "Get him as fast as you can. Tell him Kipp is here." One man was off like a shot and in a few minutes, he was back with Armstrong. He took one look and I said, "Take me to the colonel—fast!" He just said, "Come on," and we ran.

I had come out into "D" Coy. We ran to their headquarters and jumped into Major Swayze's jeep. Then we were off on a wild ride through town—no lights, down the street and around the corners wide open. Soon, we came into the main square of the town and stopped in front of the Hotel de Draak. We were out of the jeep be-fore it had stopped rolling and through the hotel door. We were shown into a big room, and there in the middle of the room at a big table sat Colonel Cromb and Colonel Wotherspoon of the South Alberta Regiment. Cromb nearly fell off his chair in surprise. I quickly told him the story. I said Lambert was still in the gin factory with a few men and would hold out as long as possible, but they were nearly out of ammo. I was wet and cold, so he told me to go into another room until he sent for me. I went into another room where there was a Dutch nurse, the same nurse who had walked along the canal with Lieutenant Armstrong earlier in the day. She gave me hot coffee and wrapped me in a warm blanket. About twenty minutes later, the colonel sent for me. He said "C" Coy. was going to try to get into the factory and I was to go with them. He said, "You'll have to hurry. They've already started." I had to go halfway across town to find the spot where we had gone through the hedge, and that wasn't easy. When I finally got there, I met "C" Coy. coming back. They had gotten as far as the railroad track but could not get over. It was like sticking your head into a beehive, there were so many bullets. They were now on their way back, bringing their dead and wounded.

I went back to the Hotel de Draak, where I was told to go with Capt. John Martin, who was taking his Bren gun platoon up to the railroad tracks. This should have been done before we tried to cross the tracks, so they could have given us covering fire as we went over. Again, they had already left and I had to catch up. By this time, it was nearly daylight. When I got to the railroad tracks, he had his guns all set up and was ready for action, even though he had had several men killed by sniper fire. I looked around and decided he did not need me there. Besides, I was beginning to get an idea of my own. There had to be a few "A" Coy. men somewhere. I thought I could get them and go back to the factory by way of the laundry where I had come out, and I was going to try it.

I started back into town to find the men. On the way, I went through "C" Coy., who were having their breakfast. I was hungry, so I borrowed some mess tins and helped myself. I had just started to eat when along came the "C" Coy. sergeant major, who proceeded to tell me to get the hell back to my own company and leave his company's food alone. I quickly told him that I didn't care whose food it was, I was going to eat, and I told him in terms he understood. He thought better of making an issue of it and left. A "C" Coy. man came in and told me that "D" Coy. had gotten across the zoom and were in the factory. A man from the South Alberta Regiment had come down from his tank to have a look around. He thought our men were across the zoom, so he walked right down to the water. As he stood looking across, a German came out of the laundry and down to the water. He called across to the Canadian and asked if he had any cigarettes. The Canadian threw him a whole packet. The German took them and went back into the laundry. There were some planks and other pieces of lumber there, so the tank man made a bridge across, and then came back and told our people what he had done. "D" Coy. was sent across and into the factory. When I heard this, I forgot about rounding up "A" Coy. If "D" Coy. was already in there, I would just go with them. I went and had a look and the bridge was there, so I went across all by myself.

It sure was a funny feeling going in there all by myself. After all, it was only a story I had heard. Maybe it wasn't right. I went into the laundry, crossed over an alleyway and into the factory. Then I started to make my way back to where I had left Lambert. It was an eerie feeling. What if "D" Coy. was not in there after all? I moved along as carefully as I could and soon stepped into a large storage room. It had a loft full of stainless steel vats all piled up. I also found a section of "D" Coy. men in there. I thought, "Good, now we can move." I stepped out in front and said, "Come on, don't stop here," and moved ahead. No one said a word. I heard something up in the vats, and I knew why. I fired a shot up into them. A .303 bullet in steel vats made an awful racket. A German jumped up somewhere in amongst them and hollered, "Kamerad, kamerad," and started to come down. Ten or twelve of them came down with their hands up. Now, what to do with the prisoners. I did not want to interfere with the "D" Coy. men, as their corporal was doing a good job, so I said I would take the Germans back. I took them back across the bridge and turned them over to some other men. Then I went back in. It had only taken me about fifteen minutes, but when I got back to the storage room, the "D" Coy. men had moved on, so I was once again in there alone. I started to go ahead, ready to shoot at anything that moved. It was extremely nerve-racking going through there all alone. I passed through more rooms and passageways, but still did not catch up with them. Eventually, I came into a good-sized room. As soon as I stepped into it, I knew something was wrong. I could feel danger. I stopped and looked it all over. It was quite a large, square room. In the far corner, another small room had been built. It looked like an office. I could just *feel* that something was not right. Then I saw it! The door leading into the small room was not open. If the "D" Coy. men had gone through, they would have looked in the room, *and* they would have left the door open. It was a small thing, but I knew it was not right.

I stood and looked at it for several minutes. Then I saw that the door *was* open, just a crack. I tiptoed over very quietly and put my eye up to the crack. Indeed, it was a small office, and there on the floor lay a dead German, just as he had fallen. I began to feel better. The "D" Coy. boys had come this way. But something told me, "Be careful. Just take it easy and make sure." I stood and watched him for three or four minutes, hardly breathing. Then, as I watched, the dead man opened his eyes. I watched as he rolled his eyes around, looking all over the room. He saw nothing, so he turned over and sat up. I kicked open the door and put my rifle on him. He was a very surprised German!

I told him to come out of the room with his hands up. He must have understood English because he did just that. It was then that I saw he was wearing a Luger in a holster on his belt. Ah! The colonel had expressed a wish for a German Luger and now I had it for him. The German was a sergeant in the 6th German Paratroopers Regiment. I could also see that he was a very dangerous prisoner. Just by the way he watched me, I knew he would jump me if he got the chance. We were all alone.

I gave him no chance. I stayed well back from him and told him to take off the Luger. He took it off and held it out to me, but I would not go close enough to him to take it. I told him to put it on the floor and step away from it. I did not search him further. I just picked up the Luger and prepared to head back to the zoom.

Just then, a man from Battalion Headquarters came in. Why he was there, I don't know. I guess he had come up just to look around. He had no idea what danger he was in because he was not even armed. I made sure he knew how to fire the Luger, then I handed it over to him and told him to take the prisoner back. I gave him very strict orders. After he delivered the prisoner, he was not to give this Luger to anyone else. He was to take it straight to Lieutenant Colonel Cromb, give it to him, and tell him that Sergeant Kipp sent it. Later, the colonel thanked me for it.

Meanwhile, I went on, trying to find "D" Coy. I knew I must also be getting close to where I had left Lambert and the men of "A" Coy. I went through several more rooms before coming out into an open spot. I found the "D" Coy. men there, but I never noticed that one of them was missing. The men were just standing there when I arrived, so I stepped up and said, "Come on, don't stand here." I saw an opening out into another part of the factory and I thought it looked familiar. I went around the end of a brick pier and found myself in the laneway I had gone out the night before to make my escape. I took four or five steps and looked back over my shoulder to see if the men were coming. In an alcove behind the pier stood five or six Germans, and lying dead at their feet was one of the men from "D" Coy. What a shock! Here I was with my back to them and my rifle pointed in the wrong direction. I froze. The German officer raised his gun and sighted me—he could not miss; he had an automatic gun and I was only about eight feet away. One more second and I would be with the dead "D" Coy. man. I was going to try to turn around, but there wasn't time. If I made a sudden move, he would surely shoot right then and there. I was told later by some "A" Coy. men, who had hidden in a small shed nearby after they had run out of ammunition, that they had watched as I stepped out in front of the Germans and the officer raised his gun to shoot me. They said he had tried to shoot, but his gun would not fire.

I was not aware of this. My first thought was to duck to one side and get turned around, but I knew I would never make it. I let go of my rifle with my right hand and pointed behind him. He hesitated and I nodded my head for him to look behind him, and much to my surprise, he lowered his gun and turned completely around. Behind him was the first aid station I had gone through the night before when I had escaped through their lines. All that was there were two wounded German soldiers on stretchers and the dead "D" Coy. man. He looked, then turned back to me. He had been fooled, and now the shock was on his face. I had gotten turned around and now I had my rifle on him. All I had to do was squeeze the trigger and he would die. But he also now had his gun on me.

There was not six feet between the muzzles of the guns. We just looked each other in the eye—neither one of us daring to blink, each with our fingers on the trigger and the slack taken up. If I shot him, his reflexes, when the bullet hit him, would fire his automatic weapon. If he shot me, my reflexes would fire my rifle. At six feet, we could not miss. We would both die, and we both knew it. So there we stood. If either one of us moved, it would be all over. Death was a fraction of a second away for both of us—all it needed was one wrong move or just the blink of an eye. I can say he was one cool customer! Never taking his eyes off me, he said something out of the side of his mouth to his men, and they turned and went down the lane, out the door and were gone. Then he slowly turned, took a few steps and broke into a trot down the laneway. When he came to the door at the end, he stopped and looked back at me. He stood for a moment, then raised his hand in a goodbye salute. I raised my hand in a salute and goodbye to him. He went out the door and was gone. I started to breathe again!

I heard a noise behind me and I spun around, ready to shoot. A door opened in a small tool shed and out came Lambert and what remained of the thirteen men who had gone in there the night before. I just said, "Lambert, you bastard!" They looked like ghosts. All of their ammunition was gone and when it had run out, they had hid in the tool shed.

Wally Balfour told me forty-five years later that he was never so glad in all his life to see anyone as he was to see me that day. He had come out from somewhere, and what a story he had to tell! In the fight we had had the night before, he had gotten lost. He ended up in a small room and he heard Germans coming. In the room, there was a bench up against the wall and he crawled under it. Two Germans came into the room. It was pitch-black, so they lit a candle and sat down at a table and talked for a while before they left. He had not budged until I came. When he heard us talking, he came out.

The "D" Coy. men finally came around the corner and only then did they know at last why I was in there. I led the company out of the factory, and when we got back over the bridge we sent for the "A" Coy. jeep. When it arrived, we all piled in and went back into Bergen. Of the thirteen men who had been in that fight, only eight of us were left, but remarkably, we thirteen had inflicted heavy casualties on the enemy, which numbered twenty-seven in all.

The Germans were shelling the town with heavy mortars when I walked up the street. There were shells landing all around me. It was now October 29, and with the sickness I had had since the 20th, I was all done in again. This battle had lasted more than seventeen hours, and I was sick to begin with. I paid no attention to the shells—I was just in shock. I came to a door in a house. How I got there, I don't know. I just went. All of these houses looked the very same. I opened the door and walked in and went down into the basement. It turned out to be the house of Professor Luijten, where we had interrogated the Dutch underground man the night before. Luijten, his wife and nine-year-old Hans were in the basement. A shell had just hit the roof of the house, and he asked me if they should leave the house and go somewhere else. I said, "No, those shells won't hurt you down here. They're highly explosive and explode on impact. They're coming almost straight down and they won't get to the basement." There was a window well about two feet long and a foot wide. A shell would have had to make a direct hit on it to do any harm to the basement occupants.

I sat down on the bed in front of the window. They took my clothes off me and put me in bed and I went to sleep. From that time, October 29, until about three o'clock on November 7, I have no recollection of anything. I do remember that on November 7, Owen Borthwick, a new platoon officer of a new No. 8 Plt., gave me orders to bring the platoon to a small town by the name of Engelen on the River Maas. I was to have them there and meet him just as it got dark on November 8. I had now been in the fighting for three months, and

I had led the platoon myself, without help, for a little over two months, and I had never been out for a rest. I was the last man left who had come into France with "A" Coy. who had not been out.

On the first day of November, the city of Bergen-op-Zoom had a big celebration. The regiment supplied the food and the girls in the town waited on the tables. After the supper, they had a big dance. I was sick and asleep in bed at the Luijtens' house. I learned about the party forty years later on a visit to Bergen-op-Zoom. In 1984 when I went back to Bergen, we went into the municipal chambers of the town hall. A girl came out of the burgomaster's office asking for Sergeant Kipp. When I was pointed out to her, she came to me and gave me a piece of paper with a telephone number on it and told me to call that number. That night, I gave it to my host for the visit and he called the number. It was the phone number of Mr. Luijten. For forty years, he had been trying to find me. They had seen my name on a list of Canadian veterans who were visiting Holland. Arrangements were made to meet him and his son, Hans, the nine-year-old boy of 1944.

The next morning, we arrived at a café at the appointed time. A few minutes later, in came an old man. He stopped inside the door and, in a very strong voice, said, "Is Sergeant Kipp here?" He was a fine old gentleman, now eighty-nine years old. He asked me if he could have me as his guest for the rest of the day and I was turned over to him.

They took me back to the house and into the basement where he had been living in 1944. He related to me how I had come back to his house after the battle, looking very wan and as if I had been to hell and back. He told me how he and his wife, now deceased, had undressed me and put me to bed. I was very sick, but I had told them to wake me in six hours as I had to go. They could not wake me, so they called for Lambert to come, but Lambert told them to leave me alone and let me sleep. I slept for more than forty hours. He apologized for not having had any hot water to give me a bath. I have no recollection of leaving his house at that time.

We also talked of sitting on the basement steps and drinking a toast on the night of October 28, 1944. He said I was the coolest customer he had ever met. I told him I never saw the young corporal again, so I had always assumed he was killed that night. Mr. Luijten recalled with a chuckle how the like-minded young corporal and I, when answering his question as to why our nerves were so steady on that night, had instantaneously and fervently proclaimed our pride and love of country when we had answered in perfect unison, "Because we are Canadians." It was an image he had carried with him for forty years, an image made all the more poignant because one lived—and one died. He never forgot it, and neither have I.

18

ON THE RIVER MAAS

I HAVE NO RECOLLECTION of events from the time I was put to
bed by Mr and Mrs. Luijten on October 29 until about November
5, at which time I had obviously rejoined my regiment. I have no recollection of waking up, talking to the Luijtens, leaving their home or
even of rejoining my regiment. There had not been a No. 8 Plt. since
the battle on October 22. When I returned, a new No. 8 Plt. had been
organized. Since Lambert knew that I was in very bad condition, a
new platoon officer was sent to command it, and I was second-in-
command. The platoon was made up mostly of men from "A" Coy.
who had been wounded and had now returned to the regiment.
When they learned that I was still there, most of them had asked to
come to my platoon and go with me. We were now entering a
different kind of war. The Canadian line stretched along the south
side of the river, and at that time, it looked as if we would spend the
winter there. It was much easier: sleep in the daytime; patrol at night.
During this time, I caught up on a lot of rest and regained much of
my health.

Whatever had happened to me on October 22 I put right out of
my mind, and as I didn't actually know what had happened, I refused
to face up to it or to even think about it. It was not until 1984 that I
started to think about it and try to find out what, indeed, had happened. In the regiment history book were all the dates, and I did

finally put it all together. All of these years I knew about it on some level, but it was more than I could acknowledge. I know now that it was the beginning of the heart trouble that I have had for the rest of my life.

On the evening of November 7, our platoon officer, Borthwick, came to me and said he was leaving on a reconnaissance. The next night, I was to bring the platoon to a small town on the River Maas and meet him just as it got dark.

Our TCVs pulled into Engelen just at dark. I jumped out and Borthwick was there waiting for me. He had been the regimental intelligence officer, and this was the first platoon he had commanded. He was very energetic and eager for the work, but he did have a lot to learn. I got the men out of the TCVs and ready to move to our position, which was in a farmhouse about halfway between Engelen and a small village named Bokhoven.

He led off to the west side of Engelen and up to the river, with me right behind him. We had not gone far before I got the impression that something was not right. I could feel it. I tapped Borthwick on the shoulder and stopped him. I said, "Are we in the right place?" He assured me that we were, and on we went. In just a few minutes more, I knew we were wrong. We were someplace where we should not be. Again I stopped him and said, "This is not right." This time, he stopped to think about it. It was very dark and he was not used to these things. He said, "Wait here. I'll go back and have a look." In about ten minutes, he was back and said he had missed a turn and we were in the wrong place. He was taking us into a minefield and out in full view of the Germans. We turned around and went back. Soon after, we were settled into the farmhouse and would be there for several days. After we got there, Borthwick went back to Engelen and I was left in charge of the platoon, so I went outside to look around. We were sitting right up on top of the dyke, but that was about all I could see at the time. I put a guard out and the rest of us went to sleep. I took the last stand as I wanted to be out there at daylight.

Finally, at daylight, I got a look at our position. Normally, at this spot the River Maas was only about 30 or 40 yards wide. The River Maas and the Waal River are actually the same river. To the north of us about half a mile was the Waal River, a big river. Where we were was what was called the Old Maas, which was not much more than a canal. But now, the Germans had flooded all of this land and the Old Maas was about 500 yards wide and about 10 or 12 feet above normal. Right across the river was a town held by the Germans. A high dyke ran east from the town to an island, Fort Crevecoeur, and beyond that, to a big bridge across the Waal River. It had been blown apart by the Germans to stop us from crossing the river. When it became daylight, I sat out beside the house and watched the Germans moving around on their side of the river. Some men were dispatched back to Engelen to bring up our breakfast. At noon, the utensils were sent back by other men, and so on until suppertime. Then in the morning, our supper utensils would be sent back. I looked the house all over and found freshly canned fruit in the basement, so we had a good dessert with our meals. This was the farmhouse of the Kusten family, with whom I became very good friends later. Although this was their farm, they were now living in Engelen.

Later in the morning, Borthwick came back up to the house to look around and we went over the position thoroughly. Between our house and Engelen was another house and barn, and we decided to look the other house over, too, so back we went. We checked the main floor and the basement first. It was a very small house and I said I would go upstairs. I put one foot on the first step and started for the second step, but I did not do it. The old, cold chills went up my back and I could feel the danger. I backed down and said, "Come on, let's get outta here." Later, Borthwick sent our engineers to look it over and they found the second step to the upstairs was booby-trapped. If I had stepped on it, I probably would have been killed. But once again, something had saved me. For the next few days, we had a good war—just sleep and more sleep. Then we changed places with one of the other platoons and went back to Engelen for a few days.

My platoon moved into a house with the Kusten family: a mother, three daughters fifteen to eighteen years old, and a six-year-old boy named Peter. The youngest girl, fifteen-year-old Tony, had taught herself to speak English just so she could talk to us. The other girls' names I have forgotten. Tony was just a child, but she and I became very good friends. She used to carry soup to the old and sick towns-folk, who were put in a house by themselves. I would go with her every day. With her as an interpreter, I got to know some of the people in the town. I had my platoon headquarters in the house next to the Kustens. Once again, for a while, we had a very good life, and I did recover some more of my health.

The weather was changing, growing cold and freezing at night. We stayed in or around Engelen pretty well all through November. It was at this time that one of our platoons, No. 7 Plt., I think, noticed lights at night coming from the German position on Crevecoeur. They watched for several nights and then they saw lights from a house right beside them just a couple of doors away. A signals man was sent up to read the lights, and they caught a Dutchman and his German wife and seven kids sending messages to the Germans. They were sent to an internment camp, but I don't know what they did with them later.

When the Canadians started to get close to this one town, the Dutch people were afraid of getting caught in the fighting. The Germans put a big bomb under the church and then told all the people to go in the church, assuring them they would be safe there. Once they got as many of the people into the church as they could, they blew up the church and killed them all. In that town was a padre whom we got to know quite well. He would come to Engelen a couple of times a day just to thank the Canadians and ask what he could do for us. He did become a nuisance. In the Lincoln and Welland Regiment there was a word for anyone who was a nuisance. The regiment had two brothers from North Bay, Ontario, by the name of Buckley—good men, but wild as colts. They always kept things stirred up. To Lambert, they were almost a nuisance. One day when I was talking to Lambert, the padre came in. Lambert always had a name for things, and after the padre left, Lambert didn't know what name he could put on him, so he said to me, "He's a Buckley." That was the first time that name was used to describe a nuisance, and from then on, everyone who was a nuisance was a Buckley. This name became famous in the lore of the Lincoln and Welland Regiment.

Eventually, two platoons, No. 7 and No. 8 Plts., were sent to the town of Bokhoven. No. 8 Plt. was on the right front of the town on the bank of the river, while No. 7 Plt. was on the west side. Our job was to patrol from Bokhoven to Engelen, while the No. 7 patrolled to the west of Bokhoven. It was really cold. The wind and snow came right up the river off the North Sea. We lived in the basements of the houses and stayed out of sight in the daylight. If the Germans saw us, they fired at us with machine guns and mortars. At night, we put out two-man listening posts. I always checked mine twice in the night. I never sent men out one at a time, but I always went out alone. I told them that if I ever had to run from the Germans, I would not have to wait for someone else. And I never put the men in the same spot twice.

One night, it was freezing cold. The Germans were crossing the river somewhere between Bokhoven and the Argyll and Sutherland Regiment. The top brass miles behind the lines picked out a spot at the edge of Bokhoven and said, "There's where they're coming." On that night, we were ordered to watch that spot. I was to take three men, go out and stay until two o'clock. Bill Thorne was then supposed to bring out three men and change places with us. As soon as it was dark, I went out. It was so dark the men had to hang onto each other so they wouldn't get lost. Since there were mines in the area, we had to walk a path between two gateposts. I had never been out there before. We went through backyards and gardens until we thought we had gone far enough, then we turned north and hoped we were in the right place. I put my arms out straight from my sides and walked directly between the two posts. When I hit a post on each side with my arms, we lay down, two men on each side of the path. And froze! The wind and snow just howled through there, and by two o'clock, we could hardly move. Thorne did not come. We stayed until three o'clock and then went back into town. When we got there, I sent the men on alone and I went to find Thorne. He and his men were all in a house asleep. I woke them all up, then went to my own bed, and the Germans stayed home.

One day, two strangers came to the house where we were staying. No. 8 Plt. had now been moved to the west side of town and our territory was from the town of Bokhoven to where the Argyll Regiment was, about half a mile down the river. It was just bare, flat country. These two men said they were scouts sent out by the brigadier of our brigade. They wanted to stay with us, have something to eat and have a sleep, so they stayed all morning. In the afternoon, they prepared to move out and said they were going to contact the Argylls. I told them, "Don't go out there. You'll never make it." They just laughed at me. They said they had been picked as brigade scouts because they knew their job, and if anyone could do it, they could. They would not listen. It always seemed to be a habit for men who were way back behind the front lines to come up and assume they knew more than the men in the front. We watched as they headed out to the river about half past two. After they had gone only about 200 yards, we watched, too, as the Germans came out and manned their machine guns and started to fire. The two scouts hit the ground in a hail of bullets. They tried to get up and come back in, but they couldn't make it because the Germans fired every time they moved. They called for us to come and help them, but there was nothing we could do. It was a very cold day, and they had to stay out there until it got dark. By that time, they had decided they wouldn't go to the Argylls. They had had enough of this kind of war. We laughed at them; they weren't as smart as they thought they were.

On the night of November 16, "B" Coy. sent out a patrol in three boats to cross the Maas and get a prisoner. One boat was swept downstream but landed on the north shore. They couldn't find anyone, so they returned to our side of the river and went home. The other two boats crossed the river twice. They also landed on the north side both times, but couldn't orient themselves or find anyone. They tried it a third time, but this time one of them stepped on a mine, killing one man and wounding two others. Lieutenant Cartmel was badly wounded and they could not get him back in the boat, so they put him in the icy river and towed him.

On November 24, we were sent back to a town called Saint-Michielsgestel, which was to be our winter quarters. We were in a monastery. It looked like a good place to spend the winter. We were there until December 4. We had a good time—we had movies, a dance one night, and another night even put on a live show. Daytime was spent in training and sleeping.

On December 4, we went back to the River Maas and my platoon was sent back to Bokhoven. On the night of December 8, Sergeant Winterford took a man by the name of Brown and went on a patrol into Fort Crevecoeur, held by the Germans. Brown was a good man, but without glasses he was as blind as a bat. And he had lost his glasses. The fort was on an island and they came to a small stream or ditch with a plank across it. Winterford could see and he jumped across. Brown couldn't see, so he stepped on the plank. It was a booby trap and it blew his leg off. Winterford could not get him out, so he took him into a house and hid him, then came back to Engelen. By the time Winterford got there, it was too late to return for Brown. The next night, Winterford took a patrol back into Crevecoeur and brought him out on a stretcher. They had a jeep waiting to take him to the hospital. They put him on top of the jeep and started down the road along the dyke right where Borthwick had gotten lost the first night we came into Engelen. A patrol just going out met the jeep with Brown in it. The jeep ran over a mine and killed two men. One man died later from his wounds and five other men were wounded. After the war was over, I met Brown in a bar in London, Ontario. He was very bitter over it and I did not blame him. Why an almost blind man was sent on a patrol, I don't know.

On the night of December 12, two patrols were sent across the river. One patrol from "C" Coy. got across but was unable to find any Germans, so they came back. When the other patrol from "B" Coy. reached the middle of the river, their boat overturned and all were drowned but one. How he got back, I never knew.

All this time that I was in Bokhoven, I did not know that these things were going on. On December 13, Lambert sent for me and I went back to Engelen where he was. He did not tell me about all the patrols across the river that had failed. He just said, "Tonight, 'A' Coy. is going to send a patrol across the river. You pick any six men from the company that you want. You are going across." The platoon officer from No. 9 Plt., whose name was Hume, would be in charge of the patrol. We would go in two boats. He would go first and set up a firm base. I would take the second boat and leave five minutes behind him. I was to take my men through Hume's position and go into the town and get a prisoner. I picked the five best men in the company, with Jim Alexander as my second. At the appointed time, I brought my men to where the boats were. Hume was just getting into his boat. I got there in time to see him shove off. It was a pitch-dark night, and on the water it was black. Our boat was pushed over the dyke and into the water. The Germans could hear us and the sky was full of tracer ammunition. The whole sky was lit up. I counted my men as they went into the boat—Jim first and me last. I grabbed a paddle and sat down. My job was to steer the boat. We shoved off. The current was wild, but I was ready for it. I shoved my paddle down deep and kept the boat headed straight across the river. It did not seem very long before I felt a bump and we were on the north shore in German territory. Jim jumped out, followed by the rest of us.

There was a hedge about 15 yards from the river, so we dragged the boat behind that and hid it. I left two men to watch the boat and started inland. Up ahead was a road that went into town. There was a crooked place in the road. This was where I was to meet Hume. To get there, we had to cross a low spot. This low spot had filled with water and frozen on top, then all the water had run out, leaving a big spot of white ice just like glass. There was no way around; we had to cross it. I stepped on it. *Crash!* The ice broke through, and then, just like glass, the pieces tinkled down into a pile. Every step—*crash, tinkle, crash, tinkle.* What a racket! On a cold winter night, the Germans could hear every step I took. And I guess they did. Up until that time, they had been doing a lot of shooting, but it was over our heads. Now the shooting stopped. They just sat down and kept quiet. We made our way up to the road to the spot where we were to meet Hume. He was not there, so we sat down to wait for him. He should not be far away. I had had no trouble getting there; in fact, it was quite easy.

We waited, and then I thought, "Maybe we're in the wrong place." We followed the road back and found no one. We went up the road to the edge of town—no one. We went back to the crook in the road and waited. It soon became apparent that he was not coming. I knew that all the Germans were in the far west end of the town, as I had watched them for a month. I made up my mind I was not going to take my men into town like this. Down to the east about halfway to Crevecoeur, I knew there was a German machine gun. We would go down there and get him, but we could not find him in the dark. I am sure that we went right past him. We had to give that up, so we went back to the edge of town. Maybe the Germans would run a patrol past there, and we would grab the last man as they went past. We waited nearly all night. I was watching to see if the sun would soon be coming up. We would wait until the last minute.

It started to get light, so I said, "Come on, let's go." We went down the road on the run, but we had stayed almost too late. Before we got to our boat, the Germans saw us and ran for their guns. The two men at the boat saw us coming and started to drag the boat out. We grabbed it, shoved it in the water and jumped in. By now, the Germans were shooting at us. If we could go straight across the river, we would be all right, but the water had come up in the night. When I held the boat on a straight course, the water was so swift it came in over the side. We would have to angle our way across downstream.

We came to the south side—our side—but there was nowhere we could land, and we had to go farther down. It was a small boat and there were seven men in it. It sat low in the water. The water was about an inch below the gunwales of the boat. When the boat rocked, water came over the side. We were coming down the south side of the river looking for a place to land, but the dyke was too high. The Germans were shooting rifles, machine guns and mortars at us. We were all sitting as far down in the boat as we could. The bullets were all around us. The mortar shells were dropping around and behind us. We could hear them coming. They would hit the water and explode. The water would shoot 50 feet in the air, just like "Old Faithful" in Yellowstone Park. It was a wild ride—me screaming at the men, "Go! Go! Paddle, you bastards! Paddle!" and they did! In this way, we went about a half a mile down the river, right in front of the Germans and right past Bokhoven. Down there was low land. The bank of the river was about two and a half feet above water. I brought the boat in close, and Jim grabbed the rope and jumped out.

I held the stern of the boat in place with my paddle and away went the men in a hail of bullets. I dropped my paddle and scrambled out. Jim let go of the rope and the boat spun out into the river. The last we saw of it, it was still spinning in circles as it headed out to the North Sea.

It was about 100 yards to Bokhoven, and the men were running as fast as they could. I was bringing up the tail end, running as fast as I could. Why no one was hit, I don't know. When I got in amongst the houses to safety, the men were all there, laughing. The danger was over and we were back. I did not laugh very long, though; I was mad. We had had no trouble getting across the river. Why couldn't the others make it? Because of that, we had nearly lost our lives, and the whole thing was a failure.

We went back to our house. By now, we had a telephone back to Engelen. Art Winterford grabbed the phone and called Lambert to tell him we were back. We had been gone all night, and had already been reported as missing in action. The girl back at Army Headquarters who took the message that I was missing was Jean Love of Tillsonburg, a very good friend of mine. She told me of it after the war was over.

I was cold, tired and mad. I refused to talk to Lambert. I just went to bed. That afternoon, I went to Engelen to find out what had happened. The history book of the Lincoln and Welland Regiment tells a different story: "On the night of 13/14 of December, a patrol from 'A' Coy. under Lt. E.L. Hume crossed the river in search of a prisoner. Signal communications broke down and the patrol stayed on the north bank for four hours. At 1:45 on the 14th, the platoon commander reappeared with apologies for being absent so long and for being unable to find a prisoner." But this is what really happened. Hume's boat spun out into the river and he lost control and his bearings. They landed about 200 yards down the river from where they had started and on the same side. They got out their wireless set and reported that they were on the north shore. They would orient themselves and call back. They went up the river, and fifteen minutes after they had pushed off for the north shore, they walked right back to where Lambert was. They went back into Engelen and left us out there. Hume was given credit for leading a patrol across the river and I was not even mentioned.

Another patrol was sent to cross the river on the night of December 14. The history book says their boat leaked, so they had to turn back. The story told to me by the sergeant on that patrol was altogether different. They started out with an officer in charge of the patrol. They were carrying their boat and were told when they started that if the boat leaked, they were not to go. They decided the best thing to do was to put the boat in the water to see if it did leak. They came to a small pond of water and put the boat in to check. The officer was at the front of the boat. The men did not want to cross the river. Some of the men at the back of the boat used their steel helmets for dippers and poured water in the boat. The officer saw the water and announced that the boat leaked and that they could not cross the river. To make sure the boat did leak, another man took his Bren gun and fired a burst through the bottom of the boat. It leaked then.

The history book describes another patrol as running into a German patrol on the south side of the river. They did not. There were no Germans there. This is the story that was told to me at the time: The front half of the patrol got way ahead. The men at the back stopped and sat down. The men out in front came back after them. The men who had stopped heard someone coming and thought it was Germans. They opened fire on the sound and killed their own men who were coming back to look for them.

"A" Coy. was moved from Bokhoven back to Engelen and No. 8 Plt. took up residence with the Kusten family again. On December 20, I got word that men from the Army Service Corps had volunteered to take over our job on the River Maas and give us a rest. They came in the night and took over our position. The NCO in charge was an old friend of mine from Tillsonburg, Martin Purdy. But in the dark, I missed him. After the war was over, during a conversation with him, he told me of coming into Engelen and taking over positions from the Lincoln and Welland Regiment. We were both very surprised to learn he had taken over my position. On the morning of December 20, we moved into the monastery in Saint-Michielsgestel.

On December 16, a German officer by the name of von Rundstedt had led an attack in the Ardennes, and the battle that was to become the Battle of the Bulge was on. The Canadian army was to go in there and meet them, but by this time, as a fighting unit, the Canadian army was almost non-existent. We had had so many casualties and no reinforcements that there was no one to go. So the Americans were sent instead. There was much talk that we would all be sent back to England and train as an army of occupation, but the Canadian bigwigs would not stand for that. Canadians would stay until the war was over. They would now send the "zombies" (conscripts) over to reinforce the infantry—a trainload of ten thousand men headed for Halifax. When the train arrived, 80 per cent of them had deserted and were gone. A few did get overseas, where they did a very good job. On December 24, we were ordered out. We would take up a position in the town of Loon op Zand, about two miles north of Tilburg. Borthwick, of whom I had seen very little as a platoon officer, met us there. He led No. 8 Plt. to the north end of town and took us into a café, which would be our headquarters. He introduced me to the Van Heren family, proprietors of the café, and then told me to expect the Germans any time after the next day, December 25, Christmas Day. He then left me in charge.

19

LOON OP ZAND

THE VAN HEREN FAMILY consisted of the husband, whom we promptly called "Papa," Maria Van Heren, "Mama," Nellie Van Heren and Ria. Nellie was twenty-two years old and very pretty. She became like a sister to me. Ria was nine, and she, too, was like a younger sister. I had wonderful times with these people. They took me in and made me one of the family. Their place was home to me. As I was the platoon commander, I got special treatment. The rest of the men were bedded down on the floor of the café, which was a pool parlour and a bar, but I was given a bed upstairs in a small room that overlooked the main road where the Germans would come. I carried a Bren gun with me at all times. If I was in the house, the gun sat beside the living-room door where I could pick it up and go out either the front or the back door. At night, I kept it leaning against the head of my bed. There were only about ten or twelve men in No. 8 Plt. at that time and they were organized into two sections: one under Cpl. Jim Alexander, and the other under Cpl. E.P. Arnold. There were not any better men in the regiment than those two. Both had been wounded, Jim twice, and both had come back to my platoon. Borthwick was still the platoon officer, but he left everything up to me. He usually came around once a day; sometimes in the daytime and sometimes at night. He was still working in Headquarters Coy.

We organized patrols to go out at night. There was a German ammunition dump about two miles out in the woods and there were still Germans coming to it. The two sections took turns at night patrolling the road out to the dump and back. On Christmas Day, a turkey dinner was served in a big factory by the regiment officers and a party was put on for the kids of the town. One day, the sergeant major of the company, Connie Bastable, came to me and told me that he and the other company sergeants were living in a house down the street a little way. He wanted to know if I would come and spend some evenings with them. That night I went to see them, but I didn't stay very long. Bill Thorne and I promptly got into a fight. I jumped on him, and when he opened his mouth to holler, I shoved the muzzle of my .38 revolver down his throat. The rest of them jumped on me, hollering at me not to kill him. I told him if we were both still alive when the war ended, I would shoot him. And then I left, and I never went back. After the war was over, one of the men who was there that night, Ed MacPherson, spoke to me about it. He said, "Don't think too badly of Thorne. He was very jealous of you." I was far better trained than he was and had been promoted above him. That, he could not stand. He was one of the most hateful people I ever knew.

For recreation, they started to put on movies, and several times I took Nellie to see a movie. She tended bar most evenings. Her mother made it very plain that she wanted me to be in the bar to keep the men in order whenever Nellie was working. Other evenings, Borthwick and some of his friends came to the bar and we sat in the living room around the table and had a few drinks. Even Lambert came to the house some evenings for drinks. We had some good times there.

One day, Lambert was not around at all. That night about nine o'clock, he came into the café with some of the company officers. That day, he had been flown to England and presented with the Military Cross, a decoration for bravery, for leading the attack into the factory at Bergen. He had put in for a medal for me at that time, but they would not give me one, and he had gotten into a big fight over it. He said if I was not given a medal, then he would not accept his, but he was ordered to accept it. That night when he came in with his officers, he took his medal off his chest and tried to pin it on me. He said that was where it belonged. For my part of that battle, I was given no recognition whatsoever, even though I was the one who went back in and got our men out. "D" Coy. was given the recognition for the rescue.

On New Year's Day, I was sitting in the living room when I heard planes, and then shooting. I grabbed my Bren gun by the door and ran outside, looking up into the sky. There were three German fighter planes right overhead. I looked down the road and saw a Polish convoy out in front of us just going through the town. The planes circled to come back, and as I was preparing to get a shot at them, they abruptly turned and headed for Germany. Three Canadian fighter planes had come in after them, and the Germans were trying to get away. I watched as the Canadians shot down two of them, then chased the third and finally shot it down, too. They were the last German planes we saw for the rest of the war. The German air force was done. That particular day, a girl about thirteen years old was home sick from school and was lying on her bed with her bedroom window open. When the German planes fired, a bullet went through her window and killed her. That was their last attack over western Europe.

Now things started to change. Training started to pick up. One night after supper, Lambert came to me and said, "Arm yourself. You and I have a job to do." After dark, we got in the jeep and headed north out of Loon op Zand and drove to the town of Waspik. We went to a certain house and stopped. He said, "You stay here," and went into the house. It was a cold night in January and I waited for about two hours. By that time, I was nearly frozen, so I got out of the jeep and walked around the house. Behind the house was a small canal with a plank across it, and beyond that was an open field. I decided I would go for a good run to get warm and took off on the run. I had run about a quarter of a mile when I began to see a dyke on the skyline. At about the same time, I got that old feeling of danger. After all, I did not know what was up there, so I turned around and went back to the jeep. Lambert came out a few minutes later and we went back to Loon op Zand. I did not know it at the time, but I had just been up into the German territory where we would engage in one of the worst battles fought in western Europe during the war.

A couple of days later, I got orders that I was to report to a certain house in the southern part of town that night. When I arrived, six or eight men were already there. And then we got the story. On an island up in the River Maas, the island where I had gone for my run, was the last German stronghold south of the river. At the time of the Battle of the Bulge, the Germans were going to use this island to make a drive south to Tilburg. Along with another drive coming from the east, they would meet at Tilburg and catch the Canadian army in a trap. The Battle of the Bulge was over now, but the top brass decreed that the island was to be taken. This was one of the most unnecessary battles of the war.

This was the story as it was told to us. The Polish Division was to take the island, which was held by somewhere around 175 to 200 German paratroopers—some of the same men we had fought at Bergen-op-Zoom. The Poles had attacked the island about a week and a half before but had been driven back with heavy losses. A British commando regiment was then sent in to show us all how it was done. They were also beaten back, and lost a lot of men and equipment. The island now meant nothing to the Germans, or, for that matter, to us. But the Germans meant to hold it. This time, the Lincoln and Welland Regiment was ordered to take the island. We would take it and turn it over to the Polish to hold. This was *big*, and all very secret. We were told at that meeting not to talk with anyone about it. Those at the meeting were the only men in the regiment who were to know about the plan.

Now the regiment went into intensive training for this battle. It was also brought up to nearly full strength, something which it had not been since we landed in France. New officers and new men. As for me, I was once again sick and exhausted. Although I didn't know it at the time, I was undergoing an attack of arteriosclerotic heart disease. I was showing all the signs of exhaustion. I was very pale. I had lost a lot of weight, and was now nothing but skin and bones. I could not stand up straight—my back was bent, my shoulders hunched over and my neck stuck out. My chest was sore, I was very short of breath, and my nerves were once again at the breaking point. I had very little feeling for anything and a great fear of disaster. Something terrible was going to happen. I had given up all hope of surviving the war and I was living in a world of my own. I was experiencing what is known as "battle numbness." A new platoon officer was sent to take over No. 8 Plt. and I was called to the company office to meet him. I only met him once. I do not, and never did, know his name. He said he wanted to meet the platoon, so I said I would assemble them and introduce him to the men. I called them out on parade and introduced him. He was brand new. He had left Canada just two weeks before and had no idea what war was about. He gave the men a pep talk about what he would expect of them. He then ordered me to dismiss the men and said he had some words he wanted to say to me, so I dismissed the men and went to him. He proceeded to dress me down. He told me that I was a disgrace to the regiment. He said that my neck stuck out and I looked like a turkey. I was to stand up straight—if I was going to be a sergeant, I was to look like one. I was thunderstruck! I knew I was in bad condition, but I was there doing my job. I had fought in an infantry platoon for six straight months. In all that time, I had been out one week for a rest at Saint-Michielsgestel. I had been through shell shock at least three times. At that time, I had been wounded eight different times; all slight wounds and I was never evacuated.

My first impulse was to go to Lambert and tell him I would not have that officer in my platoon, but then I thought, "This man will take care of himself." He went to Lambert and complained about me. Lambert immediately ordered him to go to his quarters and told him to stay there until further notice. He was kicked out of the regiment and sent back to the holding unit. It probably saved his life. But that was the end of me. It knocked the fight right out of me. *I was done.* The next day I walked down the street of Loon op Zand. I hardly knew what I was doing. Lambert saw me, came over and started walking down the street with me. Then he said, "I don't know what to do with you. I have put you in for a promotion to lieutenant, but the higher-ups say no, the Canadian army already has more officers than they need." It was a very great honour to be put in for a promotion such as this. It only happened about twice all through the war and it was something to be very proud of. I thanked him and said, "Don't worry. I'm all through." Subconsciously, I knew I would not go to the island of Kapelsche Veer, the island we were to attack. I could not face another attack. I truly believe I would have shot myself to end it all. I went back to the café. That afternoon, the company runner came to me and told me I was to pack my things and move. I was to be transferred to Support Coy., where I would have an easy job. It was just six months since I had come into France. I knew then what a condemned man on death row feels like when he gets a reprieve. I had just got one.

I moved down to the Support Coy. position at the south end of the town. I was told to find a place to stay until it was decided where I would go. Every officer in the company came to me and asked me to go to his platoon. I thanked them and said I would wait and see where I was sent. For the time being, I just wanted to be alone. There was a big empty house there, the people who owned it having moved to a safer place. I moved into it all alone, locked all the doors and made my bed on the floor. I had been there several days when the runner came one day about four o'clock and told me I had been assigned to No. 5 Plt., the anti-tank platoon. I was to be the platoon sergeant. I moved into their place, which was another café.

That night, I made my bed on a pool table and about half past nine, we all went to bed. We had just gotten there when we heard a buzz bomb being fired across the Waal River a few miles north of us. Sometimes, these things would go wild. We watched them being fired every day, and every once in a while, they just went out of control, and no one knew where they would go or what they would do. Instead of going up in the air, this one stayed down low. We could hear it coming—the motors on it shook the whole town. Then the motor shut off, and we knew it was coming down. We all collectively stopped breathing. And then out in front of us, there was a tremendous explosion. We all started to breathe again. Some of the men got out of bed and went outside to look. It had been close. When they came back, they said it had hit a big empty house about 80 yards from the café. It was the very same house I had just moved out of at four o'clock that day. All that was left was a big hole in the ground. Once again, something or someone had intervened to save my life.

The training continued with ever-increasing urgency. This was to be a big show. Monte Cassino in Italy was put on with a brigade much larger than a regiment, but for this show, our one regiment would get more support than was used at Cassino. The support for this could be termed as massive. This island was to be taken at all costs.

A sixty-man flotilla of fifteen canoes would go down the river after dark and land at the small harbour on the bank of the river. They were sent out to an old airfield to train. On one of the canals there, I was put in charge of a party that was to stay and guard the canoes. I was not to leave them and no one else was to get in to see them, in other words, no unauthorized person. It was a good spot to train not only the canoe party but also the infantry companies for the assault up the dyke on the island.

One day, one of the companies came out for a practice. I sent the men of my party out of the airplane hangar because, in this practice attack, they would be using live ammo. As there were Dutch civilians around, I did not want to leave the building. They could very well be Germans in civilian clothes, so I stayed in the hangar. The infantrymen were given orders they were not to shoot at the building, and the practice got under way. Those men shot at everything. The bullets came right through and bounced all over. It was almost like a hail storm. I crawled under a Bren gun carrier and stayed there. Everything in the place was riddled with bullet holes, and I thought I was going to be riddled, too. We stayed in that hangar for a week. It was the middle of January during the coldest winter on record in Holland. We had put up a canvas cover in one corner of the hangar. For heat, we cut the top off a 5-gallon can, filled it with gas and set it on fire. We got as much smoke as we got heat, and by the end of the week, all one could see of us was our eyes. We were just covered with soot. After our week at the airport, we went back to Loon op Zand, where we spent our time with more training. At night, we went out and practised manhandling 6-pounder anti-tank guns, moving them into position and then out again—very hard work, but something that got easier with practice. Then the day of the attack was set.

On the night of January 25, 1945, the men were told, "We go tonight, and attack at daybreak." That night, two of my men from No. 8 Plt. came to see me. They asked me to come back and lead the platoon. This was going to be a bad one and they had never gone into battle without me. When I had left No. 8 Plt., Borthwick had gone back and taken over as platoon commander. He was a good man and officer, but in all this time he had never led a platoon into battle. I had been in battle for six months with "A" Coy., and for four of those months, I had led No. 8 Plt., and now they were going in without me. I did not know what to say. Now that I was with No. 5 Plt., I would have a job in support. I was very tempted; I very nearly said, "Yes, I'll be there." I could not say no, so I said, "I'll think about it." But the decision was taken out of my hands. Before morning, I was given orders that I was to be in charge of getting the wounded out. In the middle of the night, the men left in their TCVs to take up positions for the attack. I moved up to Waspik so I would be ready in the morning. The men were told the fight would be over and they would be back in Loon op Zand for breakfast. The actual battle should take less than an hour.

20

KAPELSCHE VEER

KAPELSCHE VEER WAS a small harbour on the north side of an island, which was 6,000 yards long and 1,700 yards across at its widest point. The island was formed by the River Maas on the north and the Oude Maasje, meaning Old Little Maas, on the south. There was a dyke about 300 yards in from the Maas, and the Germans were dug in on the north side of the dyke. Their headquarters was a farmhouse situated on the dyke, with tunnels running out of the basement. The harbour came right into the house. The island was held by 120 to 150 men of the 10th and 17th Paratroop Regiments. The Germans had been informed that we were coming and on the night of January 25, they had been reinforced by another 150 men.

By 7:30 A.M. on the morning of January 26, the men were in position, ready to attack. We all knew this was going to be a bad one. My old platoon commander and friend, Lieutenant Armstrong, said, just before they pushed off, "This will be my last one." The men thought he meant he was going on leave when he came back. "A" Coy. was mounted in TCVs or a type of amphibious TCVs called water buffaloes. Their job was to take the farmhouse. "C" Coy. would then pass through and meet up with "B" Coy. coming in from the west. A smoke company would lay down a smokescreen for our men to go through. The smoke went down; the water buffaloes went in; and "A" Coy. was on the way. As they came up out of the Oude Maasje onto the island, a man with a Bren gun killed two Germans in a machine gun nest on the dyke. The men poured out of the buffaloes and disappeared into the smoke on the run. I saw them go when I came down to see about getting the wounded out. In about two minutes, most of "A" Coy., the company I had just been transferred from, was wiped out. Even if there was a thick cloud of smoke over the whole island, the Germans could still shoot through it. "A" Coy. raced down the top of the dyke, fighting and killing as they went. They bayonetted the Germans in their slit trenches; they threw in grenades, they jumped on them and fought hand-to-hand. A German had one of our men to the ground. The man was fighting for his life. Just as the German was about to put a knife into him, another one of our men put his rifle to the German's head and blew it off. They killed as they went, but now there were only a few left. "C" Coy. swept through right into "A" Coy. and they were wiped out, too. All of their officers were either killed or wounded.

Lambert and two men had gotten through it all and managed to get way out in front. They had not only reached the objective, they had actually gotten inside the house. The Germans came up out of the tunnels, throwing grenades. The two men managed to escape and get away, but Lambert was killed. A grenade exploded between his legs, and he went down, presumably dead. When they came out, they told me about getting into the house. The wounded men were now streaming back. Major Dandy of "C" Coy. was one of them, and he gave the order to get out. The men all came back to where I was taking them out with a boat. We lifted the wounded in until we had a boatload, then paddled the boat across and unloaded where ambulances were waiting. There was no kind of order—the men came in crawling, hobbling, carrying or being carried. We were swamped with them. I ordered them to stay back and not bunch up, and not to bring the wounded in until we could manage them. One man from "A" Coy. came back in a state of shock. He was laughing as he told me, "I just got mine. I'm on my way home." He had dropped a grenade into a slit trench with two Germans in it, and in the excitement, he jumped in on top of it. It blew both of his feet to pieces. He was about a foot shorter when he came out than when he went in. I bet it was a shock when he came out of it. Five men came in and stood in a circle. I hollered, "Don't bunch up," but it was too late. The Germans only put one shell on my position, but it came down right into this circle of men. It killed four of them and very seriously wounded a fifth, taking out one of his eyes. After the war, he was a bartender in one of the hotels in London, Ontario.

I have no idea how long it took us to clear everyone out of there, but eventually I was the only one left. I was soaking wet, as I had been in and out of the canal several times. I was told all of our men were out, but I had to make sure. I tied up the boat and went down the dyke past all of the dead. As I got near the house, I could see movement. I would have to go and see what it was. It turned out to be four "C" Coy. men and one German prisoner. One of the "C" Coy. men was very badly wounded and they were carrying him out on a stretcher. The German was the only prisoner taken and he said he was very lucky to be alive. And he was. It was very cold—down around zero—and he was wearing Dutch wooden shoes with no socks. He said it was the only way he could keep his feet from freezing. I asked them if there were any more men in there and they said no. They said Lambert was dead, but I wanted to go back after him. I got to within 60 yards of the house, but I could see no movement there and our artillery had started to shell it. Maybe I could have made it in, maybe not. It only took our artillery a few minutes to demolish the house completely. I knew there would be no one alive in there now.

I was alone on the island. The best thing to do was to get out. When I got back to the boat, the "C" Coy. men had gone across, but they had left a rope for me to pull the boat back. I retrieved the boat and went back and into the town of Capelle. I was ordered to go to Waspik and rejoin my platoon. My shoes were full of water and I was wet right up to my neck. The snow was a foot and a half deep. I knew if I went to Waspik in that condition, I would freeze, so I said I would go when I got some dry clothes. I got a Bren gun carrier and went back to Loon op Zand and got dry clothes. I then returned to Waspik and went up on the dyke with No. 5 Plt. "A" Coy., "C" Coy. and most of "B" Coy. were either dead or wounded. There may have been only thirty or forty men left. "B" Coy. was bogged down, and "D" Coy. and Support Coy. had been ordered in along with what few men were left from "A" and "C." The Germans had counterattacked and killed a lot more of them. As the Canadians went up the dyke, the Germans came up out of holes behind them and shot them. They said the Germans came in waves and went right through them. I found Bill Thorne with a bullet hole right in his forehead. He was dead. I always said it had saved me the trouble.

One of our men, Captain Dickie, had been taken prisoner. As the Germans were taking him away, his German guard kept poking him in the ribs with a bayonet. Dickie hauled off and punched him, so the German shot him.

After I had found my men, I went for a walk up the dyke to try to find out what was going on, and I came into "D" Coy.'s position. There, sitting on the side of the dyke, was Jim Bell. Everything was quiet, so I sat down beside him and we spent the afternoon talking.

There was a big bustle going on. We had only a few men left. All of Support Coy. was ordered in, and most of Headquarters Coy., too—clerks, cooks, drivers and everyone. Some of these men had no idea how to handle a rifle. Even though they had been in the army for several years, they had never been trained to fight. The "A" Coy. clerk was handed a rifle and told to get up there. He said he had never fired a gun in his life. Regiment Sergeant Major Cox, whose job it was to make sure ammunition and weapons got to the front, disappeared. Later, after the battle was all over, he was picked up in a bar miles behind the front line. After the war was over, he came to the reunion—walked in as big as life. But he was told in no uncertain terms that he was not welcome and he never came back.

That night, the night of January 26, I went back to my platoon, took up a position with the men and settled in. We were dug in on the south side of the dyke, and the Germans were on the north side. We could hear them talking, and they could hear us. If we had reached over the top of the dyke, we could have held hands. The snow was a foot deep and it was sub-zero weather. To keep warm, we dug holes and trenches in the side of the dyke. Some men froze their hands and feet and had to be evacuated. Up at the east end of our line, the rifle company carried on skirmishes with the Germans all night. They attacked the Germans, and the Germans attacked them.

On the morning of January 26, when the attack had begun, the boat party took to the water. They were to be at the harbour when the main attack started. The previous night had been very cold and some of the Argylls were there to help them get away. The water on the river had started to freeze, which would stop the canoes if the ice was heavy enough. So the Argylls had spent most of the night lighting and sending fire pots down the river to keep it from freezing. These were pots filled with gas, set on fire and shoved out into the river. I talked to one of the Argylls later who had been out all night lighting fire pots. He said it was the worst night of his life, but they did do a good job. The Germans were ready though. They had machine guns on the north bank of the river. As soon as the canoes took off, they came under fire. Men were killed, men were wounded, boats were upset and men were drowned. They were dressed in white snowsuits and all bundled up. As soon as they hit the water, they had no chance. It was dark and they got separated. Any boat that could make it across landed on the shore between the river and the Germans on the dyke. Some got through, but both Germans and others were killed trying. That whole exercise was a disaster.

We had lost a lot of men, and the Canadian army had no replacements for these men. They went into army depots and sent out men who had never been trained. I talked to one who had been a cook. They were good men, but had no idea what to do. A bunch of them came in and they were put out amongst the regular men. The idea was that we could keep an eye on them. I recall one who was just a few feet from where I was. He moved in and said he wanted to see a German. Before anyone could stop him, he raised his head up over the dyke, and a German shot him right between the eyes from about four feet away. Another one could hear Germans talking on the other side of the dyke, so he threw over a grenade, but did not know enough to pull the pin. A German picked it up, pulled the pin, then reached up and dropped it over the dyke on our side. It killed the man who had thrown it. A tank tried to get in close to help us. It was a new officer in the tank and he was standing up with his head out of the turret. A German put his rifle up over the dyke, fired over our heads, and shot and killed the officer. It was his first and last trip.

Several days passed by with the forward platoons inching ahead, taking out Germans one slit trench at a time, sometimes digging their way forward to get close enough to toss a grenade in on the Germans in the next slit trench. On the morning of January 26, when "B" Coy. had made their attack, they had several flame-throwers mounted on Bren gun carriers. I don't know what happened to the rest of them, but one of them was stuck at my position. The right track was on solid ground, but the left track had broken through the frost and it was in a big hole. There were only a few men there who knew how to operate these flame-throwers and I was one of them. I looked it all over and wondered if I could get it out. If I could, I would take it up to "D" Coy. and use it. It was loaded with 40 gallons of oil. I started the motor, but it wouldn't budge. The left track was sitting in water and it just kept going around without getting a hold on anything, so I left it. In the morning when everything around it was frozen solid, I tried again. I tried to back it up—no go. I tried to swing it in a circle and get it out that way—almost, but not quite. I was not in very good condition when I came up there to begin with, and lack of sleep was only making things worse. Plus, digging holes all night to keep warm was hard work. Several men were dug in maybe 40 yards from the dyke. There was a canal running from the dyke back to the town of Waspik, and these slit trenches were back beside it just behind the flame-thrower. My chest was getting sore again and I was very light-headed. I moved off the dyke and into an empty slit trench about three feet deep. I did not have a blanket, but at night I got down in the hole where it was warmer, and I could sleep and not freeze. About 10 feet from my hole was another one occupied by a man named Gunner Jones. Gunner had a .50-calibre machine gun set up there.

On the afternoon of January 28, I was up on the dyke watching across the river and I could see a column of men heading towards the river. They were all dressed in white snowsuits. When this battle had started, all of our infantrymen were wearing white snowsuits. The Germans came down to the river and put boats in the water. There must have been about sixty to eighty men. We had an artillery spotter with us who could call down artillery on all of our fronts, so I went to him and pointed the Germans out to him. They were on the water now and coming across the river, but he would not call down fire on them. He said, "They're Canadians. They're wearing white snow-suits." I said, "There are no Canadians on the north side of the river." We argued, but he would not listen, so I got a Bren gun and went down the dyke about 50 yards past our position and tried to fire on the Germans. But they were too far away and I couldn't reach them. I watched them come across the river, march the 300 yards to the dyke, and then up onto the dyke right towards us. About 100 yards from where I was, there was a curve in the dyke. They were out of sight now, but once they came around that curve, they would be right on top of us. I ran back to where my men were and got two men, Joe Monaghan and a man named Foreman. We took grenades and my Bren gun and ran to meet the Germans. They were coming up the north side of the dyke and we were going down the south side. We went about 200 yards past the curve in the dyke, and then we could hear them right opposite us. We stopped and started to throw our grenades, and as Monaghan and Foreman threw grenades, I got up on the dyke and poured machine gun fire into them. After the men had thrown all of their grenades, they turned back. Right across the river from us, the Germans had several good-sized ships with machine guns in them, and I was right in plain sight for them, only about 600 yards away. They poured machine gun fire at me until I had to get off the dyke. I tried several times to get back up, but the fire was so intense I had to quit. But at least I had broken up their attack. Just a few more minutes, and they would have been right on top of us. I went back to my slit trench very mad at that artillery officer. He could have sunk the whole lot while they were crossing the river. He got a medal for his part of this battle. I got nothing.

Just like on October 22, my hypertension had gotten so high, I was going to start screaming again. I was also feeling very light-headed, so I stayed in my slit trench until I started to feel a little better. Down the dyke about 300 yards there was a wooden gate, and we watched as the Germans crawled up in behind it to where they could see us. But they did not try to attack from there again. That night, they tried once more to come up around the curve, but we had a Native Canadian down at that end of our line. It was a moonlit night, and every time they tried to come around, he drove them back. I went to sleep in the slit trench and slept all night.

The next morning, I woke up to someone hollering, "Come on, Sarge, it's breakfast time." I started to climb out of the trench. Down at the wooden gate, the Germans were watching, and they had set up a mortar. And they were good with mortars, too. At 300 yards, they could drop a bomb right into a slit trench. I'd seen them do it. I was almost out of the hole when I heard them fire. Gunner had not gone even 10 feet, but he dropped to the ground, for there was no time for him to get back to his hole. I heard the bomb come, and then there was a big bang—very close. I looked out and Gunner was standing there, white as a sheet. The bomb had hit his .50-calibre and there was nothing left of it. He had been out of that hole for less than two minutes. I looked down at the gate. There were at least half a dozen Germans in behind it watching us. About 300 yards back towards Waspik sat a Sherman tank with a 6-pounder gun on it. I would go back and get them to put a shot or two in there. I got up and started to run. I had only gotten about halfway when I heard them fire. The bombs were coming, three of them, and fast. I could tell within a few feet where a bomb was going to hit. The first one came down behind me. I never stopped. The second one was in front and to the right. I could hear the third one coming and I knew it was going to hit me. I was right on the bank of the canal that went to Waspik, so I dived over the bank. I got over, all but my right leg. It was sticking up in the air. The bomb hit right where I had been, almost in my very tracks. Something smashed into my right calf. I looked at it and there was a hole in my boot and a piece of steel in my leg. I was all shook up from the explosion, but I was in luck in more ways than one. About three weeks before, when the Poles had come in, they'd had to leave some of their food behind. Sitting right there was a box of frozen beef, obviously frozen ever since they had dropped it. So while I was resting and getting myself together, I had a good feed of frozen beef. I stayed there for about ten minutes before I climbed out and went on to the tank, which was about 600 yards from the wooden gate. I told them to have a look at the gate, so they got out their glasses and had a look. Sure enough, there was a whole bunch of Germans in there. They wound their gun down and made a direct hit—gate and Germans flew all over. Then just for luck, they did it again. That took care of that problem, and I went back to my slit trench. I was really shaken up that it had been so close. That was the ninth and last time that I was wounded.

My leg was paining me and I had taken just about all I could take. That afternoon, I was ordered out. I went back to Waspik, where I ran into Jim Marr. Jim was a dispatch rider, so I said to him, "Jim, take me back to Loon op Zand." I got on behind and he took me to the doctor, who put me on a stretcher to go to the hospital, but I had other ideas. As soon as the doctor went out, I got off the stretcher and left. I went back to my home with the Van Herens and rested there for a while. Later, I went out to find Jim, and when I did, he said, "Where've you been? They're looking all over for you." I said, "Take me back to Kapelsche Veer." He said, "I can't. You're to go to the hospital." Jim was one of my best friends, but I had to put my foot down. I said, "Jim, I'm a sergeant, and you're a corporal. Take me back. And that's an order." Jim got his motorcycle and took me back to Waspik.

When I got back to Waspik, it was pitch-dark and starting to rain. I stayed there all night. In the morning, word came back that the battle was over. We had finally taken the position. We would be coming out, and the Poles would take over. The rain had turned to ice and everything was covered. We could hardly stand up. All of the regiment vehicles were in Waspik and they had to be taken back to Loon op Zand. Some of the drivers had been killed; others badly wounded. I had been ordered to get Support Coy. back to Loon op Zand. As men came off the island, I just grabbed them and said, "You're a driver, and you're a driver." Some of them had never been in a carrier before. There were carriers, trucks and jeeps. I told them, "Get in the vehicles and get the motors running." When all was ready, I got into the first carrier and gave the signal for the others to follow me. It was a paved road with ice an inch or more thick. Steel tracks do not go very well on ice. Some vehicles were in the ditch, some were turned around and some just went in all directions. I told my driver to keep going, and the others gradually got straightened out. We could only move at a snail's pace, but everyone eventually got to Loon op Zand. We parked on the street in the Support Coy. area. I just said, "Everyone get to bed." What a sorry-looking bunch! We were all exhausted.

On January 26, the day we attacked the island, we were to have been back in Loon op Zand for breakfast. It was now five days later. I went back to my home at the Van Herens' and went to bed. The next day, I was sent back to the island to help pick up our dead, but thank goodness, someone else had already done it. I saw them; that was bad enough. Armstrong had his head, from his eyes up, blown off. Lambert, they could not find. The German dead were not picked up until spring.

There are many strange stories from the war. The following is a story told to me by a man named Smith. "Smitty" was only eighteen years old. He is listed as being killed January 26, 1945. *That is wrong!* He was killed on January 31. He was a member of my old No. 8 Plt. When "A" Coy. went into Kapelsche Veer, Smith had just returned to the regiment. He had been in the hospital with pneumonia, and so he was left behind. After I left the first aid post, I went back to the café and the Van Herens'. Smith was in the café and I talked to him there. He told me that on the morning of January 26, shortly after eight o'clock, he had gone to the kitchen to get his breakfast. Lambert's office was in the same building as the kitchen. Just as he got to the kitchen, Major Lambert came out and walked with him down the street. Lambert said, "I have come to get my razor. I am going away," and he went into his office. We had two Dutch boys—two brothers who had put on Canadian uniforms and attached themselves to "A" Coy. We called the one boy Johnnie. Johnnie told me later that he also had seen Lambert. I talked to another Dutch man who had been across the street at the time, and he, too, had seen Lambert go into his office. He also said that there were others who had seen him as well. Lambert went into his office, but he did not come out. And when they went into the office to talk to him, he was not there.

I thought this was a very strange story. Two eyewitnesses had seen Lambert take an exploding grenade between the legs, and go down, presumably dead, shortly after eight o'clock that same morning. I asked Smitty if Lambert had come into town from the north, but he did not know. He had not seen him come into the town. All of a sudden, he was just there and no one had seen where he had come from.

Smitty insisted that his place was up on the island with the rest of the men from his company and that that was where he was headed. I ordered him to stay in Loon op Zand until he was sent for. The battle raged on, night and day. On the night of January 30, the Germans had had enough. They had packed up in the night and left across the River Maas. We had won the battle at last, but at a terrible cost in dead and wounded. On the morning of January 31, Smitty had gone to the island. As the battle was over and the enemy was gone, he thought it was safe to stand on top of the dyke and look things over. A sniper shot him in the stomach from 500 or 600 yards away. Smitty was the last man to be killed on Kapelsche Veer.

On January 31, the island was turned over to the 8th Polish Infantry Battalion, and the Lincoln and Welland Regiment returned to Loon op Zand. Our dead were gathered up and taken out for burial. Major Lambert's body could not be found. Then the rumours started. He was seen here and he was seen there; he had taken all the war he could take and had left.

The most persistent of these stories was that he had been seen in Bergen-op-Zoom by some of our men. He had been wearing civilian clothing and when our men tried to talk to him, he said he did not speak English. This story sounded so plausible that I resolved to go to Bergen and see for myself. I reasoned that if I spread the word in Bergen that I was there, then he would make himself known to me. Or maybe he would not talk to me because if he were actually there, he would then be a deserter cut off from the regiment. But I was still certain that he would make himself known to me. He had been my company commander. We had gone through a lot together. I had been his right-hand man.

On further reflection, I decided not to go. I had the story of his death from the two Able Coy. men and I had also gone to the house looking for him. I knew that he had not gotten out of that house. He was dead. Both of the Able Coy. men were gone from the regiment. The two Dutch boys were also gone and Smitty was dead. I was now the only man in the regiment who knew that Lambert had gotten into the house. However, as no one ever asked me if I knew anything about him, I told no one about it.

In the spring of 1945 after the snow was gone, a crew of men went to the island to clean up the mess. It was then that Lambert's body was found. And although no one ever said it, I have no doubt that it was found buried in the rubble of the house.

I do not claim that Lambert was seen in Loon op Zand that morning. I was not there. I do not know who or what they saw. But that was the story they told to me. And they all told the same story. They had all seen Lambert go into his office. They had all heard him say, "I have come for my razor. I am going away." Yet Major Lambert was dead at that time.

This story would eventually become very well known amongst our troops. Later, after the war was over, I heard it again from someone I did not know from another regiment.

In 1984, I went back to the island and talked to a Dutchman who lived there in a new house. He told me that he had lived there in an old house in 1944. As a nine-year-old boy, he had come with his father when they picked the Germans up. He said he had seen a pile of 200 dead Germans, and that there were many more than that. As for the Lincoln and Welland Regiment, we had had 50 men killed, 133 wounded and many sent out with frozen hands and feet. The exact number of our casualties was never known. It was set at about 249 men—we had made that attack with about 300 men.

It took a long time to recover from Kapelsche Veer. There were very few original men left after that. All of my old friends were gone, either dead—Lieutenant Armstrong, Captain Dickie, Major Lambert, Slater, H.H. Smith, Ely Snake and Sergeant Thorne—or wounded—Lieutenant Borthwick, Owen Dandy, Lieutenant Hume, Wally Balfour, Brown, Chowen, Erwin, Gagnon, Hill, Ledingham, MacDonald, Walsh. All were gone.

21

CATCHING MY BREATH

ABOUT THIS TIME, I was sent as an instructor in an NCO's training school in Udenhout, a small town about four miles east of Loon op Zand. The regiment was returned to the River Maas to a town named Elshout. They were there for two days and then returned to Loon op Zand and prepared to go to Germany. On February 22, they moved into Germany through Staatsforst Cleve, a forest at Cleve. There they would start the drive to clear the Hochwald forest and make way for the crossing of the Rhine River.

I was in Udenhout and did not know they were gone. If I had known they were going, I would have left Udenhout and gone with them. When I heard they were gone, my first thought was to follow them. This was the first time I had been left behind. After much thought, I realized I had been left behind to rest and recuperate. So I decided to make the most of it and stay where I was. I think I spent about two weeks in Udenhout billeted in a house with some Dutch people whose names I never did know. I had a lot of spare time, so in the afternoons I would take a Bren gun carrier and go to a rifle range outside of Udenhout. I would take several cases of ammunition and three or four Bren guns, and fire these weapons until the ammo was gone. I fired rifles and Bren guns from the hip until I could hit a target 500 yards away with every shot. There was a range there with moving targets to simulate a battlefield. A target was raised as we went through and I could knock them down with one shot. I could take a Bren gun, shooting from the hip, and cut off an eight-inch tree 500 yards away. One day, someone started a fire in a small woods about 400 yards away. I put it out by firing at it with a Bren gun. I would have a man on each side of me with a case of grenades. They would throw them as far as they could as fast as they could, and I would explode them as they threw them, with either Bren gun, rifle or revolver. I fired thousands of rounds every day. Up above the rifle range, there was a small clearing. Germans would come out of the woods behind it and watch as we practised. They did not bother us and we did not bother them. I put in a lot of days out there, but because the Germans were watching, I stopped going out alone.

At night, I would go next door from where I was staying and play cards. Another sergeant from the Lincoln and Welland Regiment lived there with an old man and his two daughters. They were big, red-haired twins. Each weighed over 200 pounds—not fat, just big. The sergeant slept downstairs and the old man and the girls slept upstairs. The girls left the outside door unlocked and we discovered that, in the night, German soldiers were coming in and going upstairs to visit them. They would sneak in and sneak out before daylight. Between that house and the house where I stayed, there was an alley about two feet wide. One night, I had left the house and started down the alley to my house. It was pitch-dark. I bumped right into a German soldier headed to where I had just left. He ran one way and I ran the other. I went straight up to my room and went to bed. He was not there to bother me.

Another night, we sat around the kitchen table playing cards. I heard a very small squeak, and out of the corner of my eye, I saw the doorknob start to turn. I just pulled out my .38 revolver and fired at the doorknob. The bullet hit just below the knob. I jumped up, ran to the door and opened it. It was too dark to see anything, but I could hear Germans running out in the field behind the house. I fired a couple of shots in that direction, but did not hit anything. That broke up the game and we all went to bed. I guess the girls went to bed alone that night.

On a Sunday afternoon, I took a bicycle and went to Loon op

Zand to visit the Van Herens. I stayed late and had to come back to Udenhout in the dark. It was about eleven o'clock before I got back into Udenhout. Just at the edge of Udenhout, there was a crossroad. As I was coming from the direction of Loon op Zand, I had my .38 in my hand at the ready. Just as I was coming to this crossroad, guns started to fire and a hail of bullets zinged up the road in front of me. I jumped off the bicycle and into the ditch. There were bullets going all over the place. I could tell by the sound they were German guns. There were several machine guns and some rifles, all firing right past me. However, I could see they weren't firing at me. I had just happened to come along. Another minute, and I would have either been through the crossroad or right into the bullets. I could see the guns about 200 yards down the road. They would fire a while, then they would stop, and then start all over again. I watched for my chance, and then jumped on my bicycle and pedalled furiously into town. My house was way down at the far end of town, but I was down there and in my bed in very short order. The next day, I asked the school commander about it. He said it was the Argyll Regiment out there, but the Argylls were not there on a Sunday night firing German weapons. I left the school shortly after that and went to Germany. I got there just in time to return to Holland with the regiment.

We arrived at Best, a little town southeast of Tilburg, on March 13 and were there until March 29. The time was spent in training. Since February, the regiment had lost more than 250 men. There were a lot of new men now to train. I had been issued a motorcycle now, so I had a very good time. No one cared what I did, so I just did as I wanted. I rested most of the time, either in Best or in Loon op Zand, which was just a few minutes away by motorcycle. The Van Herens kept a bed for me in their house. So like this, the war went on. I had fought my war. Now, like an old horse, I had more or less been put out to pasture.

22

THE WAR IS OVER

THE REGIMENTAL CONVOY moved off to join the divisional column at quarter past seven on the morning of March 30 and
passed through 's-Hertogenbosch, Grave and Nijmegen on the way
to Cleve. We left Cleve at quarter past five on the evening of March
31, and crossed the Rhine River by "Blackfriars Bridge," which was a
Bailey pontoon bridge named after a bridge in London. We were
finally on the last push to end the war.

About this time, I was told I was to go on two weeks' leave to
England. I was very tired. By now, the war did not mean much to me.
At last, all the fight had been knocked out of me. I had been in the
front line nearly eight months. The only part of the war I had missed
was the two weeks I had been at Udenhout. When I went back to
Headquarters to go on leave to England, my old friend Jim Marr was
there waiting for me. Jim and I had always gone on leave together,
and, with a small group of other men, we were to be taken back to
prepare to leave. At a camp located in the Siegfried Line about five
miles behind the front lines, we spent several days cleaning up.

Jim and I decided to go out and see if we could find some eggs.
Everyone had a craving for fresh eggs. We went to several farm-
houses, but didn't have very much luck. The people simply would not
sell the eggs. Finally, we came to this one farmyard and we could hear
chickens in the barn. I went to the house while Jim hid behind the

barn. The farm was owned by an old German couple, and I went right into the house and sat down to visit with them. They spoke no English and I spoke very little German, but, somehow, we managed to have a little talk. They told me they had six sons in the German army. They had their pictures all lined up on the wall. They had not heard from any of them for more than two years. I sympathized with them, and they cried a bit. I kept them busy for about fifteen minutes, then left. By that time, Jim had gotten into their chicken house and was waiting for me with about three dozen eggs. We took them back to camp with us. We thought we had enough eggs to last us several days, but just then we were told to get ready to leave in the morning. We had to have a bath and wash our clothes first, so we got a big tin can and built a fire to heat water. We put our clothes in the can to boil, took out water to have a bath, then dropped all the eggs in the can with the clothes and boiled them. We did not share them with anyone else. We ate them all—all three dozen of them.

I don't remember much of the trip to England. We went up to Glasgow in Scotland and stopped there for a couple of days, then started to work our way south. We would ride the train for a few hours, then get off in some town and look it over, and then get back on the train.

We stopped in one town and decided to have a drink, so we went into a pub. There was an old woman sitting at a table. We got a drink and sat down. Soon, the old lady started to act funny. She would look at us, mutter away to herself, then grab something out of the air and inspect it. Then she'd throw it away, grab something else, look at it and throw it away, too—all the time looking at us and muttering away to herself. After a while she said, "I see a *K.* Your name starts with a *K.*" By this time, she had our attention. She continued to mutter and grab things that were not even there. Eventually, she started to talk to us and told us she would be able to tell me the first letter of my first name. By this time, we were ready for another beer, so we bought her one, too. After a while, she said my first name started with a *C,* and after a bit more, she told Jim his last name started with an *M* and his first name started with a *J.* How she did it, I don't know, but we bought her another drink. After a while, the bartender told her to either shut up or get out. He said he didn't know how she did it, either, but he was not going to have her bothering us.

About this time, another Canadian soldier came in. He got himself a drink and sat down. He took one look at us and said, "Lincoln and Welland, eh? Do you fellas know a Sergeant Kipp in your regiment?" We said, "Yes, we know him. What do you want him for?" He said his brother had been a major in the Lincoln and Welland Regiment and had been killed, and he wanted to know how he had died. He said he had met some Lincoln and Welland men in London and they had told him to get in touch with me. All he wanted to know was, "Did he die easy or did he suffer?" I told him that his brother had died very easy; that he had died instantly, and did not even feel it. He said they were from London, Ontario, and we stayed and talked to him for a while. His brother was only about 30 yards from me when he was shot and killed at Olendon in France. He was shot in the leg and the bullet went up into his stomach. He died a horrible death and he screamed right up until the end. There was a rumour that the bullet had come from behind him. But I did not tell the fellow any of this. I guess he still thinks his brother died very easy. He thanked me and we all left.

We travelled in this way down to the south of England. Then Jim left on his own to visit some friends of his, so I went to Tunbridge Wells and stayed there for a while. One day when I was walking down a street in London, I saw a staff car coming down the street flying a flag. We were always to salute a car with a flag. I knew some high-ranking officer was in it, so I turned my head to the right, up came my arm, and I found myself looking right at Colonel Cromb, the colonel of our regiment. He had been on leave to Canada and was just coming back. He saw me, too, and started to wave his arms at me. I thought he was going to come right out the window. In a split second, they were past and he was looking out the back window and waving. I stopped and waited, thinking he might come back. Cromb and I had become very good friends, and that was something unusual, a sergeant and a colonel being good friends. Later, when I met him again after the war had ended, he said he had wanted to come back and talk to me, but he had had a strange driver and he was afraid she would report him for stopping and talking to a "non-commissioned" on the street.

When Jim came back from visiting his friends, we met in Tunbridge Wells, where we had a few days to wait for a ship to France. We took up our abode at a small inn out in the country, which was cheaper than the hotel in town. The only drawback was that we had to go into town to eat at the hotel. However, this was no bother as we could catch a bus into town right at the door of the inn every morning and then back again at night. We had often heard of the class distinction in England. There were three classes of people: the upper crust, the middle crust and the "no accounts" below that. The middle crust looked on Canadians as being no accounts. After all, we were colonials. The first morning, we cleaned up and went out to catch the bus around half past nine. We boarded the bus by a door at the back end and sat down in a seat across the aisle from a couple of old English "biddies." They gave us a disapproving look, got to their feet and went to the front of the bus. The rest of the people on the bus smiled or laughed a bit. We paid no attention and went on into town and headed for the dining room of the hotel. Inside sat a retired major of the Imperial Army having his breakfast. As soon as we walked in, he sat right up straight and grew red in the face. After all, how dare we have the temerity to come in there where he was having his breakfast. We smiled at him and said, "Good morning." We got no answer. He picked up his morning paper and put it in front of his face. We watched him out of the corners of our eyes, and soon he very slowly lowered the paper and looked over it at us, with just the top of his head and his eyes showing. We both smiled and waved at him. He would not finish his breakfast; he just glared at us over the top of his paper. When we finished our breakfast, we made a point of going past his table and speaking to him.

The second morning we got on the bus, there they were, the same two old biddies. We took the same seat as the day before, and again, they got up and moved to the front of the bus. But by this time, we had caught on as to what it was all about. When we went into the dining room, there sat the major, and, like the day before, he glared at us over the top of his paper until we left. On our way out, we made sure we again went by his table and spoke to him.

When we got on the bus the third morning, the two old biddies were in the same spot once again. But this time, we handled it differently. We thought we'd have some fun. I sat down in our usual seat in the back of the bus, while Jim went to the front of the bus. Tut, tut. They had nowhere to go. The next morning, the two women were not on the bus, and the major did not make an appearance in the dining room, either.

We had now been gone nearly a month and the war was starting to wind down. There was still a lot of fighting, but at least we could see the end. Towards the end, I had missed a lot of the fighting, but I did not care about that. A few days before we returned, the regiment had crossed the Twenthe Canal and had a big fight. For the next week or so, I did not do very much. I was a kind of troubleshooter—sent here and there, wherever I was needed. I took up ammunition and food and did all sorts of jobs. This was the best way to fight a war. This was a lot better than being in a rifle company. I was finally getting lots of sleep and enjoying life.

The last big fight I was in was at the Kusten Canal on April 16, 1945. The regiment was preparing to cross the canal, and I had not been given any special job. No one expected so much resistance, and it was not long before "C" Coy. was in trouble and bogged down before they could get across the canal. I was sent for, told to go see what the trouble was and to give them any help I could. I got Ron Vinkle and his carrier, and away we went down a road that ran parallel to the canal. Between the road and the canal was a wood about 80 yards wide, but there were also some open spaces we had to pass. The wood was not very thick and the Germans could fire right through at us. As soon as they saw us, they opened up from the far side of the canal. We roared down the road through a hail of bullets—all around us and bouncing off the carrier. I hollered at the top of my lungs, "Go, Vinkle, go!" and we went, just like a bat out of hell! I got excited and stood up and pounded the front of the carrier. Vinkle was down as far as he could get and still see. I was hollering, "Go! Go! Go!" He looked up at me and yelled, "Sit down, ya damn fool!" and I realized what I was doing and got down out of sight. We went about seven or eight hundred yards like this before we ran out of their range of fire. I stood up to see just where we were, and right there, by the side of the road, was one of the section leaders of No. 4 Plt. lying in the ditch. I hollered to Vinkle to stop. This was the sergeant who had hid in the bushes back in France while I did the job he had been sent to do, and he got the medal for it. Here he was—hiding again. I got out of the carrier and went over to him and said, "What're you doing here?" He said he was observing his Bren gun section, who were 100 yards up the road in front of him. This was my chance. I called him everything I could lay my tongue to. I soon explained to him that his job was with his men, not hiding behind them. When I was finally done with him, he was very glad to go up with his men, and I saw to it that he got up there with them, too.

We came out to a clearing and stopped. There, down on the bank of the canal in a big hole, was "C" Coy., and they were under heavy fire. I made a run for them through the bullets. The hole was surrounded by a dirt wall about four feet high. I dove over the top and rolled in. They were trying to get a boat out into the water to get across. I talked to the company commander, Major Dandy. He said he thought they were going to make it, and they did. They just pushed the boat out over the top and several men at a time followed it. Once they got it in the water, they were down out of danger. They could take the men across a few at a time. Once across, they could hide behind the dyke over there, then follow the dyke along for about 300 yards until they reached some houses. They had just got inside the houses when the Germans attacked. They thought they were gone for sure and had to fight most of the night. It was so close that Dandy ate his order papers to prevent them from being captured. I went back and told the colonel they were across, but that they had lost a lot of men.

I was shown a spot on a map and told to get some men and go there and wait. One of the quartermasters, whose job it was to get food up, would meet me there and we would take food and ammo to "A" Coy., who were across the canal and also bogged down. After dark, a jeep came up to where we were waiting in a small house. Everything was in packs, to be carried on our backs. The quartermaster was not very brave—he was close to the front and did not like it one little bit. When all the packs were on our backs, we had one pack too many, so he said he would go back and send us up another man. One of my men was a great big corporal. Our packs were on and we were ready to go. I looked at the corporal and he looked at me. I grabbed the quartermaster and the corporal grabbed the extra pack, and we put it on him. He hollered, but there was nothing he could do. I said, "Let's go," and we started out, the corporal pushing him every step of the way. We loaded him into a boat and took him with us. That was the closest he ever got to the war.

The next day, I took my platoon over, and we set up our guns in a hedgerow just outside of town and stayed there all night. In the morning, I got orders: "Leave your guns in position and bring every man into town." This was very strange—we did not leave our guns alone anywhere. I questioned the runner, but he said he didn't know what was up, just that that was what we were to do. So I took the men in. The whole regiment was lined up in a field outside of town. We had just gotten there when from town came a party of people: the colonel, several headquarters officers and two women—a girl in her early twenties and her mother. They started walking through the ranks of men, looking at them. We wondered what was going on. Then came a couple more men—the burgomaster and someone else. He was waving his arms and talking. He stopped the first party, and we could see he was very mad. After a few words, they all left, and he was sure giving the girl and her mother a tongue-lashing. Then the story came out. The girl had said one of our men had raped her the night before and they had come out to identify him. But the burgomaster soon put a stop to that. She was a German sympathizer. He said she had looked after half the German army and was nothing but a prostitute. She would have picked out a man at random, and the penalty for rape was to be hanged. At that time, we had crossed a small spur of land and were back in Holland. That was about the last big fight I was in.

We pushed ahead into Germany and were swinging to the east.

Our objective was Oldenburg and we were almost there. The Germans were fighting hard. We could not figure it out—the war was practically over. Maybe we were going to see the end of it after all, and now we were being extra careful.

Our rifle companies were pushing up a side road. About four o'clock, they came to a large concrete roadblock in the centre of the road that was defended by German troops. Our men attacked and took the position. The Germans immediately counterattacked and took it back. By the time it got dark, the position had changed hands several times and was now in the hands of the Germans. Our platoon had lost quite a few men, including the officer, and it was now commanded by a corporal. I was a sergeant with plenty of experience, so I was sent up to give them a hand. We decided at this time that there was no sense in attacking the position again and risking the loss of more men. Instead, we would wait, and by morning the Germans would be gone anyway.

As we were settling down for the night, we could hear someone coming up the road behind us. It was very dark, but soon we could make out a small party of three or four men loaded down with packs. We stopped them, and they identified themselves as demolition engineers on their way to blow up the roadblock. I advised them to just sit down and wait for a while. I said that the Germans had control of that piece of property at this time, but that it would not be long before the Germans would leave, and then it would be safe to go up and do the job. I can only suppose their leader was an NCO, as it was too dark to see for sure. At my suggestion, he promptly reared up on his hind legs and, in no uncertain terms and tones, informed me not to try to tell them how to do their job. They had been sent up to do a job and they were going to do it, and I could mind my own business. They did not need any help or advice from me.

Well, far be it for the infantry to turn down a bit of help in a situation like this. We wished them luck, and while they shuffled off up the road, we crawled into our holes and pulled our heads down. Someone was about to get a lesson in manners.

The roadblock was less than 30 feet in front of us. They shuffled towards it. Suddenly, a Schmeisser cut loose. The bullets went over our heads in sheets. In a few minutes, down the ditch came the party of engineers, this time not walking, but crawling on their bellies. To our inquiry as to when it was going to blow, they gave no answer as they headed back down the road in the direction from which they had come. In the morning, the Germans were gone. We went through the position and never lost a man. The Royal Canadian Engineers were indispensable. They were a good outfit. We could not have won the war without them. Thank goodness most of their NCOs were smarter than the one who led that party.

We kept pushing farther into Germany. Sometimes, we would go up a road and there would be German soldiers sitting along the road or out in the fields, watching us. I asked one why he was there. He said he had gone to sleep and his pals had left him. When he woke up, we were there.

One day, I was sent to take an anti-tank gun up to the front. We went up with the infantry and set up our gun, then went into a house to spend the night. It was very dark that night. After dark, the infantrymen were all called back, but no one told us and we were left there all alone. We had a man outside on watch while the rest of us were sleeping on the floor. The house was occupied by two women and a boy—a mother, her daughter-in-law and her grandson, who was about eight or nine years old. They went to the basement for the night while we occupied the upstairs. We had a lamp lit so we could have some light. We were all asleep when one of the men woke up. There, standing in the doorway looking at us, was a German officer. He had been in the basement all along and after we went to sleep, he had come up to have a look. The two men just looked at each other. Then, the German went back to the basement and our man lay back down and went back to sleep. In the morning, he said to me, "I woke up last night and there was a German officer with his arm in a sling, in here looking at us." He said he went to the basement. I went to the women and asked them about him, but they said no, they were the only ones there. I took a grenade, opened the basement door, and told them I was going to throw it down. Then, the daughter-in-law said yes, it was her husband down there. He had been wounded in Russia and was now hiding in the basement. It was his home we were in. I told her to go and tell him to stay in the basement and we would not bother him. She went to the basement and spoke to him, and we never saw him again. Then, I found out we were up there all alone. But by then it didn't matter, the infantry was coming back and going on up the road.

A few days later, I was again sent with a gun up into a forward position. We had taken a small town and were on the outskirts of the town at the very last house. About 100 yards to the right of us was another road running out of town and parallel to our road. On that road was a farm, with the barn sitting in a field between the two roads. It was just only slightly farther out of town than we were. It was a nice warm sunny day, and I went out to the south side of the house to sit in the sun and get a bit of sleep. I had just settled down when out of town came Sergeant Jones. Sergeant Jones was the senior cook in the regiment—a hateful little being. I had only met him three or four times, and every time, we had gotten into a row. His favourite words were "You're on the peg," meaning he was going to lay a charge against you. Why he was up there, I don't know. His job was way behind the front. He had never been this close before. He saw me sitting out in the sun and stopped. He hollered, "Has anyone been over to that barn after eggs?" I answered, "No, no one's been over there yet." We would have been, except that there were Germans in it. We were watching them, and they were watching us. Jones went past the house where I was and started across the field to the barn, which was about 80 yards away. I did not get up. I just waited, and I did not have to wait long. He had just entered the field when a German machine gun cut loose. In about fifteen minutes, Jones crawled up the ditch and headed back to town. He sure gave me an awful look. I just laughed at him. That taught him a lesson. The German had just fired a few rounds over his head to chase him back. After dark, they left and we moved on up the road towards Oldenburg, fighting from one small town to the next.

The Germans knew the war was lost, but they kept on fighting. Some gave up very easy, but not many. Then, on May 2, No. 13 Plt., along with the platoon officer, were all taken prisoner—26 men in total. The next night, May 3, just after dark, we came into an area where we were to stop for the night. Orders were given, "Park your vehicles," and we were told that the cookhouse was set up at the edge of a small woods. We were just getting ready to go find it when we heard several shots being fired in the woods, and then a lot of yelling. It was very dark by now and we wondered what was going on. Soon, a couple of men came out of the woods on the run. They had gone in search of the cookhouse and had gotten lost in there. Then they came upon a lineup of men who were waiting to get supper. Ah, this was it, they thought, so they fell in line and were moving up with the rest of them when they discovered they were in a lineup of Germans. The Germans discovered them about the same time. Who fired the shots, I never did find out. A platoon of riflemen were sent in to find the Germans, but they had gone. They had been camped on one side of the woods, then we came in and set up camp on the other side.

The next day, May 4, was very quiet. Patrols were sent out but could find no Germans. They had just petered out. I went over to "D" Coy. to find Jim Bell. The war was just about over and we were both still alive. Jim had been promoted to quartermaster. When I found him, he was just going to get his dinner and we walked down the road together. We were talking about our friend Bill Nicholson, who had been killed on the Leopold. "D" Coy. was lined up for their dinner. Suddenly, a man in the lineup started running towards us, calling my name, "Charles, Charles, Charles." We stopped and looked at him, and then, all of a sudden, I knew who it was: Russell Howell. We had gone all through school together in the same class. As I walked down the road, he had recognized me. I asked him where he was and he pointed to a barn, so I said, "I'll come and see you this afternoon."

That afternoon, I went over, and there he was. There was a hole in the wall of the barn and Russell had a Bren gun set up in the hole. He lay down on one side of the hole, and I lay down on the other. Every so often, he stuck his head up in front of the hole and looked out to see if there were any Germans. I nearly fainted the first time he did it. Lucky for him, there were no Germans there. Then someone said, "There's a German." Off to the right front was a house maybe 200 yards away. We all looked and saw a German come out of the house and climb up a small tree to look around. He looked around, then climbed down and went back into the house. Then way off to the right, we could see some Canadian tanks manoeuvring into position, and they were being very careful. Then we discovered that there was not only a German in the house, but also a Tiger tank behind it. The German had been climbing the tree to keep an eye on our tanks. Several times, he came out and had a look. I had always wanted to get a tank. I made up my mind—this was it. I had my supper, got myself a PIAT gun and a couple of bombs, and went back up to the "D" Coy. barn. I sat down to wait until it got dark. As soon as it was dark enough that I could not see the house, I would go after him. Then we heard the tank's engine start. It was nearly time for me to go, but the German was watching, too, and he was smart. Just as I got to my feet to go, out from behind the house came the tank. All we could see was the fire from its exhaust, and all I could do was watch it disappear down the road, so I went back to my platoon and went to sleep.

The next morning, May 5, 1945, everything was quiet when we got up. There was no hurrying, not even any guns firing. This was very strange. It gave me a funny feeling. Then orders were given to move and we moved on down the road. About half a mile down the road, we caught up with the Tiger tank. It was sitting in the middle of the road—out of gas. We only went about two miles and moved into a farmhouse with a barn attached. No one was told anything. We were just to wait here. I went into the house and found one of our wireless sets in there, so I turned it on. The quartermaster came in with two bottles of navy rum—one a 26er, the other, a bigger bottle—for our platoon. Something held me there: "Don't leave the wireless set." I just sat there, and then someone came on the air and announced that the war had ended. What a shock! I knew it was coming, but I still wasn't ready for it. I could not believe the war had ended, and I was still alive! I opened the 26er and took a drink, then another. I just sat there and repeated, "The war is over, and I'm still alive," over and over and over, taking a drink from the bottle every so often. That stuff was enough to kill anyone—heavy black navy rum, and nothing to go with it. I was so shocked, I sat there for at least an hour. I should have been out stone cold from the rum. I was a bit tipsy, but that was all. At one in the morning, the following message had been received by telephone: "Offensive operations cancelled forthwith. Cease fire 0800 hrs. 5th/May/45. All units stand fast until further orders."

One of the first things I did was take out my .38 and unload it. I thought, "I won't need this anymore." Then I took the big bottle out to the men and told them it was all over. And I sat down—and laughed. All over the world, people were celebrating. But we could not believe it. In the front lines, there was no celebration. I spent that day in plain, dumb shock. I never expected to see the end.

Still, I was a long time getting over the shock. It was weeks before I came out of it. I sat down and wrote a letter to my wife, and then went into my shell. Nothing meant anything and nothing mattered. There was nothing important. The war was over; I did my duty as required, and that was it. Weeks passed by, and I did not write to my wife or anyone. I just could not write. I had letters from her, and finally, a letter from her asking why I did not write. What was wrong? I wrote her a short letter saying I would write when I could.

What a change there was in the regiment. There were very few of my old friends left. Most of them, like Bill Nicholson, had been killed. The regiment was now made up of strangers. Of the four of us who had gone to the regiment in 1943—Bill Nicholson, Jim Bell, Jim Marr and me, three of us were still alive. By war's end, I was an acting sergeant major, Jim Bell was a quartermaster sergeant and Jim Marr was a corporal.

During this time, I had been wounded nine different times—all slight wounds. I was known as something of a legend in the Lincoln and Welland Regiment. I had been through more war than any other man in the regiment, and I had single-handedly accounted for more Germans than any platoon in the regiment. I had fought in the front lines for six months non-stop without a rest. No other man in the regiment did this. And although I was never given a medal, I had more citations for medals than any man in the regiment.

Jim Bell and I were eligible for decorations, but we were left out. We were the only two men in the regiment amongst those who were eligible who did not get them. Jim and I talked about this later and recalled the day we went to the regiment. The four of us were all qualified instructors and had been sent to that regiment for a purpose. We were not made very welcome. I remembered our first day there, when we were paraded in front of a major who had asked us to revert to the rank of private, and we had refused. He had said: "You will report to Able Coy., and you will get *nothing* from this regiment." It was a promise made, and a promise kept. We got nothing from the regiment. Jim and I were very pointedly left out.

On my journey home, I arrived by troop train in London, Ontario, on December 10, 1945. I was one of the first men to step off the train. I stopped and looked around for a moment, and then I saw my mother and Margaret standing in the crowd waving to me. For so long, I had thought I would never see them again. One of the first things I asked them was, "Where's Dad?" I was then told he had had a heart attack a few days before and was home in bed. As soon as we arrived home in Ingersoll, I went right up to see him and spent about an hour with him. I never saw him alive again, as he died that night. It was a terrible shock.

I had planned on staying in the service, but this threw a wrench in it all. One thing I did not want to do was be a farmer. But in my state of shock, the war would not be over for me until I was back in our farmhouse north of Delmer. Jim Marr and I were discharged from the service together on January 17, 1946. We were curious to see what had been put on our service medical records, and before we were discharged, we both asked to see them so we could make sure they were correct. We were told in no uncertain terms that the medical records would most certainly be correct and that we were not allowed to see them. The officer in charge, a higher-ranking officer, was called in, and he gave us a direct order to sign the medical records as is. We had no choice. We signed them then and there, sight unseen, and then we were discharged from the service.

I went into a farming partnership with my brother Bill, who had just been discharged from the air force. I had not done manual labour like that for six years, and as I had been diagnosed with a heart problem in October of 1944, I soon began having problems. Soon after I arrived home, I started to have fainting spells. My chest would get sore and heavy and I felt as if I had indigestion. I was generally alone when I had these spells and I never told anyone, so no one knew.

Eventually, Margaret found out and insisted that I see a doctor. I did, and, only six months after the war was over, I was diagnosed as having arteriosclerotic heart disease and informed that there was evidence on my heart of previous heart damage, incurred while I was in the service. Even though my doctor had told me that although I was young in years, my heart was like the heart of an old man—it was so worn out, it could not do its work—like most survivors of traumatic events, I went into denial, and I refused to accept the fact that I had a heart problem.

Farming was too strenuous and I had to give it up. I could work only part-time. I have never been able to do an eight-hour day's worth of work. My wife, Margaret, got a job, and, for the next twenty-five years, she worked to support our family and pay the bills.

I started having flashbacks of the war. I would wake up and fight the war all over again. It was as if I was on a magic carpet; I just sailed from one battle to another—Bourguébus, Tilly, La Hogue, Verrières, Grainville-Langannerie, Saint-Germain, Butcher Hill, Olendon, Ghent Canal, the Leopold, Bergen-op-Zoom and Kapelsche Veer, to name but a few—with all their shock and horror. I would be awakened by a loud bang like a rifle shot or a grenade exploding. I would be in a terrible sweat. Perspiration rolled off me in large drops and trickled down my body, and I would be seized by an overwhelming fear that something terrible was about to happen. My head was full of dandruff I could not get rid of, and my hair came out in handfuls. I went through periods of very deep anger, with no apparent reason. I would be drawn up tight—every muscle in my body drawn so tight I could not move. Every muscle, straining and straining. Then I would realize what I was doing, and relax. I was nothing but a bundle of nerves. I had lived by a gun so long I could not give it up. It was the first thing I looked for in the morning, and when I went to bed, I put it within reach. I have often said I would have walked down the street without my pants on but not without my gun. When there was thunder and lightning, I went to the basement. And to this day, it bothers me to go into a restaurant or a public place and sit with my back to the people. I want my back against the wall, so no one can get behind me. It's the same driving a car in heavy traffic. I get hemmed in and start to feel panicky. To this day, there are still times when I tighten up and fight those old battles. When a bunch of us goes up north to our hunting camp every year, my nephew, Joe Williamson, says I wake up some of them in the night with the noises I make, and that sometimes they lie there listening to me fight the war all over again in my sleep. I always feel guilty whenever I think of all the friends I saw die, and the fact that I lived through it all to come home. Why me?

Many days, I could not work at all. In February 1960, I collapsed and was sent to Westminster Hospital for six weeks. I was diagnosed as having myocardial infarction, arteriosclerotic heart disease and hypertensive cardiovascular disease, and was questioned about my heart problems from the past. There was no way I could talk about it at that time. From the trauma I had gone through, it just would not come out. The trauma of those days is beyond comprehension. I could not describe the day-to-day fighting, the holding myself ready to kill or be killed, every minute of the day, twenty-four hours of the day, with no relaxing of the tension I was under. To relax or forget was to die. No way would I go back to my war days. I did not talk of, or even think of, these things. To do so would make me break out in a cold sweat. Those things I had put out of my mind when they happened. I kept all these things to myself. My wife knew about the sweating and dandruff and not sleeping, but all these years, I never told her anything else. In 1984, I talked to my younger brother, Don, who had been badly wounded with the Essex Scottish Regiment. After that, talking about it started to come easier. He suggested that I should try to do something about it.

However, in my quest for help with a pension claim, on more than one occasion, I have been sworn at, called a liar and ordered from doctors' offices and told not to come back. In fact, one Tillsonburg doctor who could have helped me did just that. Once, many years ago, when I had gone to see him, I noticed he had a whole wall of books on the Second World War in his office, so I presumed he was interested in that subject and would be just as interested in anyone who had fought in the war. Wrong. When I broached the subject of my health problems to him and told him of my difficulties in trying to get a pension, he abruptly informed me that I had done nothing in the war that would make me exhausted, swore at me, and told me to get out of his office and not come back. Even my family doctor in Tillsonburg would have nothing to do with helping me. He said he was interested only in the present and cared nothing for the past. The fact that since the war, I have been able to do only very light work, and then only at my own pace and schedule, seemed to concern no one but me.

Still, I did continue to try to see doctors who could help me with a pension claim. And there were some doctors who were willing to help. In 1984, a doctor had asked me to obtain my service medical records from the war. It was not until then that I discovered, to my dismay, that many things that had happened to me during the war were never entered into my service medical records, including the heart problems I had had in 1944. Once, I contacted a doctor in Toronto who had me come to Toronto for a heart examination. He found that I did have two very old scars on my heart, but as there was no record as to when they came to be there, they could not put an absolute date on them. I knew they had been put there in October of 1944, but as there was no record of my heart problems on my medical service records from that time, the Department of Veterans Affairs refused to accept them as evidence on a pension claim.

I do not blame the army doctor though. He was a very good doctor, and, at that time, he was in almost as bad a shape as I was. And after all, I had not gone back to see him as I had been ordered to do on October 27, 1944. I received very little medical attention for any of the things that happened to me in the war. I grew up in a depression and we had no money to see a doctor. Seeing a doctor was a last resort. I never got over that. I still go to a doctor only as a last resort. There were different times during the war I should have gone to the doctor, but did not. To go to the doctor would have meant leaving my men, and that I would not do. The only way I would have left was if I was being carried. As a boy growing up, we took care of our own scratches and scrapes with home remedies. Most things would heal themselves if left alone, as my slight wounds did. It is a myth to say that when an infantryman went into shock, he was taken to the doctor for treatment. In all my war, I never saw a man taken to the doctor for treatment for shock. And I saw a lot of bad cases of shock.

No human being could go through ten months of fighting as I did and come out unscathed. Every battle, and every time I saw a man die, whether friend or foe, left a mark on me. But it took me years to accept the fact that I even had a heart condition, and that many more to talk about it. But, as the years passed, my heart condition grew ever worse and there was simply no denying it. Eventually, I had to have a pacemaker put in. Without it, I could not live.

According to the Department of Veterans Affairs, I soon learned I was not a hero who had fought for my country. All I was, was a liar and a lead swinger, trying to get a pension so I would not have to work. As recently as June 1999, I attended yet another hearing on this matter and was told by a member of the panel hearing the appeal that he would concede that I had experienced a heart attack back in 1944, but that what was at issue was which came first—the trauma or the heart attack. Apparently, three solid months of fighting in the front lines, day after day, nonstop, is not enough time to experience any trauma. At the time of this writing in 1999, I am still fighting for a pension for the heart problem I incurred in 1944. I think of my father's words to me on the day in 1939 when I went to London to enlist: "You are young and tough, just the kind of man they want in the army. And when you come home with your health in ruins, they will do nothing for you." *

---

* Since this writing, Charles's appeal of earlier negative decisions on the matter of a heart disability pension was finally granted. He first submitted an application in 1985. (He did actually broach the subject to them in the 1960s, but they wouldn't even talk to him about it back then.) They finally said yes, but only to "partial" entitlement for a disability pension, and the issue was then what percentage that entitlement should be. They made three payments to him before he died.

Epilogue

FACE TO FACE

AFTER THE WAR, the Lincoln Memorial Bridge, named for our regiment, was built across the canal in Bergen-op-Zoom on the spot where I had swum across, all alone, to bring back help for the rest of my platoon trapped inside the gin factory, on the night of that terrible battle of "madmen fighting in the dark."

Now jump ahead to May 1986. I'm approaching the Lincoln Memorial Bridge. It's late morning and I'm nervous. Understandably, since I'm about to meet a former German soldier I last saw here in October 1944. We desperately tried to kill each other then, and battle recollections are running through my head. I'm fighting it all over again.

This has come about because of a lengthy exchange of letters between me and Lt. Carl Heinz Holst, formerly of the German 6th Paratroop Regiment. A 1984 visit to Bergen-op-Zoom by me and other representatives of my regiment had prompted local resident Zaak Roosenboom to send my name and address to a German who had visited in 1981 and told similar stories of the intense fighting there. When I showed Roosenboom the spot where a German was killed in the old liquor factory, he had replied that the German visitor had also noted it, saying one of his best friends had been killed there.

Amazed to receive that first letter from Carl, I had replied promptly, thinking this was a chance to hear from someone who had fought against us. It was interesting to hear the other fellow's story, and when he proposed we meet—this time in peace, not trying to kill each other—I decided to go ahead. I asked my brother Bill to come with me, and by the middle of April 1986, our plans were complete. We had arranged to place wreaths in the war cemetery at Bergen-op-Zoom on May 4, the Dutch memorial day, and spend the rest of the week touring war cemeteries, old battlefields and other sites in France and Belgium.

The day before our pre-arranged meeting, my brother and I made sure all our clothes were in good shape and put an army shine on our shoes in an extra effort to look good. As I said to Bill, "We licked these guys once, let's try to look like we could do it again."

Now, as the hour draws near, the burgomaster and his assistant ride up on bicycles to join us. I have invited them to be with us, along with Dutch friends Hans Luijten of Breda and Jon Vroom. About 50 yards from the bridge, another group of men comes from behind the old laundry building and advances up the street. Just like in 1944, they from the north and us from the south. There are seven of them, and I have no idea what to expect.

The Germans stop at their end of the bridge and our group stops at our end. Then one man steps onto the bridge, and I go out to meet him. We meet in the middle and stand looking at each other. I don't know what he's thinking, but I'm wondering what this man, Carl, whom I tried to kill, is like. He introduces himself; I do the same. We then step forward and shake hands. The next few minutes are one big blur, the Germans gathering around to shake hands. The next thing I know, my brother is tapping me on the shoulder to remind me I've forgotten to introduce the burgomaster. Introductions are made all around, and names promptly forgotten.

Three of the Germans were in the fight in 1944, they tell us. Their CO of that night is one of them, a man named LeCoutre. I present Carl and LeCoutre with key rings made from .303 bullets of 1944 with their names and the date of the battle inscribed on them. I congratulate them on living through it to receive their mementos. In one of Carl's letters, he had stated that twenty-seven Germans were killed in that fight.

We stay on the bridge for about half an hour, getting to know one another and taking pictures. One German, who has a tape recorder, stays by my side to get every word I say. Eventually, we visit the factory, and they point out where three of their men were killed and then buried in a flower bed behind the house.

I point out my escape route, showing them the green door where I came out of the factory. The Germans cannot comprehend how I passed through their lines without being detected, and, to tell the truth, I don't know myself. Carl finally locates the spot where we had shot at each other, and we have our pictures taken there. He recalls getting behind us and shooting at us, and someone calling him a bastard—that was me—and then getting out when we shot back. I tell him of the German soldiers calling us Canadian pigs and saying they were going to kill us. We had replied that we had sharp knives and dared them to come in and try it. They get it all on tape and say they're going to print it in their regimental paper.

We spend an interesting hour or so at a local café, then drive south to look at other battle sites. At a big white house in Mattenberg, they tell me about what they called their "White House" being bombed. One day they received word from their intelligence service that the British were on their way to bomb the house. They left everything and ran out of the house, heading for Bergen-op-Zoom. They just got to the road when the planes came in. They sat in their cars and watched as the house was destroyed, then went back in and set up headquarters in the basement. They stayed for nearly a week before we came in and chased them out.

After a long day, we arrange to meet the next morning at the Canadian war cemetery. Once there, the Germans want to place a wreath at the cenotaph. I have mixed feelings about this. After all, some of the Canadians they killed are buried there. I give it a lot of thought, but after talking to them and getting their thoughts on the war, I decide to go along with it. After all, I am not their judge.

There's more picture taking, then Carl and I place a wreath. I have purposely not worn a hat so I won't have to salute. One of their party, a member of the West German government, makes a speech about peace and friendship between our countries. I can't help thinking it is more than forty years too late for the men buried there. There are tears in everyone's eyes, and one German walks amongst the graves crying openly. He says he is very sorry over it all now. They then present me with a bottle of good wine and a beautiful clock from members of their unit.

It has been a difficult two days, and I'm emotionally drained. Although we've made plans to spend a few days at Carl's place in Germany, I reluctantly tell him I'm exhausted and can't go. The Germans say they understand; I don't look very well. Goodbyes and good wishes are exchanged, and I present Carl with my story of the battle of Bergen-op-Zoom to help him with a history he's writing.

On reflection, I decide the trip to meet an old enemy was well worth what it cost me. The idea of sitting down in friendship with men I had fought against is something I believe every Canadian soldier thinks about and wonders how he would handle. I can say it's some experience. My brother and I agree the German veterans we met are just like Canadian veterans. They tell the same kind of stories as we do and are proud of the fact that they were good soldiers. As one of them put it, it was not that they disliked us or were mad at us, but they were fighting a war for their country, just like we were.

They said they didn't know anything about Jews being destroyed until the war was over, and they found it hard to believe but have accepted it as true. Carl told me his father, mother and sister all died in the Auschwitz concentration camp for opposing Hitler. What a bitter irony.

Before I met him, Carl described in one of his letters about sighting up a Canadian officer who was walking along the canal with a Red Cross nurse, and how he didn't go ahead and shoot him because of the Red Cross. I was pleased and relieved to know that about him. I wrote him back and told him the officer's name was Armstrong. I said he was a good man and a very good friend of mine, and I thanked him for sparing his life. How eerily strange and fitting that this story, too, would be connected to Carl.

All in all, I am glad I got to know Carl Heinz Holst and that we had the opportunity to meet face to face before he passed away nearly a year and a half later. His son, Marc, sent me a death notice from the funeral home, and I was saddened to hear of his passing. He was a good man. When I presented him with his bullet key ring, with his name and the date of the battle of Bergen-op-Zoom engraved on it, I had said to him in jest, "I've had a bullet with your name on it for forty years." The irony was not lost on either of us.

Life seems to be full of ironies. In one of his letters he had given a somewhat amusing and honest critique of his "old enemies" as soldiers. I quote:

We found out that, except the 101. Airborn Div. and other paras the U.S. havnt been very hard fighters. If they wouldnt have had the endless lot of material and we had a few more tanks together with hundred ME 109. the Uta-Beach would have been a fiasko. The British have been hard fighters. For my opinion harder as the U.S. And the Canadiens didnt care at all. They have been the most rude fighters I saw. That's not you are such a man out of that army. It's stated in a lot of books.

High praise from a member of a group of soldiers who had a pretty formidable reputation themselves.

But he is right about that. It *is* well documented in books, most of them written by foreigners, that Canadian troops were formidable fighters, often used as "storm" or "shock" troops when a particularly difficult objective needed to be taken or held. How strangely at odds that seems with our international reputation as a peaceful people, and so extremely polite, to the point that jokes are made about our politeness. It is the eternal enigma of our national soul. It *is* "Because we are Canadians."

AFTERWORD

I FIRST MET Charles Kipp almost thirty years ago when we moved beside him and his family into the house that his father had built and in which he was born. I remember that first meeting very clearly. He has great presence and I liked him instantly. I found him to be not only a warm, kindly man, but also an individual of great personal integrity. This is an impression that three decades of time and experience have only served to reinforce.

Thirty years ago, Charles rarely mentioned the war to anyone, but I had already heard something of his experiences from other sources, and, being somewhat of a history buff, I couldn't resist asking him about them. He showed me a scrapbook full of pictures, war mementos and, more importantly, old newspaper clippings detailing some of his exploits. I was intrigued, and over the years I broached the subject of his wartime experiences many, many times. I had always urged him to write them down and make a book out of them. For years, I told him that if he would just write them down in longhand, then I would gladly type and edit them for him. Finally, after I purchased a computer in 1991, I was able to convince him how much easier this task was going to be using a word processing program.

He started to write, and boy, did he write! The memories just came tumbling out onto the page. He told me I was going to be shocked, and I was. It was hard to juxtapose the tough, brash, "kill-or-be-killed" young soldier on the pages with the gentle, loving, grandfatherly soul next door on whom my children thought the sun rose and set. At first, I was able to keep up with him, and I would have the latest chapter ready for his perusal before he had the next one completely written. But eventually, he was pretty much finished and I was way behind. However, I was still plugging away at it and we were doing rather well with it.

Then, my family was hit with a horrific tragedy, the discovery of which by me in 1993, and later by my husband in 1995, devastated us all, including Charles and his wife, Margaret. Both my health and my looks deteriorated from that day forward. Although I had always looked much younger than my years, I aged fifteen years in three, and I was no longer the happy, upbeat, optimistic person I used to be. It literally killed my soul. The next few years were a horrendous morass of trying to cope with the myriad ongoing problems it bequeathed, along with the grief and the betrayal, not only by the perpetrator, but also by the community. I did not work on Charles's book again for seven long years. His patience astounds me. In 1999, it hit me that he was now eighty years old and heading for eighty-one, although he didn't look it. I had to come back to life and make good on the promise I had been making for thirty years to this person I admired so much and held so dear to me.

I always knew I owed Charles Kipp a tremendous debt for the horrific sacrifices he had made so many years ago to protect the lifestyle all the rest of us take so much for granted. How could I not? After all, we had had so many conversations about his wartime experiences. But as I got back into the book filled with such horrific memories, and I marvelled all over again at his post-war resiliency and attitude, I slowly began to realize I owe him still another debt beyond his wartime sacrifices. Charles was wounded nine times, suffered a heart attack in the heat of battle and continued on even though he was gravely ill. Yet his many, many acts of bravery, for which citations for medals were written up by his commanding officers and duly thrown away by a jealous and vindictive comrade, while noted by many who fought with him, have never been officially recognized by his armed forces community. The war was an experience that changed his life forever and profoundly; it ruined his health and greatly diminished his quality of life. He was never able to live even a semblance of the physical life he had enjoyed before the war. In addition, he fought the war in his head for years, suffering bouts of depression and disturbed sleep. That hurt and damage was never fully acknowledged, by the community of Canadians for whom he fought, in the form of a heart disability pension from the Canadian government. Over the years, I typed many letters for him in repeated applications for such a pension. The applications were never exactly turned down; they were just in continual limbo. Obviously, if they dragged their feet long enough, it would cease to be an issue. A lesser person would have been very bitter at the continued injustice.

Yet, in the three decades that I knew and loved him, I never detected a note of resentment or rancour, not even during our conversations about the war. He stated the bitter facts, but never once with even a trace of bitterness in his voice. While he certainly neither forgot nor accepted the lack of support and recognition from the Canadian community, he never let it break his spirit or steal his joie de vivre. No matter how frustrating the physical limitations on his life surely were, he never failed to greet the world with a smile and a friendly demeanour that gladdened the heart of the recipient. He never let the injustices damage what is essentially a beautiful soul.

I have often said that Charles was the only true Christian I have ever known, the only person I have ever met who even came close to that nebulous ideal. He was a deeply spiritual man; a profoundly good person. This came across loud and clear. Charles never spewed religious platitudes, and then behaved in unchristian ways towards his neighbours. He simply conducted his life the way one should. He lived those Christian ideals every day of his life in the way he treated others. And whenever problems and setbacks in his life occurred, he always mustered the courage to do the right thing. Just as in his wartime career, he never failed to rise to the occasion. He lived his life with such good humour, it never ceases to amaze me. The war broke his body, but neither the war nor all the petty jealousies during it and injustices since were able to break his spirit.

Over the years, Charles Kipp has been many things to my family— unsung hero, wonderful neighbour, cherished friend and confidant, a loving second grandfather to our children, an example by which to conduct our lives. I had been blind to the latter for a while, until his book kick-started my soul and jarred me back to life. I had shut down my heart and ignored my own life's rule: You never let bad people or their actions against you erode your character or blemish your soul. It's all right to be appalled by a hideous wrong done to you and yours; it's all right, too, to kick a few butts that need to be kicked, for it's that passion that causes us to work for others to see they do not have to suffer the same injustices, but never lose your joie de vivre or good humour along the way. You don't let it break your spirit. The living, breathing example of that had been right beside me all that time, only a few hundred yards away. Because of him, I know I will find my way.

We all owe a debt to Charles Kipp for the lifestyle of freedom we have today for which he sacrificed so much to ensure. But we also owe him a double debt of gratitude, for he was and continues to be a positive influence on every life he touched. I have never known a more kindly, upbeat, gracious, life-affirming soul my whole life long. He was both a gentleman and a gentle man. For all of us who have been fortunate enough to pass through this life having known him, "We certainly shall remember thee; and be the better human beings for it."

LYNDA SYKES
Brownsville, May 1999

APPENDiX

Letter from Charles to his parents

A 57319 Cpl Kipp C.D.
L & W. Regt.
A. Coy
Cdn. Army Overseas
Aug. 27/44

Some where in France
Hello Folks.

Just got a letter from you a while ago. So since I have been lucky enough to find some paper and envelopes I will answer it while I have a few minets.

We are having some wild and exciting times over hear and a lot of close calls. I have only been hit six times. But not bad enough to go to the M.O. So I am doing alright. I would like to write about some of the things we have done and seen. But I am afraid they would not let it through. Just follow the Cdn's and I am right at the front with them. The front line is the safest place. And I have got my share of the Jerrys to. I am scarred stiff when we start an attack or any thing. But just as soon as the shooting starts and I can get my machine gun talking back at them I feel right at home. The last week has been more like a pleasure trip. And you know where we are now.

Our boys say I was the first Cdn across the river that every one is talking about. But I don't know if I was or not. How are all the people at home now. Just as well as I am I hope. I catch the odd flea on me. But am getting used to them now. Say hello to every body for me.

These French people are sure glad to see us. We took one town. And I was the first one in. I could hardly get through to look for Germans. We had about half a mile of open country to get through in front of the town. Me out in the front of our Regt. I never expected to make it when I started but hear I am. The Air Force sure make a mess of things. And I am glad they are on our side

A French family that live in a house behind us just came to see us. We gave them smokes and pipe tobbacco. They are happy now. We have been eating their vegetables all day. And are they good, we even had green corn to-day. Well it is getting dark so I will have to close. I am sending a skull and cross bones the sign of the S. S. men. We are making mince meat out of them.

But there are some tough boys among them. They die before they will give up. Will write again soon. And keep those prayers going. I can use them.
C.K.

P.S. Haven't heard from Don for a while. I hope he comes to our outfit. We are making history and can't be beat.

Letter to Charles's mother from her aunt

Dec. 31, 1944
104 Spitsby Road
Boston, Lincolnshire
England

Dear Stella

You may well be proud of your gallant Charlie. May he be spared to do more good work & then to come home to you. I saw the account in a London paper, never dreaming the hero was Charlie. Uncle Charlie says the same. & I showed your letter & the newspaper cutting to Cousin Fred Disbrowe & we all send you & his Father our congratulations—I hope Donald is well & busy now. Parents of men in the Forces have an anxious time now & I should think your prayers are going up to Heaven day & night, asking that the sons may one day return safe & sound when this horrid war is over. Germany is jealous of the greater countries and doesn't like being beaten by a little country called England. and England w^d be beaten if it were not for the Allied countries of Russia & the Americas which of course include Canada—

You sent me a beautiful Christmas card quite unlike any others I have recieved—Today is Sunday, & instead of going to Church I am writing some letters for I have got a chill & some rheumatic aches & feel the fireside is the best for me & coal is rather scarce, so I am writing in the kitchen to avoid quite emptying the coal cellar. I hope to get a replenishment tomorrow as its due to me, under the present rationing law.

Goodbye—God bless you all, & God bless the Allied Armies
  Your aff^te Aunt
  Edith A. Disbrowe

Letter to Charles from Hans Luijten

Mr. F. M. Luyten
c.p.m. Luyten-Bartens
Montensbos 31
4837 cc Breda

Mr. C.D. Kipp
Brownsville Ont.
r.r.i. NOL ICO Canada
11th December 1984

Dear Charles,
Many thanks for your letter of November 4th 1984.

For us too the renewed acquaintance with the man who 40 years ago came down the cellar in Bergen op Zoom was a great joy.

We have always remembered your name, because your heroic fights made a great impression upon us, which were much talked of when we remember the liberation of Bergen op Zoom in '44.

During 40 years, we often thought of you and we shall not forget you for the rest of our lives.

I hope that the whole European trip has been a successful happening for you as may be proved from the fact that you consider to come back to Holland.

You had so many things to do that I quite understand that there was no time left to visit us in Breda too.

Should you come to Holland again, please inform us in time.

Enclosed I sent you 4 photos which were made during your stay in Bergen op Zoom.

Those photos were taken within the background of what is left of the Potaschfactory where you fought at the end of October 1944. The stories you told us about these fights have made a deep impression upon us.

The other photo was taken from the entrance of the house Bolwerk Zuid 50 in Bergen op Zoom where you slept a night. It is a pity that it is not very clear, but I will send you another one when I come across it.

You would oblige my father and me very much by sending us a photo of yourself in the uniform of these eventfull but very important days. I assume that you have kept one of them as a remembrance. I should also like to receive a photocopy of the newspaper article about the fight in the Potasch in Bergen op Zoom. At the moment I cannot find this paper.

It is hardly to be believed, that you—after three days of unconsiesness—again took part in that heavy fighting.

I understand that many of your comrades still suffer from those terrible experiences.

Let us hope that your European trip has done you some good for your present health.

Together with my father and my wife we wish you, your wife and your friend James a happy and joyful Christmas and a prosperous 1985.

With many thanks for all you have done for us, my best wishes for the years to come.

Hoping to hear from you soon,

I remain for ever

Yours Faithfully,

[signed] Hans Luyten

F.M. Luyten.

Letters to Charles from Carl Holst

CARL HEINZ HOLST   OT- Obershagen, 11-1-1985
Ringstr. 8. D - 3162 UETZE 3   tel.: ø 05147/1288

Dear Mr. Kipp!

When you saw the enclosed copyprint you'll know who is writing a letter to you. Yes, I was one of the soldiers who was fighting against you at Bergen op Zoom in the end of October 1944. Our Regiment, the 6th Para-Reg. von der Heydte, was first in Hoogerheide in the south of Bergen o.Z. and then we went back until Steenbergen via Bergen o.z.

I have been several times in that town. The last time it was in 1981. By that time I meet Mr. Roosenboom who is living behind the laundry in a nice little house. We had a good contact to another and he promised to give a notice as soon as someone of the Canadien-Sodiers would visit that place at Bergen op Zoom. So he phoned up twice and handed over your adress to me.

Meanwhile I put a notice into a veteran-magazine that I am looking for comrades who have been on that place by that time because Mr. Roosenboom told me, that you would come to visit the Netherlands during this year. And I thought it would be much interesting for you and us to have a conversation with the 'old enemy'. You'll remember the night-fights at the laundry and iron-foundry as well as the factory for spirits. As well as your tank standing on the street opposide the laundry—and a nurse with an officer inspected the frontline in the afternoon without any care of missiles etc.

Well, let me know what time you'll be in Bergen op Zoom. I am there with or without comrades.

With kind regards from 'an old enemy'
yours [signed] Carl H. Holst

Ø to Mr. Roosenboom
    Buitenvestr. 50
    4614 Bergen op Zoom/NL

CARL HEINZ HOLST   OT- Obershagen, 09-03-1985
Ringstr. 8. D - 3162 UETZE 3   tel.: ø 05147/1288

Dear Mr. Kipp!
I thougt that my letters got lost as I didn't got a reply. But by now I am lucky to receive your letter dated 26th last month. Thanks very much for it.

Your adventure in that spiritfactory had been told round our whole Regiment. Not all in the same way as you wrote as a real witness—do you know how soon storys are told in the army and what is on the end. So far as I was instructed by the Dutch people and Mr. Roosenboom we lost at that fight 27 men which died. Includet the two ore three who have been killed by the spirit in that big drums in the factory. I dont know how many prisoners you made but so far as I know not many? In my group I lost two; one was killed and the other one got woundet. Sorry, but I havnt been in that factory as you went in. As you made that night-attack at 1 o'clock (German time) I was near our Company-Office (in a house on the end of the street (Buitenvest). I was glad about it because your guns where shoting more than one series of shells to our lines and I had a shelter. Afterwards I got notice that your group came through our lines and I was surprised about your courage and angry about our men who more or less slept. As soon as I have kown all details I went back to the office to fetch some men for a counter-attack. But in that office-room the six or eight men including our officer, who was incharged of our company, have been drunk. As an excuse for the officer (Lieutenant Le'Coutré—later in the new German Army colonell—was that he got a wound on his right leg with a lot of pain. A night before he checked up our lines and forgot the watchword. As one of my man called him he didn't answer. And at once the man fired with his MG 42 (Machine-Gun). Le Coutré was very lucky that he got only one bullet in his right leg and not more. But in that days more or less everybody was drinking more as they should.—Well, there was not one man spare—so I took a MG 42 with ammunition in drums and made the counter-attack by myself. Meanwhile your boys have been in a shelter of straw with earth on the top from the Dutch. In that darknes I couldn't see anybody and so I fired directly to that place where I thought you have been. They shouted me a bastard and some other words, but that was the whole fight. That you got your men back I hear the first time. I always thought that you stayed in that place. My man who fired to our chief got killed that night. I suppose by a handgranade—one of yours, but I am not quiet sure. Then I went back to my watchtower—underneath the roof of the laundry—and look to your tank. By that time I saw that officer together with the nurse. I had him inside the sight of my MP. I couldn't belive that such a man promenade alonge the line together with a girl by that danger—and I didn't shot—also the nurse was wearing the red cross.

Red Cross—two or three days before, as your tank got position an that factory, one of our blokes got his bazooka and shot two rockets to your tank. Both shots missed it and than the tank fired to the place where the shot came from—the jutting of my watchtower. The man was killed, but the bazooka was all right. So we put out the red cross flag and pulled out the dead body from that bricks of the half dstroeyed jutting. As I used the bazooca an hour later the electric contact didn't work any more and your tank got out of it.

I suppose that this or that will be back in my memory when we meet each other and talk about that battle.

What I like to know are following things:

1. You have been a Halfplatoon leader?
2. How was your Regiment called (Number and Name)?
3. How many soldiers have been in your Regiment?
4. Are you a foot-soldier or?
5. The tanks belonged to your Company? (Platoon)
6. Did you ever hear that we killed soldiers of your platoon under-neath the destroyed bridge (over the zoom) about 200 yards to the north of the laundry at nighttime?
7. Did you hear anything about reprisals of our boys to the Dutch population(?) or about any bad things in that way?
8. Did you read the book of R W Thompson 'Eighty-Five Days' about the battle of Woensrecht? I translated it into German.
9. What time in 1986 we could meet(?) each other?

Meanwhile I transleted your letter into German and it will be printed in our magazine in a short while. I'll send a copy over to you.

About my contact to you I wrote in that magazine as well and I got some phonecalls from veterans (my Regiment) which want to see you as well. When you come over are you allone or comrades of you are coming as well? On the other hand I like to invite Mr. Roosenboom in every case because he is the man who made it possible that we will meet one time. And as well I like to invite the mayor of Bergen op Zoom as well as the mayor of Woensrecht together with the press. Do you agree with all that? For us it has a background. West Germany is the onliest country in Europe who does not belive itself that means the words fatherland etc. does not mean anything to our youth—and we vetarans are the killers. The men who killed four and a half million of Jews! The first time I heard about it was just after the war. I was a soldier and nothing else. And to document that I like to show through the press that we are not anymore enemys. Perhaps you understand my point og few. As we lost the war we build up Germany again without looking left or right—and we didn't teach our children about the things which have been. That was a big mistake, and now we are called the killers! Sometimes it is a bad feeling.

About our contact I informed our old chief Brigade General Professor Dr. Dr. von der Heydte. He has had a very bad car-accident in the first days of this year (he is nearly eighty years old) and I hope he recovers soon. He made it possible that we met (about fifty of us) with the 90.US Infantry Division (200 men) at Heidelberg last year. Enclosed you'll find the explanation.

I hope you are not to tired by reading my bad English. Please let me know how your opinion is. By the way, I got some old photos of the laundry and the meltingwork from a achive at Bergen op Zoom. It will be interesting for you as well.

With kind regards

[signed] Carl H. Holst

PS. My address please write in this way

C.H. HOLST

Ringstr. 8

CARL HEINZ HOLST   OT- Obershagen, 4-05-85

Ringstr. 8. D - 3162 UETZE 3   tel.: ø 05147/1288

Dear Mr. Kipp!

At first I have to say thank you for your long letter dated 4-4-85. One day later I received a letter of your comrade Jeff Brown, who was the leader of the 1st Platoon. I answered him with a copy to you to say that your letter arrived.

Meanwhile I spend the last weekend in Bergen op Zoom with Mr. Roosenboom. He phoned up to say that a friend of him found a very old document of my Regiment. It was a order of my old chief Count von der Heydte, by now Brigard-General, from a date 25-10-44. I had a long conversation with that Piet Withofen, who was about fourteen by that time. About my visit in Bergen o.Z. I made a notice which I send to Jeff Brown. He has a friend who is an Austrian—perhaps that gentleman is able to translate it for you.

I did not know that we blow up three church towers exept the bridges on the Zoom. Through one explosion of one of the bridge a girl about nineteen was wounded and died a few hours later. She got a stone to her left chest side. In the Marine-Hospital they coud'nt help. A sad story. I am glad that you wrote that it is untrue that we murdered your prisoned boys underneath the bridge.

I was strong shock to read that I killed one of your comrades by my shouting with the MG 42. I never had known it and now after fourty years it is a heavy to wear. Everyone of your and our boys was shouting but at most you never have known if that soldier was killed or wounded or even felt down on the earth by the shock of the bullet. But now I know that I killed a friend of you—and that is a story which still occopy my thoughts.

You see by my answer that you are a good writer es well as your handwriting is easy to read. Dont bother about it—I understand every word. And I translated your letters as well as the letter of Mr. Brown. The copys I send to several comrades of me that they know about us and the contact to our old enemy.

In Bergen o.Z. I have had a telephone conversation with the Burgermeister Mr. van Bevenberger. He knows you very well as he said and he will join into our meeting in this or the coming year. I promised to give him a note about the date. As well I had a personal conversation with the Burgermeister of Hoogerheide/Woensrecht, Mr. de Loeuw. With him I had a long conference and explained unknown things to him which happened in October 44. He will ask in a homepaper if some of the inhabitants are willing to get into contact with me because I'm willing to write a book about all the things which happened in that month of October 44. Therefore I am sending a copied plan of Bergen o.z. Perhaps you are able to draw in some details f.e. where your Platoons have been waiting for the attack and where your MG's as well as your guns have been placed. By the way, on a short areal of 100 x 100 Yards near the Rozenstraat there have been 365 granades (shells) exploded. That was counted in November/December 44. I cant remember that we have been in such a hell.

As I said I like to write a book about our story! I got some photos from the lundry and the meltingworks from the town office. But I would like to have photos of you and Mr. Brown as well from a few of your comrades if possible to have a print of it in the book. I hope you dont minde if I ask for it.

As well I like to write about our story between us both and some other stories which I'll know as soon as we had our meeting. A great help is Mr. Roosenboom in this case. I am very sure that the book will be interested only by the men who have been there and so it will be not a big busines, but still I belive it has to be written.

I agree with your mind about a won battle—luck is a funny mate and for-tuitousnesses deciding often.

I did not know that some of my comrades have been able to talk or to cry in English—I mean about the knives. I heard some more shoutings at that night but I couldnt get the contence. Of course I learned English at school but my real English I learned as a PoW in England, where I spend as a guest of King George the V three years. (It was a good time and I still have some friends in Nothumberland which I visited in the past nearly each year twice).

I full agree with your opinion that a man has to fight for his country. But today here in Germany we old veterans are the killers—more or less the same as in the US with the veterans of Vietnam. It's a bad feeling for us because we did only that what the order of the rules during the war said. Well, we destroyed a lot but after the war we rebuild more or less whole Germany with our hands. But the young generation has theire own opinion and not much knowledge about our history. The most heavy weight are the concen-tration camps and the killed jews—you habe been reading the papers from the last days about the visit of Reagan in Bonn.

Well Mr. Kipp, thats all for today. I hope to hear soon from you and that you are in good health.

Yours [signed] Carl H. Holst

CARL HEINZ HOLST
Ringstr. 8. D - 3162 UETZE 3

OT- Obershagen, July 4th 1985
tel.: ø 05147/1288

Dear Cliff!*

If I had to write my letters by hand it would be a real hard work. And in this way I have to thank you very much for your most interesting letter dated 10th and 16th of the last month. I suppose you never wrote such a lot of letters—except during the war to your wife—as now. And I do respect that very much!

It's a good thing that you got rain after such a lot of dry-time. I know what it means with my garden. The last four weeks we have had only rain and I thought by myself a worm winter! But by now it changed and the cherries are

---

* Cliff was the name of another Canadian veteran Carl was corresponding with.

red (a lovely taste), the strawberrys have to be picked up and the gras is growing like hell. I have also a lot of work to do. I dont know how all the things
have been done as I still was on work. I'm busy the whole day and have no spare
time at all.

In about fourteen days I'll make a brake off for a few days. I'll visit together
with my girlfriend the town Hamburg (I was born there). And Mr. Sjaark
Roosenboom/Bergen op Zoom called to come. My girlfriend (she is called
Teichmann) will accompany me to that visit. Two or three days we will spend
in Belgium near Gheel (also in working up a time from the last war). There is
living a young men who writes a book about the fights of Gheel and Beerin-
gen. I have been there in September 44. And this Chris van Kerckhoven is a
very nice chap with a lot of knowledge about the fight around there.

Years ago as I was stil married I used to go to Denmark for fishing. But if
you would ask me what type of fish I couldnt tell you. My son likes this job
very much and has a permission to fish. Years ago he tryed to fish trouts in
the river Tyne between Newcastle and Carlisle (North GB). Perhaps you remember I have got still friends up there from the time as I was a PoW.

Enclosed you'll find a copied map of Bergen o.Z. Could you be so kind
and draw with a red or green pencil your way from the south to Bergen? I
would be very obliged to you.

About the SS and the Hitlerjugend-Div. I'll write later. First I have to
read the book of Panzermeyer. It's a book which was written by the permission of the British Ocupation Army—that means it got's prooved. I'll try
then to explain some things. Of course I cant argue against your experience
during your fights in the Normandy. I havent been between this SS-Army.
But I agree with you in case of the Wehrmacht etc. We found out that, except
the 101.Airborn Div. and other paras the US havnt been very hard fighters. If
they wouldnt have had the endless lot of material and we had a few more
tanks together with hundred ME 109, the Uta[h]-Beach would have been a
fiasko. The British have been hard fighters. For my opinion harder as the US.
And the Canadiens didnt care at all. They have been the most rude fighters I
saw. That's not you are such a man out of that army. It's stated in a lot of
books. —As I said that the Wehrmacht in the Normandy was weak—the
most of the soldiers have been older than 30 years and a lot have been sick by
stomage etc. Sodiers of the third class.

How was your meeting with Cliff. I hope you didnt talk the whole nights.
But when you get older and you have time to think, all the old stories are
coming back. The war was measured to our life a very short time—but it is
like a knive you never get out of your body—so is my feeling to it. And I like
to talk about it—and now I like to write my experience down. Perhaps I feel
better afterwards. Cliff was realy lucky to get out of all by that very hard

wound on his shoulder—more or less a wonder.

Have you ever heard about the documention of Frederick Winter-botham? The war in Africa as well as the submarine-war so as the Normandy have been lost by the action Ultra. The British found out the German code and have been able to tranfer every wireless message—even from Hitler or the German Marshalls as Rommel or Model and Goering.

I wish in the same way like you that we might meet each other in a shorter time as one year. But I know it's not easy by that lot of cost for the air-trip etc. And we all not in such a very good position. Still ich hope to see you and your comrades soon.

With kind regards

[signed] Carl H. Holst

PS. Your letter has been tranleted and send in copies to five other veterans of our regiment. Cliff gets a copy of this letter.

D.O.

CARL HEINZ HOLST   OT- Obershagen, June 4th, 1986
Ringstr. 8. D - 3162 UETZE 3   tel.: ø 05147/1288

Dear Charles;

This letter should have been written half a month ago. But I do not feel well since a few weeks time. So please excuse if I'm late.

At first I have to send the regards of all German which have been in Bergen op Zoom. Every one of my friends phoned up or wrote and said that they are very glad to have seen you and spoke some words with you and your brother. Lt. Col. le Coutre wrote a long letter. He explained that he is very thankful to me that he had the chance to meet you. It was a very deeply occurrence for him—and also for myself. Therefore I have to say thank you for your visit!

I hope you came back in a good condition! As we went to Schijndel we talked about your health. We could see that you are not in the best disposi-tion. It's a pitty, but we are not any more in the bloom of youth—and the long trip from Canada to Europa—and the time-change—and the strange way of living missing the normaly things of life—I understood that you have been tired and not been able to ride further sevenhundered Miles. Here at home everything was ready for your reception (five days I was eating the same meal), but I understand that you have been unable to come.

Thank you as well for the cartride with the dedication. It's standing in my sitting room cupboard and reminds me to our meeting.

A few days ago I reveived the first pictures. It-s a map which is circulating and I ordered a lot. As soon as I get them I'm sending some over to you. As well I have to send two or three to the lord-mayor of Bergen op Zoom. One of his clarks was visiting me in our hotel at Ossendrecht. They want to write about our meeting with pictures. As soon as I get that story I'll send a copy to you.

At the moment I'm translating your war-diary. It takes some time to be translated in a good German language and will be the stock of my book. Thank you very much for your hard work!

Meanwhile I recieved from Sjaak Roosenboom a book written by General Whitaker (by that time a Lt. Col.). He was our enemy in Woensdrecht and Hoogerheide. He met Baron von der Heydte at Germany in 1983 and wrote a lot about our Rgt. I send him a few lines to get into contact with him. Also I hope to meet von der Heydte in the end of this year. Von der Heydte is very sick and I do not know how long he will be in this world.

On one of the pictures is a Jewish couple from USA? Do you know the name and where they came from? Are they refugees from Germany? And please give me the name of your friends in Bergen op Zoom. If I do not write down the names I forget it—I'm getting old!

I am sure that your grand-daughter is happy that you are home again—as well as your wife. Please let me know how you arrived and how the way back was like. In the hope that you are feeling well I say goodbye—Aufwieder-sehen—for today!
[signed] Your Carl

PS. My regards to your brother!

From an unknown Canadian newspaper, October 1944

Essex Soldier in 'Lost Patrol' Fights Off Boche
By BOYD D. LEWIS
United Press War Correspondent

WITH THE CANADIAN FIRST ARMY AT BERGEN OP ZOOM, Oct. 19.—Allied troops owned the bridgehead over canals north of this Dutch city today be-cause 13 men of a Canadian "lost patrol" including Pte R. J. Brow of Essex, Ont., and commanded by an American captain, held out for 16 hours in a cavernous stove factory that was filled with vats of deadly acid.

AMERICAN OFFICER

Capt. Owen Lambert, La Jolla, Calif., led the Canadians against a greatly superior force of Nazi paratroopers who surrounded their precarious position in the factory. The Canadians were members of a famous regiment which we shall call "The Pinks and The Swells" because their real name might inform the enemy. They challenged the enemy by shouting:

"Come in and taste our knives, you riff-raff—we are Canadians."

The "lost patrol" gradually was whittled down in a hellish battle of hand grenades, while fighting like madmen among the acid vats marked with the skull and crossbones.

"When things are that bad, you just don't give a damn," Lambert said, as he and four of his patrol came straight out of the battle line, muddy, wet and unshaven, to tell their story. "We were positive we'd had it. We'd been gone so long, we'd been crossed off as dead or captured."

Only 13 men remained of a force sent last night to wade or swim two parallel canals and seize a foothold among the factory buildings.

IN DEAD OF NIGHT

"We were surrounded in the dead of night in a factory the size of a football field," Lambert said. "Jerry was blasting holes in the walls with bazookas and throwing grenades in. It's lucky for us that Jerry's grenades aren't any damn good. If they were, we wouldn't be here. They shatter in tinkling little pieces as if he'd thrown a vase at you. I had one burst right between my boots."

While Lambert related the story, the men sat in a semi-circle, occasionally interrupting to supply bits of detail.

"I ordered the men to run all over the factory, shouting and yelling like hell to make Jerry think we had a regiment," Lambert said. "We never fired two bursts from the same spot. As a matter of fact, we fired damn few bursts. Our Sten guns and rifles had clogged with mud so badly getting across the canals that most Stens wouldn't fire at all or would just go 'pink!'—not enough snap to detonate the cartridge.

"You'd have to yank the rifle bolt for five minutes to get the breech open, then take five minutes more to get it shut, then maybe it wouldn't fire. We were caught with our Stens down. I knew we had it if we couldn't get reinforcements.

"We were calling paratroops every dirty name we could think of. Whenever we'd yell 'come in and get killed … We ain't special troops, we're pinks and swells … Come on in, you riff-raff, and taste Canadian knives,' he'd fire a grenade and give his location away, and that would be one less Nazi."

HELP SOUGHT

Lambert sent Sgt. Charles Kipp, a keen, bronzed boy from Ontario, to try to get back to the regiment and bring help. Kipp walked down the middle of the street "like he owned the town," swam one canal and waded another without being recognized. A platoon led by Major M. J. McCutcheon, Niagara Falls, Ontario, and Kipp fought their way back across the canals and through streets and fields littered with dead paratroopers killed by Lambert's men.

"When I saw Lambert coming out of that building with the other fellows dragging along after him, dead tired but grinning, I thought, 'My God, they're ghosts'," Kipp said.

Lambert, with tears in his eyes, said:

"You see how it is up here. Kipp has been under my command only a month, but you can know a guy for a lifetime in one month of fighting like we've had across Belgium and Holland."

Members of the patrol who helped Lambert tell the story were Cpl. J. E. Erwin, St. Catharines, Ontario; Cpl. E. P. Arnold, Hunstville, Ontario; Pte. Harold Cader, Penetanguishene, Ontario. Others in the battle were Pte. Brow, Essex; Lance Cpl. Walter Balfour, Lindsay, Ontario, and Pte. J. E. Kitcher, New Toronto.

From the British newspaper the *Daily Mirror*, October 30, 1944

13 "Lost" Men Fought Battle among Vats

BECAUSE thirteen men of a Canadian "lost patrol" held out for sixteen hours until they were relieved we now hold a bridgehead over the canals north of Bergen Op Zoom.

In a big stove factory, surrounded by a greatly superior force of Nazi paratroopers, the "lost patrol" issued a challenge to the Germans to "come in and taste our knives, you riff-raff. We are Canadians."

The patrol was whittled down in the hellish battle and came straight out of the line, muddy, wet and unshaven, to tell their story.

They fought like madmen in a grenade battle in the dark, dodging among vats filled with deadly acid used to treat stove metal.

"When things are that bad you just don't give a damn," said Captain Owen Lambert, commander of the patrol. "We were positive we'd had it. We'd been gone so long we'd been crossed off as dead or captured."

The thirteen were all that were left of a force sent to wade or swim the two parallel canals and seize a foothold among the factory buildings.

"We were surrounded in the dead of night in a factory the size of a football field," Lambert continued. "Jerry was blasting holes in the walls with bazookas and throwing in grenades.

"It was lucky for us Jerry's grenades weren't any damn good. If they were we wouldn't be here. They shattered in little tinkling pieces, as if Jerry had thrown a vase at you. I had one burst between my boots.

"Our grenades were much better. I know that because the area around the factory was littered with dead Germans—but we didn't have nearly enough. We didn't dare waste a grenade. When it was all over we had two left.

"I ordered the men to run all over the darkened factory, yelling like hell to make Jerry think we had a regiment. We never fired two bursts from the same spot. As a matter of fact, we fired damn few bursts—our Sten guns had clogged getting across the canal. We were caught with our Stens down.

"We were calling the German paratroops every dirty, filthy thing we could think of, and maybe we laid it on a bit too thick because he came for us as if he didn't mean one of us to get away alive. Whenever we taunted him he'd fire and give away his position.

"I told the sergeant to crawl out somehow and get back to the regiment to tell them we were still alive. After he'd gone we sat around waiting for the end—we felt sure we were goners and that was that."

Then the sergeant took up the story—Sergeant Charles Kipp, of Ontario.

"JUST KEPT ON"

"It was a clear moonlit night. After I left the factory, leaving my gun and remaining ammunition behind me, I took a bearing on the church steeple in Bergen-op-Zoom and started off down the middle of the street. I was challenged three times by Germans, but I just kept on.

"After I had swum a canal, a voice which I recognised as Canadian challenged me, and he sure sounded good. I never thought I'd live to hear another."

Sergeant Kipp reported to the brigade commander. Two efforts were made to break across to the surrounded men. Both failed.

A major and a trooper finally managed to improvise a bridge across the canal at a point where it was only 25ft. wide, using a door broken off a nearby house and timbers hauled from the wreckage of a shelled home.

Finally a group of men led by Sergeant Kipp fought their way across.

"I saw Captain Lambert coming out of the building with the other fellows dragging after him, dead tired but grinning," said Kipp. "I thought: 'My God, they're ghosts.' I was so happy I nearly cried."

INDEX